Advance Praise

Captive Audience

"If Mann doesn't quite elevate reality TV to an art form—and that's unlikely his intention—he makes a persuasive argument for readers to sit up and take notice. The cultural implications are perhaps more potent than we'd like to believe. An immensely captivating consideration of reality TV and a moving reflection on marriage."   —*Kirkus Reviews* (starred review)

"I'm an ardent admirer of Lucas Mann's work. *Captive Audience* shows us how to do 'media criticism' the right way or rather the wrong way, the more electric and exciting way: the target is never out there; it's in here. A galvanizing, illuminating, and nervy book."

—David Shields, author of *Other People* and *Reality Hunger*

"I was initially drawn to *Captive Audience*'s smashing critical analysis and savvy pop-culture apologies, but what I ended up cherishing most of all is this book's vivid portraiture. Mann has written a soulful recounting of not just a decade of watching reality TV as it has evolved past entertainment into something more complex, public, and even sinister, but a story of doing so alongside another person—a beloved life partner, nonetheless, with whom his shared reality also evolves and deepens. Who could have imagined that one of the most evocative love stories I've read in ages would be mixed into heady investigations of *Joe Millionaire*, *Cops*, and *Vanderpump Rules*?"

—Elena Passarello, author of *Animals Strike Curious Poses*

"There is no cultural critic in America like Lucas Mann. Perhaps that's because he turns on the television and sees what you don't—in the vulgar and striving world of reality television, he finds beauty and heart in the ambition that drove these overtanned and underfed people to perform for us—and that brought us in to watch. Mann's voice is filled with empathy, irony, and a tenderness that will make you laugh and then ache, sometimes within the span of a single, perfectly constructed sentence. *Captive Audience* is the definitive book on the aging but perennially renewed genre of reality TV, and there isn't an author alive who could have written it better."

—Kristen Radtke, author of *Imagine Only Wanting This*

"Epistolary writing is custom-made for immodesty and over-sharing, the kinds of filterless self-display, as Lucas Mann shows us, that we happen to want from reality TV stars. But in this epistle to his wife, Mann explores their shared enthusiasm for reality television and proves there is insight and virtue to be found in examining the desire to be seen. He gets closer to that dimension of intimacy and love, in fact, than any spotlight-seeker yet who has beguiled us from our most private screens."

—Gregory Pardlo, author of *Air Traffic*

"What other book goes so boldly into the insatiable need to be seen? Who else is as tough on his own perceptions? I already knew Lucas Mann was a wonder of a writer, but *Captive Audience* is his best book yet: a tender, humane, comic, brainy, unsettling achievement." —Paul Lisicky, author of *The Narrow Door: A Memoir of Friendship*

Lucas Mann

Captive Audience

Lucas Mann was born in New York City and received his MFA from the University of Iowa, where he was the Provost's Visiting Writer in Nonfiction. He is also the author of *Lord Fear: A Memoir,* which was named one of the best books of 2015 by the *Miami Herald, Kirkus Reviews, Paper* magazine, *Largehearted Boy,* and Oprah.com, and *Class A: Baseball in the Middle of Everywhere,* which earned a Barnes & Noble Discover Great New Writers selection and was named one of the best books of 2013 by the *San Francisco Chronicle.* His essays have appeared in *Guernica, BuzzFeed, Slate,* and *The Kenyon Review,* among others. He recently received a 2018 National Endowment for the Arts Literature Fellowship. He teaches creative writing at the University of Massachusetts Dartmouth and lives in Providence, Rhode Island, with his wife.

www.lucasmann.com

Captive Audience

Captive Audience

ON LOVE AND REALITY TV

Lucas Mann

VINTAGE BOOKS

A Division of Penguin Random House LLC

New York

A VINTAGE BOOKS ORIGINAL, MAY 2018

Copyright © 2018 by Lucas Mann

All rights reserved. Published in the United States by Vintage Books,
a division of Penguin Random House LLC, New York, and distributed
in Canada by Random House of Canada, a division of Penguin
Random House Canada Limited, Toronto.

Vintage and colophon are registered trademarks
of Penguin Random House LLC.

The Cataloging-in-Publication Data is on file at the Library of Congress.

Vintage Books Trade Paperback ISBN: 978-0-525-43554-9
eBook ISBN: 978-0-525-43555-6

Author photograph © Matthew Celeste
Book design by Christopher M. Zucker

www.vintagebooks.com

Printed in the United States of America
10   9   8   7   6   5   4   3   2   1

For Ottavia

Captive Audience

1

{REQUEST FOR AUDITION}:

Hi (: I am _____, I am a 17 year old with a story.

I want to quit feeling like I am not important. I want to be somebody in my life, I do not want to be remembered as some face in the yearbook, I want to be heard. Currently, I make youtube videos, and I have 317 subscribers. I know it is not a big number, but I am finally being heard by some people and I love it. I just want to make people happy, in any shape or form. Putting a smile on people's faces is my dream! If I could be casted on this show, my life would be complete. I just want people to know me more than just some girl who likes makeup. I want people to know who I am. My family is not against this, but they do think I should focus on school, which I agree with but this is my dream.

Height: 5 feel 5 inches

Age: 17

Gender: Female

Dream: This.

Please help me reach for the stars, this is my dream and if it comes true, I can't even imagine my life. Help me out (: Help me be heard.

—from www.castingcallhub.com

I have, for a long time, suggested that we get rid of cable. I have even suggested that we throw out our TV altogether so that we may eat at our actual kitchen table and play more Scrabble. I'd say these suggestions come biannually, on average—they used to be more frequent, then ebbed, and are now increasing again. They have been going on for the better part of a decade. They arise, as most of my impulses toward change do, out of feelings of shame. They arise when we open up our home and visitors see the way we live—by which I mean what we watch and the frequency with which we watch it—and make remarks that I take to be scornful:

I cannot believe *you guys have all the channels.*

Or: *How can someone retain so much information about Bravo?*

Or: *How do you do it? If I had cable, I think I would forget how to* live. *It's just too easy to let your mind get lost in the slush and forget to look up.*

The relationship between television and life is loaded. The relationship between television and love is, perhaps, even more so. *Life,* the way I think the term is most commonly used, is about action. Go out and *live* is the kind of thing people say to those they deem flawed—ride something, climb something. Engage. Or it can be used as an insult to those who have nothing valuable to offer: get a life.

Love, the way I think the term is most commonly used, necessitates the same action. Loving passively is as shameful as living that way. When we love fully, we are *doing* something to make that love valid. It's a conscious process; it's active. Two people see each other in a way that elevates the act of sight to a challenge that must be confronted. Two people refuse to take their eyes off one another; that's the idea. When we love fully, we are meant to engage.

For a long time, when you would refuse to give up television, I would pretend to be grudgingly acquiescent, as opposed to relieved. You would placate me and say that our watching was your fault, that I was merely implicated by association, the same way it is when I buy ice cream and offer you some—those aren't your calories if you didn't seek them out. We would, as a way to avoid any long-term legislation, briefly turn off the TV and spend the following hours in a sort of mutual meditation, leaning over the table at dinner, sometimes by candlelight, taking in the contours of the face in front of us, as though it had changed from the previous day, and the one before that, and the countless expanse of days that stretched out behind us (nearly every day of our adult lives), making us forget what it felt like to not know that face.

The literature of love, both the bad kind and the good, hinges on this type of sustained gaze. And, though the word *boredom* rarely comes up, it seems crucial that lovers put themselves in scenarios that would otherwise be boring and then very pointedly not feel bored. I'm thinking of Keats here, in one of those gorgeous poems to Fanny that I once read aloud to you in college, the last time neither of us owned a TV. I read to you of Keats wishing only to be:

> . . . *gazing on the new soft-fallen mask*
> *Of snow upon the mountains and the moors—*
> *No—yet still stedfast, still unchangeable,*
> *Pillow'd upon my fair love's ripening breast. . . .*

People used to live at such a slow, sensual pace. This is the kind of thing I still say on the nights when the TV is off. Nostalgia is all wrapped up in slowness. How long we used to linger. The capacity we used to have for sustained care, sustained concentration, sustained quiet.

My favorite book about love is John Berger's *And Our Faces, My Heart, Brief as Photos.* Berger wrote it in 1984—an early–MTV era book—but he wrote with a slowness that implies timelessness, that makes a piece of writing feel resonant, or maybe the word is *authentic.* He was an aging icon in the French Alps then, describing the way his life had moved, the way he'd seen the world change, but at its core the book is a missive to his lover.

He writes of when he is without her, thinking of her, how she shifts in his imagination:

> *In the country which is you, I know your gestures, the into-nations of your voice, the shape of every part of your body. You are not physically less real there, but you are less free.*

How strong a gaze; how long lasting—until his love (who remains unnamed throughout) becomes the image of herself, a creation of his mind and memory as much as the person he knows. There is a bending of reality in this sentiment, and in turn a sort of dehumanizing, but in Berger's hands it doesn't feel gross. Instead, it is a way of seeing I aspire to. It's the elevation of a person to art: to speak to the one I most care for and hopefully witness a grander sentiment (Love! Timeless love!) whisper out from the intimacy of that address. But Berger wrote these words long before anyone ever wrote the word *mansplain,* and I wonder now if he might ask for a do-over. And I wonder, too, if I should try to find a better way to capture and perform my own love. You don't need me to tell you what's there, what's been there, like it's a show that only I've been watching. And yet I do, uncertain, trapped in my own voice, hoping you see at least a sliver of your-self in the portrait, frozen in sustained care.

We went to the Alps once, with your sister and a bunch of other leather-clad Europeans. All that money blown to spend New Year's partying at high altitudes. Everybody else went ski-ing, but you knew I couldn't, so you let me avoid the embarrass-ment by staying behind. I spent a week binge-watching over bad Wi-Fi, and that experience of waiting for the screen to unfreeze while cold rain pecked at the windows of a moldy chalet only ratcheted up the claustrophobia. I watched. Sometimes I walked until I got bored, then returned to the screen again. I waited to hear you come in the door, and we'd put our cheeks together so I could absorb some of the cold from you.

On New Year's Eve, everyone did coke and got into predictable arguments when the coke ran out, and later we lay in bed unable to sleep. The shadows of the mountains were maybe visible through our window, framed in moonlight, but we weren't looking. We watched each other's faces and waited for the laptop to buffer. Finally, we were able to watch *The Real L Word,* a show about actual lesbians in LA, developed to capitalize on the success of a show about fictional lesbians in LA that I never had any interest in watching. It's a program we've only ever sought out in transit—in a motel in Pennsylvania, mid-move, U-Haul packed in the parking lot, dog whimpering at the sound of trucks passing outside, or in a semisecluded corner of O'Hare Airport on a night when all connections were grounded for tornadoes.

Sometimes it's nice to match moods, to decide on that mood matching together. There's a restlessness to *The Real L Word* that appeals only in restless moments. There's a pulsing crassness to the way the most intimately personal is made to feel branded. The women fuck desperately in some scenes, and with the lights on, no pretense that they're unaware of the cameras. They look up, let us see their faces, and then plunge their heads back between legs. In nonfucking scenes, every word is loaded with as much pressure as sex; anything said about anyone can be taken as a slight. It's easy to get a sense that they don't know one another at all, or maybe they really do and this is how shallow knowing someone looks when there's a camera around—another loaded thought.

We were on the futon in the dark, in the Alps, listening to the coke fights die down, and there was Whitney on-screen, fucking white-dreadlock Whitney, movie makeup artist-cum-minor celebrity, confessing in the confessional room after a pretty graphic tryst with her on-again-off-again.

Lust is easy for me, she said in front of a bright-red curtain, for some reason. *Love is hard. Lust is exciting. Love is scary.*

We looked at each other, like always. We didn't say anything, but let Whitney's cutaway line hang between us as a question or an invitation. I saw your face, pale, and my face reflected in your dark eyes. It doesn't take much to approximate profundity. At least not to me.

I've written about a lot of things, or it seems that way to me, but ultimately they're all kind of the same thing. I write about loneliness, or dissatisfaction, or incompleteness. I have tried, in different (though not very different) ways, to make sense of the things that hurt. What is harder, and what I have avoided, is trying to honor the truth of everything that doesn't hurt: that I am not alone; that (although I'm reluctant to say the exact phrase because of *Jerry Maguire*) I am closer to feeling complete because we are together; that often, in our little house in front of our big TV for hours until my eyes begin to sting, I am satisfied.

This is tough to reread after writing it. It seems an impossibly small statement to make, one meant to be offered only semi-sincerely, and a bit drunkenly, at special-occasion dinners.

Barthes says that love, as a subject, has been driven *to the backwater of the "unreal."* Then, he strives to distinguish between *unreal* and *disreal.* The unreal is the fantastical—*Tristan and Isolde, It's a Wonderful Life,* that kind of thing. In its grandness and sincerity and removal, the unreal is easier to explain, always familiar. And so it's the love story that is easiest to find in any book or movie or TV show, allowing the audience to linger in swelling impossibility.

The disreal, though, is that instant ghost of lived experience, the flickering, perceived moment, unsayable—*if I utter it (if I lunge at it, even with a clumsy or overliterary sentence), I emerge from it.*

My problem is that I am immersed in it, and because I'm immersed in it, I can't think of anything else to utter. We are in one place: our home; we see one person: the other. What else is there to say? I want to believe that I'm not interested in fantasy. I am interested in the disreal, not the unreal, both in the art that I seek and the love that I live. But if you look at any life long enough, with enough vested interest, how do you not begin to push toward the fantastical?

Whenever you catch me looking at you, you say, *What are you looking at?* Which is a really loaded question. You know what I'm looking at—you, the person in front of me; what else could I be looking at? But what you're asking for is the difference between image and interpretation—is what I see more interesting than what is really there, or what you think is really there? And all I can ever say is *nothing.* And then you roll your eyes and we become exactly what the world would expect us to be. And now I've gone from Roland Barthes to a sitcom punch line. I turn back to the TV.

It's hard to trace an exact history of the "reality show." The term is often applied retroactively—roots can be found in *The Real World,* back in the midnineties, or in *Cops* in the late eighties, or in early eighties variety shows like *That's Incredible!,* or the seminal seventies docudrama *An American Family.* One thing remains consistent: it's always been a tortured lineage, a confounding term.

The best parsing of the language I've read is this, from a book called *Trans-Reality Television: "Reality show" as a phrase is self-confessing.*

In proximity, the two words begin to chip away at each other's meaning. *Reality* should not be a performance; a *show,* if it's any good, should probably be exaggerating something. The resulting promise of the phrase, then, is an impossibility: *transforming facts to the level of the spectacular.*

I like that the implication isn't that we who watch so faithfully are being bullshitted, but rather that we are willfully bullshitting ourselves to get what we want. We are promised a dynamic that cannot actually ever exist, and we accept that.

More than accept it. The genre means a lot to us, to me. I've never expressed that sentiment with even a gesture toward sincerity, because it's embarrassing. But I think I mean it. Sincerely. At least for now I do.

Far more than I've read Berger (or Barthes or Baldwin or Sontag, or any of the others on the grad-school syllabus that I claim shaped how I see the world), far more than we have walked through museums together (and really, how many times have I had the patience for more than one wing and the café?), far more than we've sat and listened and harmonized to the songs that we so seriously call *ours,* we have watched and internalized and discussed televised showings of spectacular reality. *The Real Housewives of Atlanta* (and New Jersey and New York and Beverly Hills and, to a lesser degree, Miami and Orange County), *Keeping Up with the Kardashians, The Real World, Road Rules, The Real World/Road Rules Challenge, Love & Hip Hop, Sister Wives, Basketball Wives, Breaking Amish, Storage Wars, My 600-Pound Life, My Big Fat Fabulous Life, Shahs of Sunset, Married to Medicine, Botched, Say Yes to the Dress, Deadliest Catch, Million Dollar Listing, Intervention, The Little Couple, Vanderpump Rules*—there are many more that I'm forgetting offhand, and there have been many that came and went and briefly held some importance for us, and there are many more being produced right now that we will soon adopt. These are the narratives that have underpinned our lives. These are the stories that we choose to live alongside.

When you live alongside anything for a long time—any person, any character, any narrative structure, any screen flicker—you become a part of it and it becomes a part of you. A part of what—and also how—you remember.

We're on your bed next to the window in your dorm room and we're nineteen. I'm running my hands along your tattoo, your first one, and you tell me to stop because you don't like your body, and I tell you that I do. You don't believe me.

We ask for everything about each other, the kinds of details that other people wouldn't know, as though that will confirm the importance of our conversations. My first memory was of a red vacuum cleaner on the gray carpet of my mother's apartment on East Sixth Street. I was scared of the noise it made. It was a cramped basement apartment, and every sound was loud. I was frightened often. This was Alphabet City in the late eighties, and outside our windows I could see and hear the pacing boots of methadone patients waiting for their morning fix.

"Oh, I can picture you," you say. "Were you blonder? Were you chubby?"

I was, both. And I want you to picture me that way: a cherub in a hard, looming world.

I do remember the vacuum cleaner, and that the carpet was gray. I have heard about the methadone clinic from my mother, mostly cheerful stories about me getting free lollipops. I don't remember it, but I can picture it now, too.

You are running your fingers through my hair and smiling at what isn't an outright lie, just an interpretation, the beginning of a character that I would rather you see, another in a quickly building collection—Q: *How many partners have you had?* A: *Plenty.* Q: *Wait, did you come already?* A: *{Indecipherable, hopefully erotic grunt}.*

You say you remember almost nothing. You didn't speak as a child, you say, like not ever, because you moved to different countries and had to start learning language all over again. You remember an overall feeling of loneliness but hardly any images. Oh, here's one, you say. Coming back from the beach in Italy, drinking peach nectar out of a carton—how sweet and thick and simple it was. Oh, and you had a boy's haircut. Oh, and you were bullied for your weirdness, and your silence, so you preferred to be alone—most of the memories you have are of that pain. Oh, and one more thing: you were a liar. When you did speak, it was never the truth. And there was one particular lie you told that was too big, too painful, and you'll never talk about it even still.

This scares me a little but mostly turns me on—a repressed past; an untellable secret; dark, brooding eyes under a strange, little-boy haircut; lonely; sucking nectar out of a carton. It becomes instantly important to know that there is something unknowable about you.

I keep thinking of your secrets and the lonely anger, and all those redacted memories for a while, and then I forget about them as other details emerge to pay attention to. But these plot points linger, always, making each new scene a little more enthralling, and then they resurface, brief, overpowering—reminders that we can see so much of each other, know each other as best we can, and yet always, underneath, there is the unknown.

A few years later, at a party in Brooklyn, you're talking and drinking and laughing, and then suddenly you're silent and flushed, looking over my shoulder, down a crowded hallway. You've seen someone from your childhood, from an American camp you were sent to when you knew no English, and your face is the face of a silent girl, alone and enraged. At first you ask me to hide you, but then she comes up and says, "Oh my God, how crazy to see you! Remember camp? Don't you miss camp?"

I watch you glare at her, silent for a moment, and then you crescendo into emotion. You say that you don't miss it at all. You tell this girl that she had been so cruel—does she even remember what she did to you? She says, "No, not me." You stand closer to her and say with a new force, "Yes, you."

There are others around us at the party, turned stiff and awkward, but you don't see anybody else. The camp girl says she doesn't remember it the same way, but then she squeaks through an apology. You don't accept. The crowd watches; I watch, and watch them watch you. I am transfixed—by the coming tears, by your rage, by this beautiful soap-opera haze that has fallen over the hallway.

On the way home, you don't bring it up. You are silent again; you hold your body in what looks to be a performed, anguished seethe, and I keep stealing glances at you as we walk. Years have passed, and I still remember it, a vivid, pleasurable return each time—those mysteries in you, the pain turned to brief power, probably overblown in my mind but always potent.

2

Hello, I just want to say if I was merastically chosen as one of the lucky few. You would definitely have one very entertàining show. Don't take my word for it. Please call anyone who personally knows me. If you find your self on a very lenghty call. Don't be alarmed. You c theres nothing special about me other than having a very unique personality. Life stories that are a very entertaining to say the least, also hàrd to believe, my over the top passion\ personality\very all in attitude along with outside the box thinking. Has always been both a we3kness and a strength. My love for outdoors and ability to bring thing To light Has always been the most visible well received character list so call please.

—from www.castingcallhub.com

I would say that we're both obsessed with the actual, or at least the actualish. This is strange because we have both dedicated our lives to art forms that will never achieve anything close to that effect. You're a stage actress, which artistically is most closely related, I think, to the sand painting that Tibetan monks do— everything is exactly as it is for just a moment, and then it's gone. When I go to see your shows, I never know how to answer with any certainty on the way home when you ask how this performance was different from the last. Or if you were closer to something right, something real. Even though the realness existed in the moment, all-consuming, it's impossible to say after the fact. I liked it, decided to believe it, registered and treasured gestures that felt recognizably yours, and then the whole thing disappeared.

I write about real things, but of course there's a limit. Write about what you're looking at and you probably fuck it up; write about a memory and you're probably a liar. The only thing that is incontrovertibly actual, actual in that it remains so, is the ink or the pixel, whatever fingerprint of content I can get. My words are pasted into endless, nonphysical space, and I search there to see if they've been shared forward into the nothing—so many events played out in front of me reduced to selfish squiggles, pleasurably decipherable at best.

The history of filmed narrative, on the other hand, is the thrill of the actual. Some part of any shot was really there, and stays captured there—a person really stood in that place, saying those words, and the proof is on the screen in front of us. That's why we watch, and that's why everyone watches, and that's why everyone always has. Actually, let me back up. I've realized that's why *I* watch, and maybe you feel that way, too. Even in our weekly allegiance to something fantastical like *Game of Thrones,* the actual is part of the draw for me. Regardless of the CGI dragons, the place they call Westeros on the show exists outside of the story. It's the Croatian coast, or Malta—someplace Mediterranean, anyway; I remember waiting through the credits once to find out. The point is, it exists. You can go there. Every grain of sand is a grain of sand in the world that we live in, and every footprint made by every actor is a true indentation among a million grains. I like to fantasize that—depending on the winds and the remoteness of the location—the footprint could still be there, and, hey, we've been talking about taking a big trip.

When we watch the many reruns that we watch, we are revisiting a reality preserved just as it was. The people on-screen, actors or nonactors, were in an exact place in an exact moment, and there they are still, over and over again, on demand. This

is, to me, enormously reassuring—like hikers' cairns, marking
the course of a life lived mostly stationary. How many times have
we argued over whose impression is accurate and then rushed to
replay the scene for proof of exactly what was? Sure, there are dif-
fering interpretations, meanings to find, tastes to adhere to, but
beneath all that the action happened as it happened. They spoke,
they moved, just so: there it is; we can see it. That feeling is its
own kind of drama, more powerful sometimes than any plot.

Remember when we followed Tony Shalhoub down Sixth Avenue for like half a mile? Kept a few yards back and just watched
him walk? He was drinking an iced coffee and talking on his
cell phone. Black jeans, black T-shirt. We were transfixed by the
act of seeing him, and it's not like either of us were ever huge
Monk fans, and honestly, I hated *Wings.* But we'd seen him so
many times on-screen, and then seeing him offscreen confirmed
how real he'd been every time we watched him. Does that make
sense?

Tony Shalhoub looks exactly like Tony Shalhoub. I whispered
that to you, or something like it, and I remember we giggled
like coconspirators on an idea not yet fully conceived. He really,
really did look like that.

The first scrap of American film ever copyrighted and projected
for the public was five seconds of a man sneezing. On the surface,
it seems an arbitrary subject. I like to imagine how many ideas
must have been discarded before they settled on it.

A man simply standing? Too lifeless.

Talking? With no sound, how compelling could that be?

In an embrace? Too staged; forcing the humanity a bit.

Too much action could be overwhelming (and indeed, about a
year later, French audiences fled from the Lumière brothers' short
film of a train pulling into a station).

So instead the great ancestor of all American screen characters is Fred Ott, a tech who happened to work at Edison's laboratory in New Jersey, a good sport with a photogenic mustache, who agreed to take snuff and then sneeze in front of a giant camera. For that one act he remains a celebrity, though some might also recognize him from his follow-up film, made a few months later: *Fred Ott Holding a Bird.* I can watch him right now, a piece of cultural history presented free of charge by the Library of Congress.

He's dressed nicely for the occasion; he wears a tie and a suit jacket. He's still in his overcoat, too, which lends a certain feeling of the haphazard, the uncomposed—if this were staged, it's tempting to think, surely he would have been there for a while and he would have taken off his overcoat. But the staging is apparent in other ways. Ott induces his own casual behavior. When he snorts the snuff, an impish expression turns up his lips. He is aware of being watched, and excited to perform, and all that is conveyed in less than a second, because then his head rears back and his eyes close and he sneezes in the manner in which I'm sure he always sneezed; it's a perfectly reasonable sneeze, one that anyone anywhere will forever be able to recognize as a sneeze. He seems to look at the camera, just for a moment; then the film cuts to black.

There were no TVs then, of course, but there were also no movie theaters, and the viewing experience more closely resembled television's. One by one, viewers were allowed to peep into the little windows at the top of Kinetoscope machines to watch the image of this stranger, this neighbor, sneezing. For five seconds, they were alone with him. They saw him perform a tiny part of the reality that they participated in each day without questioning it. How many times had they watched a sneeze? How many times had they sneezed while being watched, unaware of the gaze upon them, never considering how it might look in those moments when their eyes closed and they lost control, head whipping forward, air and snot rocketing from their nostrils?

I like to believe that, up until right then, the line between performer and audience had never been so blurred. Or the line between the staged and the truthful. Or the line between participating artist and objectified subject. Not even the line between art and commerce, because the whole point of the film was to advertise what Edison could do with this new technology: We can capture reality unawares; look at this willing reality we've captured! Five seconds in the dark, with Fred Ott sneezing the way we all sneeze.

Ask me the most memorable moment I have ever seen on TV, and I will tell you about an early season of *Survivor,* a show I never even liked that much.

This bald guy, a rock climber, a ziplock-bag-of-almonds type, was helping to build a fire on a beach on a South Asian island, and suddenly some smoke blew up into his face. He accidentally inhaled and it knocked him out. He fell forward into the flames and then the cameras rushed to him. He was burned so bad he was melted. His fingers were shapeless, beginning to stick together. What a scream he screamed. I was maybe fifteen, and I'd never heard a scream like that. In my memory, I still haven't again. This was back when the novelty of unvarnished pain was surprising. Fifteen years later, it's no longer surprising but the appeal remains.

I remember how aware I was of how much I was drawn to the scene when I first watched it. I loved it because I saw the guy hurt, and I saw him dealing with hurt, and I saw other people confronting the rawness of what it's like to be around someone so hurt. He lurched toward the ocean and came out of the water like a blacksmith's iron, and again the camera closed. He sat in the water some more to cool, and I could hear him say, "It keeps intensifying," his face scrunched.

Medics broke the fourth wall and entered the shot, conveniently labeled on the bottom of the screen in the show's trademark jaunty yellow font. They put him on a stretcher, and he screamed until they drugged him. Then came quick cuts to the other cast members hugging one another, crying, hyperventilating. Then he was put in the helicopter, almost passed out, and the show aired his final words of the season: *You guys know what's right; you know what to do.*

His eyes were pale blue and stoned cloudy, weirdly beautiful. He looked right at the camera and showed us that beauty. I remember thinking he didn't have to look at the camera, but he did—maybe someone asked him to, or maybe it felt like the only appropriate thing. Maybe he was lucid enough to reach for one more moment when he was centered in the shot. Then the doors closed on him as his eyes drifted shut.

His fellow cast members waved and blew him kisses, made ridiculous proclamations:

We love you. (They'd only known him for a week.)

We'll catch some fish for you, buddy. (What?)

Looking back, what's striking is that at the same time the show was forced to expose the beams of its structure and break from its coherent, constructed-yet-unacknowledged narrative, it also transcended into a far better piece. Seeing the crew react, seeing a helicopter appear that had always been available, somehow only heightened the intensity. The cast members, these "survivors," instantly weakened, looking right at the camera for help: Fix this, please; survival is terrifying. The set felt like a set, not an endless expanse of coastal Filipino wilderness but a stamp of land painstakingly selected, contained, and constantly monitored. And when the careful construction was laid bare, it wasn't a disappointing revelation—the show was free to become about itself as a show, a vehicle for something horrible and human, about danger and pain and a person's willingness to display that for whatever reasons.

I remember calling my parents into the room as the bald man writhed. None of us could look away. I remember feeling lucky to be witnessing what I was witnessing.

I recently reread a piece by Andy Denhart, one of the few television critics who seems to actually like reality, or at least is willing to explore how such shows might succeed. For him, success hinges on *the promise of consequence.*

In Denhart's reading, those who perform are saying, "Look at what I risk for you." And those of us watching are saying, "I want to see you get hurt." Or, "I at least want to know that it's a probability that you'll get hurt." This is a pretty common idea—how I assume people watch NASCAR to wait for a crash, or how I know I watch Internet clips of a moron about to jump off a house onto a trampoline because that trampoline is for sure going to break. Safe, primed, narrativeless vessels for our worst impulses.

But those are moments set up explicitly for horror. We look because we're fairly certain something has just gone wrong, or will very soon. That's not poignant or potent, necessarily. It's just confirming a pleasurable expectation, scratching an itch. I'm not trying to separate myself from that instinct; I just think it's different from what I'm getting at here. It's a shallow pleasure, born from a guarantee. It leaves no room for *anything* besides the promised carnage.

I didn't come to this *Survivor* episode for pain, not exactly, and that's not even why I return to it. I return for how quickly the drama plays out, and how ever ready the apparatus of humanity is to perform it compellingly. I return to the evergreen realization that if anyone allows themselves to be watched for a decent period of time, *something* will really hurt and, even though pain is forever imminent, that hurt will be a surprise. This becomes its own narrative: the diffuse potential for something to go wrong, for a seam to crack on the carefully composed surface of the person or show, and also the potential for those in trouble to reach so gracefully for words and actions to express the trouble, as though those words and actions had always been there waiting.

In conversations about the stageyness of reality, people like us, the fans among groups of ardent nonfans, are invariably asked how we find authentic emotion in there among the artifice, the gloss. But that's a question you can ask anyone about anything that moves them. Emotion doesn't dissipate amid the stageyness. Whenever a stage is built and people are asked to stand on it, there remains a pulsing unknown. Will the stage break? Will the people told to stand on it break down because of the glare on them? And how will they try to save themselves while I watch? Every moment is weighted with threat.

The fire-falling scene is surprisingly hard to find, but I find a clip on YouTube. It's being used as a music video for someone's ambient, didgeridoo-driven house music. The comments on the video range from the obvious (*Ouch*) to the pacifying (*I know him and he's a great guy and his hands are okay now*) to the very specifically vengeful (*He killed a female pig the episode before this; got what was coming to him*). People take what they want from the material.

I take those eyes before they shut. I take the way he seems to acknowledge the camera on him and speaks to it, to me. There is so much feeling there, offered up. And if it's offered up, is it wrong to accept that feeling as a gift? Is it, instead, just a guy living up to the duties in the exploitative contract he signed? Maybe. But then the narrative fills in around him—compatriots who love him in that moment because what else can they say? Who promise to catch him some fish to eat upon his impossible return.

Robert Flaherty is one of the founding fathers of documentary, one of the first to film a narrative of another person's life. He became an icon of the form the moment he voyaged to the Arctic to turn an Inuit man into a tragic hero in *Nanook of the North*. The word most often used to describe his work is *ethnofiction*, which has mostly fallen out of fashion. Ethnofiction attempts to express the uneasy combination of the anthropological and the contrived within a film—asking a group of people to serve as themselves and representatives of other people like them, performing a version of their truth on the fly, at an outsider's conception and direction.

I've been reading some of Flaherty's craft essays, little missives from a director trying to figure out something no one had figured out yet. I like this passage:

> *When shooting a scene I always look at it through several different lenses, and frequently I shoot a subject with different lenses from the same position. There is usually one shot that is right. The greater the focal length of the lens, the smaller the field, and, as a consequence, with the longer telephoto, the photographer is easily able to eliminate unnecessary details and to give his picture the emphasis he wants . . . good photography, like good writing, is largely a matter of emphasis.*

I know there's nothing particularly revelatory about this statement now, but I like the frankness with which he wrote in 1934 about a topic that has since become so shrill and convoluted. I like the idea of life rolling in front of him when that was still an uncharted experience to have, and then him calling cut, finding a better lens, a more intimate, more voyeuristic one, through which to see how he wanted to see, demanding that his subject do it again.

In the same essay, he talks about the long-focus lens providing him with *the elimination of self-consciousness,* in reference to *Man of Aran,* my favorite of his movies, about the people who scraped away at survival on a desolate island off the west coast of Ireland.

An Aran Islander, Flaherty wrote, like Nanook, like anyone, felt freer to be naturally himself when the camera was farther from him. He could get used to being a person *and* a subject. Again, no great revelation. But, even through the paltry technology available to him, Flaherty was playing around with what it means to *be,* naturally, with a camera lurking, how to coax out or conjure that *being* and then capture it. What it might be used for.

I first watched the shark fishing scenes of *Aran* in an enormous lecture hall in college. Flaherty had to instruct his subjects on how to enact this tradition because they hadn't needed shark oil in decades. I don't remember if I knew that as I watched; what I remember is how the waves moved in front of the camera, and how that made me feel like the camera and I were also bobbing hard on the chop, the way a stopped train feels like it's moving backward when another train passes outside the window. I was seduced by that first, near-accidental sleight of hand. The waves swelled at the lens and then ebbed away, then a cut to a crew trying to pull a boat safely to shore, then another wave, from another time maybe, then back to the people, a family scrambling down the black slate seashore to drag a straggler out of the water, then crash, then people, then crash, and on and on like that. The wave means danger. Even if we don't see it actually doing much damage, it could—there's the wave and then there are the people in the same physical space on-screen: a narrative.

When the last person is helped out of the water and fishing nets are collected where they've washed up, the shot changes. The camera is steady, clearly safe, shooting from a vantage point high up on the shore, but zoomed in on the faces and torsos of a father, mother, and son as they drag a valuable net to safety. The audio is dubbed; we see their mouths moving over what I imagine to be breathless, indecipherable Gaelic, but the sound is clear: English spoken with a decently performed brogue, away from the action.

When the son, centered in the shot, looks up at his father, a man's voice says to him, *We're all right now.* Then the mother, trailing: *We are, thank God.* Then the scene follows them along the shore—parents watching their son run ahead, holding each other's hand, letting go, then clasping again, as strings swell.

In class, after the screening, there was an argument about who actually spoke the dialogue, and who wrote it, and whose point of view it expressed; if any of it meant anything, filtered through so much stylized deception. I believe the phrase "classic noble-savage horseshit" was used by a pale guy in a bowler hat in the front row. Most people agreed with him, and I figured I would, too, but I didn't at all. My instinct to bristle with journalistic indignation, to aim for the comfort of the moral high ground, had disappeared into pathos.

I thought that if Flaherty himself wrote the words, then he meant them. He *felt* them. *I* felt them. A close-up of a wave crashing, then a close-up of three faces, each with a seeming lack of self-consciousness, the way he wanted it, each formerly in danger and now briefly, blissfully, safe—what better to think or say over that shot than *We're all right now?* When someone we love looks at us, whoever we are, wherever we are, what do we want that look to say other than that right now there is no wave crashing?

This morning we were walking the dog, and I was saying how my T-shirt felt tighter than it used to, and that made me acutely aware of my fatness, like ground meat inexpertly fed into too small a sausage casing, a phrase I've honed and used often. You didn't acknowledge my statement; you just said that you, in fact, could no longer bear even to look at yourself. Really, you said, it feels disgusting to be you.

I didn't say but nearly said that just because you're a woman doesn't mean you get some kind of exclusive ownership over hat-ing yourself. That's not the kind of thing I want to hear myself say out loud, but I think it sometimes—a panicked reach to validate the volume of my emotion next to yours. We stayed silent for a few blocks, then talked about the neighbors who don't put their bins back after trash day and how such recklessness can make the whole neighborhood look unloved. Imagine caring so little, we said.

Last night we jostled for mirror time with the IKEA-bought naked bulbs that frame the vanity turned up to full brightness. We touched our own bare torsos and said, Look at this, and then, You're not looking; you can't even bring yourself to look.

That's not true, I said first. I love the way you look.

And then you said, I love the way *you* look.

And then, in unison, I don't believe you.

This is a conversation we have more than maybe any other, and it seems more constant than it used to, but maybe it was always like that. Repetition of emotion does nothing to dull it. We who see each other every day demand each other to look again; we say that we are exhibiting our flaws and we ask each other to confirm them, but I at least am sucking in; I am trying to look anything but what I think I look like, and if you ever told me what I imagine to be the truth I would be unspeakably hurt.

The greatest intimacy I can think of is allowing one's self to be seen. Naked, especially, but also just in general, bared in any way. The first girl who ever saw me naked—this was in high school—lay next to me on a tiny lake beach the day after I lost my virginity to her (she not to me; it mattered at the time). She wasn't looking at me; that's what I remember the most. I was lying next to her, bared, and she was looking out at other bodies, watching them run and dive and surface in still water. They didn't even notice her watching; they didn't seem to think about being watched at all. I picked a fight later that night, and in the heat of it I said something about her being unwilling to look at me, and she said, *I've* never *complained about your body,* and it's still the most hurtful thing anyone has ever said to me—the way she spoke the words, the self-congratulation and pity in her tone.

Sometimes I think we work because we understand the stakes of eyes on body, everything that is risked and everything we plead for. How many times the same question can be asked without losing its importance. When we watch together, each alone in our own eyes, our own breathing, I know we share that.

Early on in his book *Ways of Seeing,* John Berger describes the nude portrait like this: *To be naked is to be oneself. To be nude is to be seen naked by others and yet not recognized for oneself. A naked body has to be seen as an object in order to become a nude. . . . Nudity is placed on display. To be naked is to be without disguise.*

Now I want to talk about Mercedes Javid, whom everyone calls MJ. MJ is a wealthy Angelena of Persian descent, and for these demographical reasons she and her posse star in a show called *Shahs of Sunset.* We like her and feel as if we know her a bit. We know these details at least: She's a realtor who rarely seems to work but loves to party. She can often be rude to female friends but is fiercely loyal to her gay best friend, Reza (despite the fact that, at least to me, he seems to turn on her way too easily and somehow never gets called on it, which is bullshit). Also, she has been called fat many times on national television and in various cruel corners of the Internet.

We enjoy (have enjoyed for four seasons now) the abandon with which she eats and drinks on camera, and the delicate and transparent balance of bullying and pained sensitivity that she displays. I have begun to think that she behaves in ways that I like to believe I don't but probably often do—aggressive, chest-puffing performances of shamelessness that are rooted in insecurity. She can be confounding, hilarious, pitiable, unforgivable, all in the span of a minute-long lunch chat.

In one brief scene of *Shahs,* MJ poses for boudoir portraits. She tells the camera, tells us, that these photos are a gift for her new man, a for-his-eyes-only reward. Specious premise, yes. The result is that we watch her nearly nude, posing for a private reveal. We have what somehow feels like unique access. We do not see what the photographer sees, we see (or are made to think we see) what is behind that pose: the self. She's posing, after all, to be desirable for this one particular dude, but not us—we're just there, leaning in, seeing her effort directed toward a different lens, effort for him and also herself.

She holds one arm across her breasts (so large that their large-ness is kind of a running theme of the show) in a manner that is a practiced homage to Marilyn Monroe and every other bombshell who has posed this way. The photographer's murmured encour-agement is constant. MJ takes a strong, practical tone and says, *I want a lot of length from my chin to my breasts.* From the corner of the room, champagne in hand, a friend yells, *You don't want your tits in your chin; we get it!* MJ laughs, a glamorous guffaw. At one point she offers a breathy question—*So what am I supposed to do?*—which is meant, I think, to seem falsely demure, like mak-ing fun of demure women, but is, at its core, a bit demure.

Her body is made up and oiled, her hair styled and sprayed into immobility, except for one strand that arcs down to her chin. Her body has changed a lot over the course of the show, due to a combination of diet changes and plastic surgery, and the ratio between the two is a hotly contested topic. We have seen these changes, each accompanied by pointed commentary, a reliable conflict generator in any scene. Her body has been made, very publicly, an object to both celebrate and defend. The contrived scenario of the filmed photo shoot, the double exhibition, feels like the ultimate defense.

At the end of the scene, MJ, wrapped in a silver negligee, leans over the camera screen, surrounded by friends, photographers, and makeup artists, and says, *I'm so pretty*. She says it with both certainty and surprise. This is the moment that feels most naked to me, so brief. This is a second portrait, that of a woman viewing her original portrait and finding defiant pleasure in the image, performing her pleasure for a second set of cameras, for a second audience, one made to feel as though the performance has ended.

We didn't say anything about the scene when we watched it because what is there to say? It's not exactly easy to talk about finding value, maybe even comfort, captured in the image of someone else's staged narcissism. And what else to call it? She was on TV flaunting herself, framing herself just so—how can anything be captured when it's being given away? She is *professionally* bared, and what an easy job that is to scorn.

Still, there's triumph in the gesture; that's what I thought as we watched. Triumph that also felt like intimacy, since she let us see and feel along with her, even if that intimacy came planned, edited, painstakingly produced. I let myself think that I found her there, buried in the pose of self-observation. I was moved. She not only showed herself; she showed herself seeing herself— each layer a risk and thrill. You cannot be more exposed than that, I thought.

By a pond, on a little patch of beach, on the first vacation we ever took on our own together:

It was a Massachusetts kettle pond—I made us drive dirt roads through the woods to find it, an Emerson homage dulled a bit by reliance on GPS. When we found it, we were the only people in sight. It wasn't high season, still cheap, chilly and overcast.

We stood next to each other on the little patch of beach, a moment that felt instantly distinct, in its silence and slight adventure and proximity to nature. I began to take off all my clothes, sucking in as my shirt came off, running my fingers over the ribs I was working so hard to make apparent. Goose bumps hardened my skin, which I liked. I raised my eyebrows at you and you were reluctant, but you joined me in stripping.

We said *Brrr* to each other, and you wrapped your arms around yourself, but I pried them off and replaced them with mine. We hugged close and I looked down at the space between us, and at the places where our flesh pressed. I ran to the water and stumbled in. From the cold, I begged you to join me, and you did, slowly, your body in perfect pantomimed resistance as more of it disappeared into the murk.

You said, "This is kind of gross," your teeth chattering, but you stayed with me.

We told each other we were beautiful, and our protests back were half-assed, for once. We settled into the water and shivered, and I tried to keep smiling. Then you gasped and pointed past me at people milling on the docks below the fancy houses on the opposite shore, looking our way. You fled, and I watched the water drip from your ass. I held my hand over my dick on the way out, and you laughed at the goofiness of that pose as you tried to cover yourself with crossed arms. I moved my hand, briefly.

"Who cares?" I tried to say like I meant it. "Let them look."

We sprinted to the car. We sat hidden behind the doors, scrubbing off wet sand. I was already thinking of how we might remember this scene, which couldn't have lasted more than ten minutes. I wanted it so badly to be preserved as a happy memory, but I didn't know how to say that, or why it mattered.

3

{REQUEST FOR AUDITION}:

Growing up I was always the shy and quiet kid. I never considered
myself beautiful, and I feel like the opportunity would give me the
boost I need to help with my self-esteem and confidence issues. If
considered for a position I would give it my all at all times.

—from www.castingcallhub.com

When I feel guilty about all the watching, what makes me most
uncomfortable is the way other people look in front of the TV.
They look vegetative, near dead. The body and the mind seem
to be wholly at rest. Despite the fact that this is so often how we
look, and despite the fact that I enjoy it, I have these flashes of
shame; it's hard to allow myself to embrace seeing you that way,
acknowledging the joy in the image. I admire you onstage, in
workout clothes, on the phone with your boss carefully enunciat-
ing your words, biting your lip when you read—each of these is,
in some way, a pose of work.

Once, when I was a boy, my mother told me that scientists said
you burn more calories when you're sleeping than when you're
watching TV, because even sleeping is more active than watching. This was the ultimate condemnation. I've never checked on
whether she was telling the truth, but I have remembered the
claim and relay it often, the information almost always unwel-
come. She said it to get me to go to bed during a *Real World*
marathon, and it worked. TV was, technically, making me fatter
than I would be as a boy who turned off the TV and got a good
night's sleep. I would never look like the people I was watching

if I kept watching them. That night in bed I tried to think of bad things as I began to dream, to ensure an optimal amount of tossing and turning. At least a nightmare would be a workout. At least I would be doing something.

The first TV show I remember seeking out, watching in reruns every day after school, was *American Gladiators.* That can't be an accident. All that accusatory, Reaganish optimism. All that slick, hard flesh. Blade and Gemini and Nitro flexing and taunting for so many years, wearing American flag–themed unitards and telling the story of the physical dominance that hard work can provide, looking into the camera and telling me—fat, inert, little-boy me—that this was manhood to emulate. Sometimes, by the end of an episode, I'd find my whole body clenched, as if that were a type of participation. A commercial would jostle me out of this fugue state, and I'd feel some combination of exhaustion, inspiration, and shame, a physical sensation that is still quite recognizable.

The joy of watching reality TV has always fitted neatly into that dumbest cultural cliché: *guilty pleasure.* The guilt here references the participation in something so lowbrow, so vapid. But to me that's always a less vivid guilt than what I feel as a watcher of other peoples' actions—heightened awareness of my lack of effort, when those performing are, at the very least, effortful. Whatever the cultural value attached to the people on-screen, they're *doing* something. I'm watching them *do,* and in watching the content of their lives I'm sacrificing some potential content in my own. I don't think I'm escaping into other peoples' efforts; I think that watching them makes me stew in what I'm not doing, what that nothingness feels like. I could be what I am seeing, or maybe I couldn't, and maybe I don't even want to be that, but ultimately how can anyone know—there are so many ways to be.

There are so many ways to be, so how does one begin? We've never spoken that question, but it's the one I feel most often, or if not most often, at least most acutely. It's the one that can never really be answered, and maybe that's why it's so easy to stay still, wrapped up in the non-act of watching someone else try.

I've been trying to find scholarship on reality TV (looking for gravitas, I guess). There's a growing body of work, particularly from media and gender studies scholars like Brenda Weber, Helen Wood, and Beverley Skeggs. Many essays I've found, though, lead me back to a cultural critic named Mark Andrejevic, who wrote about the genre in the early-to-mid-2000s, when it was really beginning to boom and scholars were just starting to pay attention. Andrejevic dubbed the form *the work of being watched.*

He saw it as the perfect storm of an alienated, subjugated labor force. The workers provide no valued skill; instead all they have to give are their lives, until life and work are interchangeable, both edging toward worthless.

Of course, I got huffy when I read Andrejevic, and I think it was more than run-of-the-mill defensiveness. It felt like he just didn't see what I think (or hope) we see on-screen. Written into his argument is a crucial assumption about the reality performer, one that has persisted: she is not *doing* anything. Instead, something is being done to her; specifically, she is being watched by people like us. She's just living, existing on-screen, and she can't exist artfully, or even intentionally. So the performer's contribution is *only* sacrificial, like selling a kidney, if the kidney had no biological value to anyone.

To Andrejevic all reality TV does is provide *the invitation . . . to become famous by play-acting the role of the celebrity.* This means that we *focus attention on the* apparatus *of celebrity production rather than the intrinsic qualities of the star. The aura of the individual talent is undermined.*

He frames reality stars as the embodiment of Daniel Boorstin's warnings from the 1960s: a coming culture of manufactured illusions, creating a new celebrity monster *who is known for his well-knownness.* Which, it's assumed, is a universally bad thing.

I'm trying to reconcile this with how I understand the world, and I think Andrejevic gives a bit too much credit to the notion of talent, and way too much to that of celebrity. Do they have that much to do with each other? Did people care about James Dean because he was a genius? Or put it this way: What is a celebrity other than someone whom many other people give a shit about? If one succeeds in becoming seen, then how are they playacting the role of celebrity as opposed to just being one?

Our stars—the housewives, the Kardashians, et cetera—are the most successful examples of playacting celebrity; they do so in service of constant, often brilliant entrepreneurship, but the entrepreneurship exists only because of the playacting. All this focus on them as mere capitalizing existers, instead of actors, and the one thing that we see them acting at is the only thing they actually are. It becomes impossible to talk about whether they're doing a good job at the thing they're attempting if nobody seems to think they're attempting anything. More than a decade after Andrejevic wrote these words, it's still hard to make a distinction between who is talented at public being and who isn't.

Fellow media scholars Beverley Skeggs and Helen Wood have pointed to the anger that persists toward successful reality performers, an anger reserved almost exclusively for female stars: *What seems* most *distasteful about the apparent success of these women is their ability to use the performances of their bodies, gestures and language* as *themselves to their own material advantage.*

It's an ever-present double bind: How can they deserve to be successful for performing nothing but what they are? But then look at them, successful, performing—what is that?

Skeggs and Wood point out that even when our stars are well

compensated for their performances, their pay exists outside of any performer's union. No matter how much they are of them-selves, no matter the life and emotion they provide and profit from, there isn't a name or institutional solidarity for their labor. Instead, the old invitation is there to reduce their actions to nothing but existence; the easy write-off that people need *some-thing* to look at—anything, anyone. Just a body willing to be depleted by hungry eyes.

I can remember the first time I watched you. You were smoking with your friend in a gazebo outside your dorm. Your dorm was in between my dorm and the dorm where most of my friends lived, so often I would hurry by you, sober and left out, then return, stumbling home, hours later. By that time you were usu-ally out there alone. There was a light with moths in it that cast shadows over the lit part of the grass.

You now tell people that even when we first looked at each other, you had inklings of what was to come. I say that when I think about it, I sort of felt the same way. I am definitely lying, and I'm pretty sure you are, too. Narratives, even the flimsiest ones, are comforting.

I can't remember much about the first time we fucked; only that we did and I loved it, and felt the instant need to try to describe and commemorate it, even just to myself. I wrote a poem about the experience that managed to include nothing sexy and leaned heavily on the image of waking up to a surprise snowfall (I blame Keats), letting that sit on the page as a metaphor for something. (Ejaculation? I don't know.) I remember the poem only slightly better than the act it clumsily commemorated. It's hard to acknowledge that spontaneous action must become rooted in meaning after the fact.

Sometimes I like to think that every moment we've lived

together is valuable. That if one second fell away, part of the meaning of all of it would be gone. Sometimes I'm terrified of the idea of remembering all the moments until each begins to sag under the weight of collective inspection.

Here are some things that my students have called Kim Kardashian, either in casual conversation, a theoretical classroom debate, or an assigned essay:

Useless. Dumb. Rich. Spoiled. Just kind of a selfish bitch. The thing that makes me wish I wasn't born when I was born. A glorified porn star. Famous for being stupid. Famous for being greedy. Probably a bad mom. Talentless. A bad role model. The enemy of all feminists.

This isn't a trying-to-be-highbrow thing. In general, they seem to find the concept of varied brows to be pointless. I've received literary-analysis papers (students' choice of topic!) on Nicholas Sparks novels. I had three students answer my standard introductory question, "Who is your favorite author?," with "James Patterson," and another tell me that studying Shakespeare over *Divergent* is pretentious, academic bullshit left over from dinosaur professors who don't know how to have fun. They exhibit little of the obnoxious desire we had to pledge allegiance to art that was unheard of or, more important, *difficult,* as if that might validate their own perspectives. Most of them don't even seem to be going through a smoking-makes-me-look-deeper phase.

They like vampires, wizards. They like fantastical tales whose endings you can predict from the first sentence or shot. But for the most part, they don't like Kim, who is not a vampire (despite a good deal of metaphorical accusation) and whose ending is still a mystery.

Before I knew who Kim Kardashian was, when I was the same age as some of my students are now, I watched her fuck Ray J,

Brandy's little brother, in their self-produced, then stolen, piece of erotica, *Kim K Superstar*. Or, to be more exact, I sort of knew who she was, and that was crucial. She was recognizable-ish, a peripheral friend on Paris Hilton's show, and therefore already famous enough for the implied desire to be more famous than she was. I remember you showing me her picture online and having some recognition of her face. I remember, too, that she sued the company that released the tape, but on the heels of Paris's star-making sex tape, as her own grew even more popular, nobody believed that Kim wasn't in on it. What a trauma that must have been for her, yet all I remember anyone feeling was the giddiness of the argument over whether she had always wanted to be seen like that, the excitement of pausing the video to try to pinpoint falseness or intentionality, a simultaneous lust, distrust, slight pity, fascination.

The sex tape itself is long and mostly boring. Kim and Ray J are on vacation, and they film each other by the pool, and then lying on an overpillowed bed in complementary terry-cloth robes. Ray J holds the camera while they kiss; his tongue is prominent in the shot. He sort of laps at her. His eyes are wide open the whole time, and at a certain point Kim opens hers as she's breathing between tongue lappings. You can see her see herself, I assume in the little camera screen that's turned back at them. There's nervousness in her eyes, what I always took to be a brief instinct to resist the recording, or at least feign resistance, but there's also the thrill of how she looks, the way her lips are moving as she kisses back, the way the camera angle stretches down along her neck to her clavicle, to the swell of her breasts barely held in rigid, tannish lingerie.

Later she's on her stomach and he's on top of her, and she looks back, and again, there are her eyes on any of us who might ever watch. The bed is noisy, and over that noise her voice rises, the nasal and perpetually adolescent whine that would soon become famous, hated, parodied: *Oh shit, baby, I'm gonna come, I'm gonna come, I'm coming.*

Sometimes I wonder if my students would feel differently about Kim if they'd met her at the start of everything she would become. It's easy to write off those who have already achieved notoriety, without seeing how they made themselves, without that generating narrative of striving, however superficial the impetus to strive may have been. It's easy to pretend, then, that there isn't any narrative at all.

When I watched Kim's sex tape, there were already ads running for the first season of *Keeping Up with the Kardashians*. I watched the premiere episode of that show, like millions of others, with the sound of her narrating her own orgasm fresh in my mind, and I remember thinking of that over the credits, as cutesy whistle music played and her family assembled. Kim entered last, the joke being that she wanted all the attention. She stood in front of her siblings and vamped for the camera. And then, as they complained about her screen hogging, her already recognizable voice intoned: *Jealous?*

She was beginning a story about reinvention and ambition that has played out for more than a decade. I remember watching and thinking I could feel her testing what exposure is like, the rush and weight and danger of being looked at and just how watchable she could be, as she navigated herself from stolen intimacies to constant self-branding, committed to showing every benign and shameful and pained detail along the way.

The best way I can think to describe Kim's behavior on-screen is empowered desperation, which I guess is another way of saying ambition all over again. She vacillates between fearlessness and self-deprecation, an amateurism both performed and authentic, that somehow still exists even though she is so far from being an amateur. Now when her origins (the origins of her public self) are mentioned, the video is often the final point made in an argument against her cultural value that usually includes some euphemism for the word *whore*. It's an argument that hinges on her being the kind of girl who is willing to do anything, an argument that was maybe never true but that has always made it hard to look away from her.

I like to wallow in the exhausting triumph of her continued watchability. How we've been there from the very beginning, and seen how she has wrangled control of her narrative, kept it pulsing with change. I like to trace the sheer prolificacy of how many selves she is willing to put in front of us—the budding diva, the harsh sister doling out tough love, the mom, the spoiled rich kid, the pragmatic richer adult, the weeper, the hard-ass, the mogul, the ditzy, the cold, the naked, the briefly sweet, the unexpectedly prudish, the controlling, the exposed, the protective wife, the muse. I am different now than when I first watched her. You are, too, and that's part of the watching. I want different things from my life, I want to be seen differently, and so there's pleasure to be found in watching her make those same demands of millions of people. How many years has she been demanding that we follow her, shifting, beckoning to us, saying, I am this now?

In 1990, in his essay "E Unibus Pluram," David Foster Wallace wrote: *Television, from the surface on down, is about desire.* At the time he was right, and in many ways he still is, but his TV = desire equation also seems pretty quaint now—bright lights making the lonely watcher want to buy, a one-way relationship. Now there's Kim, who not only makes us desire but shows us her own; her desire is the mechanism, the show, the connection, the mirror. Her desire is more interesting than the desire a watcher might feel for her or her life; she seems always to have known that.

Last Saturday you and I watched the episode where Kim sees yet another fertility doctor because she wants a second kid with Kanye, and this is one desire that seems increasingly out of reach. It was a quiet, flannelly afternoon. We'd just eaten grapefruits with those little serrated spoons we got from the wedding registry.

Kim's mother/manager (*momager,* in the contemporary professional vernacular) often accompanies her in doctor scenes, but in this one she's alone. She's wearing heavy makeup. She's newly blonde, in a simple T-shirt, trying on a weirdly Waspy maternal identity. As expected, things get difficult. The doctor drones on about the upcoming challenges, the bad percentages, and the camera settles on Kim's face as she twitches with nervous anger. She scratches her arm, then her back. In a close-up, we look to her makeup for some satisfying streaking, but there are no tears, just the effort against them, which feels more successfully emotional.

I'm so over it, she says slowly. *Like, I'm exhausted.*

She doesn't look at the doctor or the camera or the floor; she seems to look at nothing. We don't exactly pity her or understand her, but her clenched face, the way she is referencing quiet dismay, so far from the former desires of a contentedly childless adulthood that we have spent a decade watching (and living)— it's the welcoming expanse of the narrative that compels us. Her life, as ridiculous as it is, has moved the way ours do. Kind of. And it's not even fair to call her life ridiculous—it's a life.

Thirty seconds of situationally appropriate emotion, easy heartstring tugging, are anchored and bolstered by the many scenes of the many versions of herself that she's made indelible in our minds. She is in the middle of performing a whole life; I guess that's the best way to say it. A long, inevitable arc riddled with reinvention, and self-celebration and disappointment and reinvention again.

Someday she'll die, and I want to see it. I don't mean that as an insult.

For most of our lives together, anxiety woke me up early, while you slept in. When we were visiting family or friends were staying with us, I would spend hours with them in the morning talking but also listening for the sounds of you moving behind a closed door or up a flight of stairs. This could be stressful, as though I had to answer for why you were asleep, even though the only answer for why anyone is ever asleep is because they are. But I also felt a powerful closeness as I tiptoed in to wake you gently, like I was the translator between you and the morning, and I saw the first moment of so many of your days. You slept so heavily and your body radiated heat, and finally you'd blink up at me. We shared that.

Now you get up early for work, and I wake to the sound of you dressing or sighing as you scroll through e-mail. Sometimes you have to gently wake me, tapping your fingertips on my shoulder the way I once did for you. We both say that we can't believe how I slept in, that you're the one waking me, but it's been like this for more than a year. I don't know when the change will become unmentioned, then forgotten. I love opening my eyes now to you in purposeful movement, glancing at me in passing, but I also feel that something has been lost.

And lately I've been trying to remember the way you used to dance—the swift, graceful parabola of your hips, the sweat in your hair and on your shoulders, which are always bare in these memories. There was a time when you danced often, or it felt like it. You'd be at a place before I got there, and I'd walk in to the sight of you moving, cherish the moments before you caught my eyes.

You still dance, it's still beautiful, and I still watch you, though more often now you get me to join, and then have to edit yourself into some sync with my woodenness. You think I'm reluctant out of embarrassment, but it's more like nostalgia for what existed before my ubiquity caused a change in movement. When we dance, I'm buoyed despite myself, and I watch one strand of hair on your shoulder, and your best tattoo as you spin; it's a repeated deviation in the way we most often move together, a comforting eroticism.

But when I have to acknowledge the slight change, it becomes another little loss to mourn; not even a loss, really, just a near-imperceptible shift. Something lived and observed is gone; there's no concrete image of it, just the feeling of progress and absence.

4

{REQUEST FOR AUDITION}:

Hi,

I recently found internet fame through getting a guy to send me a pizza and it went viral all over social media. I have been told my whole life I need to get into reality tv, because I have such a strong character and I am a huge party girl and have an insane group of friends. If you decide to use me for any sort of reality tv, you will not regret it. I have millions of crazy stories and I am always the life of the party. I would love to get into reality tv. You can contact me at <hidden from public>

Here is a little story about my most recent internet fame trend: people.com/article/woman-uses-tinder-free-food

Thanks!

—from www.castingcallhub.com

The Real Housewives of Atlanta, Season 1, Episode 1: NeNe Leakes introduces herself: *If you just ask anybody about me,* pssh, *NeNe, she's* real *fun.*

She says this alone, after we've pulled out of the action. Her intro segment begins with a lot of really fast cuts of party shots—NeNe in a cocktail dress, hollering hello, hugging, waving, champagne poured until it spills, a brown hand with an enormous, multidiamond ring holding a Cosmopolitan, a white Rolls-Royce outside a castle-size McMansion. In the midst of the glamour montage, the image of NeNe alone is jarring. For just a second, everyone else is gone, and so are the cars, the cocktails, the jeweled hands entwining. Suddenly, NeNe is describing herself as this worldly party girl from a corner of her suburban kitchen, not particularly well lit, almost overwhelmingly familiar.

Her empty kitchen counter looks like the nicest option among the model kitchens set up in every store we went to when furnishing our starter home. The kind you can just point to and transpose into your house if that's the budget you're carrying. We weren't carrying that budget, but we made a point of saying we didn't want those antiseptic model kitchens anyway, and whisper-giggled at the people running their hands over the blandly shiny, dark granite counters, *ooh*ing at the clear glass cabinet doors. So *generic,* we told each other. All this money to look like your moneyed neighbor. We promised ourselves we would find reclaimed beach wood for the counters, an old ship light for a chandelier. And in the end, when none of that happened and we had to cash in a lot of Lowe's gift cards and fight our way through the IKEA parking lot, we still told each other that we weren't like the other young couples around us, who behaved so similarly—Ask anyone; we're fun.

As she introduces herself, NeNe has some candles lit behind her, shining off the countertop. The blinds are open, but nothing is visible in the window except the reflection of the dimly lit room. She sits on a stool in a gray cotton top, in a pose meant to suggest she's engaged in a casual conversation. She talks about money and access, about the Atlanta community of black opulence that has welcomed her (once a small-town nobody), that she shines in.

As she talks, we dip in and out of the glamour montage. Whenever the shot returns to NeNe alone, she looks unsettled, straining, apart, somehow, from the words she speaks and the scrolling clips of her life. She doesn't look like she feels particularly fun. Over the course of the episode she is repeatedly pained, or at least never at ease, more powerfully so because she refuses to acknowledge it.

We meet her husband through more quick cuts of a dinner scene—she orders mashed potatoes and bread for sides, and then he says quietly, *No bread,* and she cancels both orders of carbs and he nods, says, *Wonderful.* Then cut back to NeNe in her model kitchen, holding up her wedding ring—*Ten years of love, honey. Nothing but love and hard work.*

We're introduced to her son at his birthday party. NeNe stands with a plastic smile on, eyeing the camera as the boy screams that candle wax is getting on his cake—*Mom! Oh my God!* Then she stands silent as her husband presents the boy with a thousand-dollar check "toward your first investment," and the crowd applauds father and son. Then another cut back to NeNe in her kitchen, nodding extravehemently—*Gregg has* definitely *provided a good life for me and the kids.*

It's instantly obvious that NeNe is the most interesting, most gifted performer among the housewives. We could tell in real time, when we first met her—there was, well, *something* voraciously watchable about her. There still is. As I rewatch, I think the hook lies in her subtext, the gap between the life we're shown in montage and the life NeNe narrates from her kitchen, NeNe's resolute navigation of that gap, an unwillingness to be static or silent.

Throughout the episode, as she drives and mothers and gets made up and bullshits with friends, she is talking herself into our lives. No matter how bland the action, she voices herself toward vivid, unspecified dominance, a constant statement of her special self that also feels so recognizable—I think of De Niro in *Raging Bull* as he thumps his chest and says he's the boss. Pressure mounts.

At the end of the episode, NeNe arrives at a frenemy's party late, so as to create buzz. She's informed that she's not on the guest list. It's a simple plot construction—anticipation, anticipation, anticipation, then the cringey, satisfying twist. Really, nothing has happened other than the only thing that made sense. But it's NeNe and her rage that make the scene compelling, standing outside this giant home that looks like her own, barred from the scene inside. It's her face, as she relents and leaves. In the last shot of the episode she stands in the cold on the street, speaking with an operatic fury, both hopeless and forceful—*There's no forgiveness,* she tells us.

In *Camera Lucida,* Barthes coined the term *punctum* when trying to articulate the unintended (or maybe subconscious) personal bit of meaning that moves him in any photograph. The punctum is that stabbing sensation, that little unexpected detail that cuts deep, the wound—*this element which rises from the scene, shoots out of it like an arrow, and pierces me.*

When I first learned the term, it felt like the only thing that ever needed to be said, like a secret code I'd been given, along the lines of *agency* in my sophomore year of college. Such is the way—you learn that a word was oversaturated before you ever got to it, and then you have to relove it without the motivation of feeling unique. I didn't even come to punctum through Barthes; I came to it through Wayne Koestenbaum quoting Barthes in a master class in grad school. Koestenbaum preached punctum, and wrote about it often; a whole book, even, on every photograph taken of Jackie O. For him she was the punctum, the pain, the enigma: *No matter how incongruous the setting around her—the photograph always captured this mystery.*

Koestenbaum encouraged us fledgling writers to facilitate the punctum, and to look for it as readers of any text—that naked, subjective bit of hurt, the detail you can't help but notice, so hard to understand. It was this fault line that mattered more than anything: the place you had to find to show what makes you look, and what makes you writhe a little as you look.

The conversation exploded as we all tried to impress him with our punctum discoveries. It was, like so many writing classes, a taste contest, our observations standing in for ourselves. I mostly stayed quiet (a rarity) because all I could think of was NeNe— the furious force with which she speaks words that are meant to be cheerful; the backdrop that she advertises over the underlying anxiety that it's never enough; the way her posture, her face, her whole person convey this swirling, potent contradiction every time the camera reaches for her. It felt cheap to think of her then, one of those antipretentious stances that come back around to being extrapretentious. I'm wary of that now, too, still thinking about NeNe, finally writing about her—her magnetism doesn't need academic jargon to be validated. But it doesn't feel academic now; it's autobiographical. She's been in my life, and I still lean close to watch her, and when I first heard the word, I understood its meaning best when she embodied it.

When I left the master class, I returned home to you. We drifted back to the TV and watched NeNe (I think it was season 3 then, the divorce season), and there was that feeling. The shot, the stab—nothing that we could articulate, just simmering pleasurable tension that we shared, or it felt like we did.

She is repeatedly, glamorously wounded; refusing to wallow, but there are the wounds peeking out. Why look at anyone if not to see their wounds? To see their wounds and feel your own?

My father makes fun of what we watch. I mean, everyone we know makes fun of what we watch, but my father especially. My father's television watching is restricted to an obscene amount of Yankees games, and also Jets games on winter Sundays. Let's leave, for now, the narrative investment he makes in these real people performing in contrived scenarios, celebrities due to a wholly unnecessary skill set. Let's leave, for now, the fact that the Yankees arbitrarily don't allow their players to wear beards because that is not "the Yankee way," and that my father appreciates the purity of this aesthetic. The hours pass, the action trundles, sometimes there is a surprise, and he enjoys it.

He watched the first reality show, he told me once, but hasn't returned to the genre since. *An American Family* debuted on PBS in 1973, and followed an upwardly mobile white American family in California. My father was the upwardly mobile patriarch of a splintering American family in New York. He and his were the target demographic; PBS was betting that viewers might be interested in seeing a probing investigation into a reflection of something like themselves.

The family watched together, on the couch. My father remembers one scene the most, the one everyone remembers, when the beginnings of a divorce played out in front of ten million strangers, during the first generation when it felt like divorce was a step that anyone could take. He remembers, specifically, the way the husband looked at his wife in the Mexican restaurant after she asked him to leave. His slight sneer, the flat rage in his voice when he said, *What's* your *problem?* How viciousness exploded from cluelessness, and how pure a moment it was because he really had no idea; he really hadn't been paying attention at all.

I've begun to think that the punctum is where a person sees himself. In my father's case, this seems obvious—the way his race and age and income bracket matched up with those of a man enscreened. But I don't think the punctum is chained to mere obvious demographic relatability. It moves beyond that, expansive in what images it might encompass, yet that sensation, the stab of sudden, overwhelming recognition, has to be personal— what you see or maybe don't want to see in yourself, hidden in the image of another. Which is why it's such a risk to be moved by any detail, the same way it's a risk to love anyone: It's a public declaration of where you manifest who you are.

My father watched the unthinking expression on an angry stranger's face, oblivious to the ways that he could hurt people, confusion and cruelty blending. There was a stirring in the space between himself and the image. Forty years later that interaction has remained indelible; he can still see it, feel it. Now that he no longer watches such petty, public, personal pain, it means that it no longer implicates him, which I think is a common motivation among those who don't engage with reality shows—if you ignore it, then no part of you can be reflected in it. When he sees me watching, I know the question he wants to ask me, one he never seems comfortable enough to fully voice: You see yourself in *that*?

On *The Real World,* I've seen a man come out as HIV positive; then I saw that man marry, and I saw the hollow contours of his face as his illness worsened. I've seen a man call another man a faggot, a man call another man a nigger, many men call many women a bitch. I've seen a man rip a barely clothed woman's blanket off her, and the resulting house meeting to discuss why that type of menace is unacceptable. I've seen a sweating, weeping meathead confess to a cocaine relapse, begging his housemates for forgiveness.

I like to think, and have said out loud, drunkenly, confidently, that the show has taught me about difficult stuff, the kind of stuff that human adults need at least a cursory knowledge of. That I have returned to it for moral and educational reasons. This is a pretty generous reading of the relationship. What I remember best, and the scenes that were featured prominently in my favorite seasons, are night-vision moments either right before or right after sex, occasionally during. Moments of infused extra-intimacy when the people involved actually seemed to think, or at least tried to behave as if they thought, that no one was watching, even as their words and gestures were so conscious, even labored. That impossibility was part of the thrill, the thought of My God, I can't believe they're saying this when they know I'm right here, and then the thought that maybe they're only reaching for those words because they know there's an audience. And then the inevitable question of whether I could ever bring myself to do the same. Or whether I might sound like that in stolen moments if anyone cared to listen.

Somehow, amid the predictable booze-fueled preening, the slurred come-ons, limbs contorting sheets, there was accidental tenderness. I was watching and rewatching the ways that people try to express the desire for contact, or the desire to be wanted, or the desire to be watched; bodies rushing together, then apart, arrogance and fear and ecstasy interwoven. For a quarter of a century that appeal was repeated, amplified, as each successive cast knew more of what they were getting into and still had to negotiate what they would show and how they might be seen. I watched alone for many years, and then for many years next to you, and that tension built through each new season. Awareness could never erase the awkwardness of the body; that never failed to comfort me.

In the first episode of the Las Vegas season, every cast member gets drunk and piles into a small Jacuzzi because they are young and beautiful and they've been selected to be in a place that has a Jacuzzi in it. For a moment, after getting themselves in position, so close, so exposed, they all look around like they're not sure what to do. They are noticeably tense still with the cameras pushing in on them, although a couple of them are taking pictures of the action, as though they need to make sure it isn't forgotten, which is really cute and adds a sense of genuineness, or at least naïveté.

In this lull, the viewer can feel the anticipation of what will be half a year of exposure, the excitement of standing on the brink of something. Then a threesome breaks out—not fully, but we see two women and one man begin to kiss and rub soapy water on one another while their new housemates stare and giggle nervously and make semishocked noises. The passion ends quickly, furtively. It's like they wanted to see if they could do it.

Later in the season these same players are climbing into one another's beds, lights off, their eyes glowing into the cameras— almost alone, hidden yet on display. I remember watching and hearing them whisper, the quotes probably shifting in my mind over the years but the tone and force of them still vivid:

I want you. I love you. I don't care if we use a condom; I love the way you feel.

Then:

I'm sorry I put us in this place. If you're pregnant, will you keep it? I think we can do it. I think I do love you. I think maybe this is what I need.

Scholarly essays have identified the Las Vegas season as a crucial breaking point that led to what is truly the modern age of reality, when all hopes for educational documentation were shelved in favor of spectacle. The producers left a show about race and class and politics and engineered instead a show about vanity and sex within the same sociological premise. And not the complex issues surrounding vanity and sex; just a show about watching hot bodies fuck. Indeed, the last remaining vestige of the *Real World* franchise is *The Challenge*—former stars flown to tropical resorts to compete in arbitrary competitions before returning to their rooms, tanned and wet, for drinking, fighting, and, inevitably, sex.

Las Vegas, it is argued, left behind any interest in the substance of modern life and instead began to orchestrate this recurring fantasy that's far more reliably fun to look at. But it wasn't a fantasy. Even as I fantasized about it, it never felt like a fantasy. It never had that easy shimmer of impossibility. It was a group of people trying so hard to figure out how to be worthy of a fantasy, a roomful of young, ambitious, malleable unknowns who'd made their bodies perfect to be noticed, who had auditioned by insisting, over and over, with their own little twists on the theme, that they were pleasurably observable, that most desirable identity. It was the jittery high of suddenly embodying the parameters of a fantasy, that climax attained and potentially ongoing, and the instant anxiety of what it might take to linger there.

I return to that moment when three of them start kissing and they keep saying, *I can't believe this is happening,* even though they're making it happen. They are pulling away to look at their reflections in the mirror. The others are watching them, then turning to the camera, then looking down, ashamed to be part of the spectacle, thrilled, too, wondering silently, and later out loud in the confessional room, if they are capable of, willing to be, *this* kind of person. They flush with jealousy that, for five seconds, they weren't someone who'd been chosen for a kiss.

The creators of *The Real World* modeled their show after *An American Family* and paid homage to its auteur, Craig Gilbert. Gilbert saw his work as anthropological, and I think this is crucial to understanding everything he did and everything that came after him. In the 1960s, he produced *Margaret Mead's New Guinea Journal,* in which Dr. Mead returned after a generation to observe how remote villagers were adjusting to increasing modernity. The time span cultivated there is important, the ongoingness. There was story, a central drama to be found even in the simple fact that the subjects grew older and wearier, that things change over time and also stay the same.

Gilbert mapped out the future of what he was calling "television documentary": *It must be in a series form—repetition and involvement with characters is what holds viewers—and it must be concerned with the events in the daily lives of ordinary citizens.*

He said this sustained voyeurism into the recognizable could *break through the aching sense of being alone that most of us feel.*

The shift, then, was from the anthropology of the foreign to the anthropology of the common, from the thrill of finding recognizable humanity in far-off, unrecognizable situations to finding the bizarre, perhaps reassuring, humanity hidden in everything that feels all too ordinary.

Look at us. Look underneath us. Inside us. Look what we have become.

I have so many memories of sitting still, watching you watch, to the point that I freely substitute those memories for my own. They *are* my memories; I was there. But the emotion, the action, the animation, is yours; I'm just watching.

Dorm-cot watching—your face in the up-close laptop glow, younger in that light than I allowed myself to see you, which meant that I was younger than I wanted to see myself.

Watching that Pixar movie *Up,* drinking boxed wine—how you wept at the beginning montage of squat cartoons loving, then aging, then one dying, then grief. I still glance to see if you're crying the moment we're watching something that might be worth tears, and I can feel you glancing at me, looking for the same signals; the simultaneity of the action is comforting and anxious and collective and alone, all at once.

The main memory, played on a loop, is of laughter: the fullness with which your laugh explodes at the screen, so many versions of that laugh and the realization each time of its fullness. It seems, each time, a more genuine laugh than I can achieve—no forced exhalation, no tension of waiting for the acknowledgment or approval of your taste. I envy you when you laugh; I begin to laugh to catch up with you, and then our laughter builds together, and then I'm really laughing, a bodily response of relief that I always associate with you.

In *Ordinary Affects*, Kathleen Stewart attempts to define a person's self in the face of the onslaught of images that make up daily life: *It exists, obliquely, in dreams of disappearing, of winning or being done with it all. Forms of attention and attachment keep it moving: the hypervigilance, the denial, the distraction, the sensory games of all sorts, the vaguely held promise that something is happening.*

I like the idea of the self as a thing that needs outside animation; I recognize the sensation. The self as one of those rounded mirrors on curvy roads, taking the images of passing cars and stretching them around the glass, suddenly alive. There are too many metaphors to mix here. What I'm saying is, when I think of these words, I think of you, the same way I think of you now when I think of watching. I never liked the term *losing yourself,* in reference to a book or a movie or a show or a person. It's too certain that either something very good or very bad is happening, instead of something very common: living, looking.

It's not that the punctum for me is always you, just that the feeling is similar—a stirring, a familiar pleasure that is too hard to pin down. I don't mean to claim that I know your perspective. The act of watching you and finding myself is limiting, it's selfish; I know it. But the looking is part of living. I look, I recognize, I feel the stab.

Another image of watching, repeated: We walk the dog in the summer when the sun is coming up, and I stare at your sunglasses, thinking that I want to find your eyes behind them. But when you ask me if I'm just staring at my own reflection, I realize that I am. We laugh about that, your laughter an explosion.

5

{REQUEST FOR AUDITION}:

HEEEYYYYY!!

   I'm _____ of Nashville, Tn and VERY excited about this opportunity. A little bit about me? I am an outgoing people person and I LOVE making people laugh. More importantly I am a single mother DOING THE DAMN THING! I graduated college with ALL odds against me and yet I still manage to keep a smile not only on my face but many of those faces around me. I love to party on baby free nights and TRUST that I take full advantage of those nights kicking it with my GIRLS. You will NOT regret having me as one of your cast members. I'm claiming this opportunity. Looking forward to hearing from you!

                —from www.castingcallhub.com

I'm thinking now of Ramona Singer, my least favorite character on *The Real Housewives of New York,* who has famously used her screen time to say, explicitly, that she is a living example that women "can have it all." She has been on television, loudly, for eight seasons, as new waves of housewives have come and gone. Such staying power is no small achievement. Again and again, cameras follow her through and around everything she has: a spacious apartment on the Upper East Side; a sulky but ultimately agreeable daughter who managed to get into college; a husband who makes money but does not resent her making her own; friends of a similar race, age, and income bracket and with similar interests; the kind of alcoholism that is still fun and not, as yet, debilitating; an eponymous midprice Pinot

Grigio that has received international distribution. There's more that I'm forgetting, a new possession popping up every episode. With all that she has and that she flaunts, she reliably portrays a cartoon of the limited parameters of conventional desire. She embodies these parameters fully. Each time we tune in to her, we're forced to watch her strut and display, to reencounter the cartoon, renegotiate our own relationship to it, as she profits from our continual tuning in and the cycle repeats.

I think Ramona is well aware that she's watched ironically by many. Or if not ironically, then at least with a sneer. Ambivalence, agitation, eye rolling. We are prime examples of the kind of viewers who can only watch her while maintaining that we don't take her seriously, often cringing or actually saying *Oof!* out loud at her on-screen—that manic glaze to her eyes, the way she will career from girlish giggle to vicious insult with no transition emotion. But she is watched. And she is recognized. And her Pinot Grigio is bought (I assume). And often, when we watch, we are drinking white wine (not Pinot Gri, but still) and claiming to be full from salmon burgers and grilled broccoli, and our vanity-breed dog is next to us on our L-shaped couch, where we're entwined, not acrobatically or seductively but in a practiced way, and we're planning our next day during commercial breaks—work, evening tennis if we can fit it in, shopping, sex, maybe—and we will be so pleasantly, terrifyingly self-satisfied when we perform these tasks. And we are laughing at her, enjoying that together.

Watching Ramona at her worst (or best?), having it all, is both a constant celebration of the vapid sheen of an obvious kind of privilege and a reveal of its filthiest insides—the assumed exceptionalism, the obliviousness. Both are left there for us to do with what we will. Who are we to assume that she expects us to feel only celebration, no filth?

I was at a reading recently, and a burgeoning star novelist was introduced with this sentence: *He reminded me that realism doesn't have to just be a defense of the status quo.*

This was met with great applause. I wasn't exactly sure what the sentence meant, but the gist of it was nice, worthy of aspiration, and it was spoken with somber force by a writer I respect a lot, so I clapped too. It was the kind of room where it felt like not clapping when others clapped was a poor career choice, and I've been working on being more careerist. That's not exactly true—I've been working on being more *successfully* careerist.

The more I think about it, the critique was about how the concept of realism can be used as a weapon, or, more precisely, an eraser. What we choose to accept as conventional, even desirable, reality has the power to cut out everything else. And realism so often refers to privileged white people interacting with one another, emoting, oblivious to anything but their own feelings and possessions, but boy do they feel and own things. The more attention paid to that feeling, that owning, the more the validity of those values is reinforced.

This hit novelist had broken that fallacy of the status quo. His was a better realism, "better" meaning more ambitious, bigger tented, less trite. Yes, definitely something to aspire to. But this also suggests that a more banal or self-involved or even superficial realism is automatically a defense or a celebration of the limited perspective it chronicles. That to display it is to validate it, and to consume it is to validate it as well.

As I often do when a roomful of smart people seems to agree, I began to feel that they were all against me. I began to see myself in the perspective they scorned. Like I didn't have the courage to reach for anything that might challenge me. Like I can't handle the effort or imagination involved in subversion. Subversion is so easy to claim—I watch Ramona Singer to feast on dark subtext; I write about myself watching Ramona as self-critique. But that claim doesn't take away the consistency of my interests: her opulence, my validation, my comfort. Much like Ramona might midepisode, I felt the desire to defend myself against an attack that may have never existed.

As the night went on, I got wasted, and agreeable careerism faded into desperate contempt, a much more natural state. The crescendo: I told an editor that *The Real Housewives of New York* was as valuable a cultural artifact as *Twin Peaks,* and how's that for realism, and I felt a brief rush of righteousness, but he gave me the most withering look, muttered *Jesus,* and walked away.

I like to teach James Agee's "Knoxville: Summer of 1915" in my introductory creative writing classes. It's short, so we go around the room reading it aloud—long, elegant sentences about a summer night from Agee's childhood when he sat on a suburban lawn with his family. When I ask how it makes them feel, my students usually say comforted. Or bittersweet. Content. One said, "Sleepy, but in a good way."

I do that teacher thing where I say okay but hold the second syllable to let them know that okay isn't quite good enough. This is met with silence. Then I ask them to go through and find the images, or even single words, that feel out of place, that have a different mood to them. With more coaxing than I should probably offer, the words and phrases are eventually said out loud. I throw them up on the whiteboard:

An insane noise of violence, from the nozzle of a hose.

The *fishlike pale* body of Agee's father.

Finally the question buried in the middle of a longer, gentler sentence: *And who shall ever tell the sorrow of being on this earth?*

The idea, I try to tell them, is to pervert the comfort of comfort. I ask, Who would want to read about something that's just comfortable and cheerful, with nothing else deeper than that? With no edge? No dissatisfaction underneath?

Often there's a sense that I'm trying to force a way of seeing onto them, an aesthetic that shouldn't be compulsory, this certainty that we *must* be responding to more than just the portrait of a lovely home.

"But what does that matter if we can miss it so easily?" a student asked once, as his peers nodded. Those are just little tricks in the grand scheme of things; how could we think Agee was trying to pervert us with a few little tricks? And anyway, what's so wrong about nice things? What's so wrong about porches and yards that look like our own porches and yards, or look like the porches and yards that we wish we had? And what's wrong with our parents, whom we love and who love us, and happiness, and, again, what the hell is wrong with all that?

When we talk as we watch, we usually talk about the characters we're watching and we usually disagree. You are, I would say, generally more hopeful in your outlook. When couples that have been fighting reconcile, you tend to take them at the words of their confessionals. When I say that Ramona seems to actively hate, or at least resent, her daughter, you slap me gently on the shoulder and tell me to stop.

Be *generous,* you tell me, and I love that choice of word.

Though we don't say it, this dynamic probably has something to do with the way we each deal with the looming, unmovable structure of our own quotidianness. Jesus. That came off overwrought; let me try again: the way we rationalize the ease with which we continue to burrow into lives that resemble a detergent commercial. So when I throw tantrums at Whole Foods, it is because I want—I guess—you and all the other Whole Foods patrons to know how much I hate it there. Because if I didn't hate it there, if I wasn't even really aware of being there but instead was simply present, shopping for the week as one does, roboti-

cally wheeling everything out to the car that I proudly parked in
the one remaining shady spot, who would I be? I would not be
smirking at myself; I would instead be the kind of person who
doesn't even realize that there's anything to smirk at. Sometimes
that possibility is intolerable.

Never mind that I do the shopping every Monday, even when
you volunteer to take a turn, because I feel such unarguable worth
when I lug sagging bags through the sliding doors. Never mind
that there are so many things I genuinely like about the Whole
Foods experience—as I said last week, it's pure pleasure to see
a display of many different-colored heads of cauliflower. Never
mind that the feeling of paying for designer food, clucking about
the prices and the faux-organicness while still resolutely pur-
chasing, making precise *lists* of nutritionally valuable items and
then checking those items off, is enormously satisfying. *Lists,*
man—what greater satisfaction is there?

You don't seem to feel that pressure to show that you are at
least a bit disturbed by the lie of American bourgeois normalcy,
even as you participate in it. When this schism leads to a fight,
I get all worked up and righteous, thinking I'm just a more self-
aware person, but I suspect I'm confusing self-awareness with
self-loathing, trying to attach value, or at least a sense of action,
to the self-loathing. The unspoken question is whether you can
still desire something as you sneer at it, or whether it's a cop-out
to try to straddle that line.

We are so tired at night from our lives, and we put the TV
on and settle in together and watch lives. Lives like these: eager
couples buying homes and discussing whether they need an extra
bedroom, how close they need to be to a public park, bickering about whether he deserves a man-cave even if the man-cave
eats into potential family space. Or these: friends at Pilates class
talking about their husbands and their other friends who aren't
there, saying nasty things, not out of genuine nastiness but out

of the tiny thrill of getting away with something. Or these: people shopping in packs, showing the price tag as they turn to one another and ask for assessment or reinforcement, faces scrunching because it's so hard to know what to want.

And what do we feel as we watch? I refuse to think that we feel nothing, to conceive of so many of our shared hours as blank, in front of an arbitrary collection of shows that invite blankness. And I don't think that we feel some kind of relief or validation when we see petty dramas resembling neon versions of our own played out as if worthy of being seen.

When we watch marathons of a particular show, it becomes impossible to keep track of how many times each person reiterates to the camera that their lives are valid. It is a *fabulous* life, they say. Or: My children are *beautiful;* they're gifts. Or: I love my job. Or: These are the best years of my life. Or, if they've been transformed in a narratively meaningful way: I can really see the life I've always dreamed of now. Or (and this is a hard one not to harp on): You really *can* have it all. Taken together, spoken by people whose homes have been turned into a set, who spend their nonfilmed moments responding to blog attacks and making enough mall appearances to stay relevant, these become a near-hysterical mantra.

Nothing makes you more aware of how tenuous an ideal of a good life is than to hear it repeatedly voiced. Every time any character states that he or she is happy, the words are yet another invitation to wonder if that is really the case—a tension, mounting. I think of Agee in these moments, I do—the real housewives of Knoxville, 1915: *Here they are, all on this earth; and who shall ever tell the sorrow of being on this earth.*

We watch Ramona Singer, and I think of Agee, of comfort and pleasure and sorrow, and how the living room looks nice with the Edison bulbs dimmed but there's a water stain in the corner behind the cabinet that we should get someone to come look at, and my body feels heavy and lumpy and I don't want to be in it anymore, and I finished the popsicles while you were at work again and I'd feel better if I came out and apologized for that, but instead I'll wait to see if you have the energy to bring it up.

Ramona's life kind of fell apart during this latest season, season 6. Her daughter finally left for college, her husband cheated and moved out, and now the tail end of her character arc is full of scenes of her in leather pants and scoop-neck tops at singles mixers populated by young, bland Wall Street chums.

On the show's one-hundredth episode (a landmark worthy of a breakdown), she finally breaks down.

The setting is a very roomy beachside villa in Turks and Caicos, where Ramona has organized a group vacation for the show's cast members, a gambit that occurs once or twice a season—the removal from routine serving, as it does for all friend groups, to stir the pot. There's been a fight among a few of the women mostly focused on the drinking of Ramona's friend Sonja—whether or not she drinks too much, drinks to cope with loneliness as opposed to drinks to have fun. Sonja has already stormed off to bed and most of the other women have drifted off as well.

Only Ramona and Bethenny Frankel (a former enemy) remain, draped, drunk and exhausted, over a gigantic, gray outdoor couch on the deck. A camera zooms in over Bethenny's shoulder onto Ramona's face, with tiki-torch flames smudged behind her. Ramona throws her head back, brings it down again, and begins: *I think what Sonja misses is to have a significant other in her life who wants to share your life and is true and honest to you and you have a friendship and a great relationship sexually and that's what we all need and crave for.*

She has, through simple pronoun shifting, wrangled control of the narrative. *Sonja* has shifted to *you,* and then finally come around to what *we* all need. And the invitation is written in the conversation for *we* to become more specific: *Ramona.* She is letting us know that she needs to have a moment.

Bethenny takes the bait and brings up Ramona's freshly collapsed marriage to Mario—twenty-five years of happiness, and six seasons of smug televised happiness, all gone. Ramona has bragged very publicly about Mario's body (I mean, can you believe it—a man his age?), their money, their mutual respect, the sex (still constant!). Now, after all that, we're being invited to watch the greatest, most humanizing conflict her character has ever faced.

He's part of me, she says. *It may not be good for me, but he really is a part of me.* The second time she says *part,* she turns her eyes skyward like a Goya portrait of Christ, and crosses her arms around her own neck, gently hugging.

Bethenny, also presented with a chance to be humanized, dives in to hug her as well, and Ramona continues, looking back into the camera over Bethenny's shoulder: *It's like I'm losing a part of myself and people don't get it. It's like, yeah, I get it, I'm whole, yeah, I get it, I'm a strong woman, but for him not to be a part of me because he's been such a part of me, he's part of my soul, he's in my heart. I don't know how to fix him. I wish I knew how to fix him.*

She rears back into the couch and covers her eyes, then launches herself onto Bethenny's shoulder. Bethenny holds her, covering her face, and Ramona, realizing this, shakes away Bethenny's hands so that her face is directly in the camera again.

I want to fix him so badly, she reasserts. Then, once more, in a whisper like the last line of a country ballad: *I wish I knew how to fix him.*

The scene, if written by someone else, would end here. I would have been totally satisfied as a viewer to see a two-minute detour into Ramona's hurt parts, something simultaneously genuine and exhibitionist. Instead, she gives fifteen more seconds, that, to me, feel like that moment at the end of "I Believe When I Fall in Love," when Stevie Wonder has written the perfect ballad and could leave it there, but just to remind us he's Stevie Fucking Wonder he throws in this little funk jam, because he can make love funky if he wants to, like he's winking at the listener. Ramona winks like that.

Still lying in Bethenny's arms, she opens her eyes huge and gets louder, her voice newly assertive and condescending: *People say that, oh, you know, Ramona you're so pretty, you've never looked better, you're so smart, you're independent—yeah, I fucking know that shit.*

By now she has hoisted herself back up and is glaring at these hypothetical morons who only see her brilliance and her beauty, not her pain. Then she stops on a dime again, smiles, throws her arms up, says, *I have no idea; I just want a hug,* and collapses into Bethenny's arms once more—humble, a bit goofy, resigned. The camera focuses on their sprawling hug, then a tiki torch still burning, then finally—in a heavy-handed cut—on a Caribbean sunrise.

The rest of the episode was mediocre—a yoga class with a hot instructor, more arguing, shots of the women in their bikinis complimenting one another's bodies while speaking ill of their own. But Ramona's speech was sublime. It came on again a few days later and again we watched it, this time waiting for every turn in emotion and grinning at one another as each arrived.

I will admit that I find something really joyful in the shared experience of watching her unravel like that—Ramona, with her bulging eyes and her preternatural gift for bullying, suddenly distraught. I'm sure it has to do with her willingness to be bared, the idea that I am lording over my screen saying, Emote for me! and Ramona, like a zoo seal, is willing to perform that trick. But

it's not a simple trick. She is not merely performing sadness—
how easy that would be; so appropriate that it would feel inhuman in its neatness. Instead, she's taking her lowest moment and
inserting into it the notion that random people repeatedly tell
her she looks amazing and is amazing, before turning cuddly
and kind, ending the scene on a satisfying, near-unrecognizable
emotional note.

In a scene staged for drunken gibberish, she manages to feel
astonishingly human in ways I wouldn't have considered until I
watched her go through the whole process. She is a virtuoso of
contradictory feeling; she did it so well that it made sense.

Who grieves neatly? Nobly? Unselfishly? Who wants to
grieve without in some way getting something out of it? Without making sure that they're turned out to the camera or the
metaphorical equivalent? Without reminding themselves that
whatever they're feeling, they're feeling it well?

The Ramona-Singer-to-Guy-DeBord transition seems a bit
smirky, and also too much like justifying one thing with the
other, but there's a line I like a lot from *The Society of the Spectacle,*
when DeBord refers to stars of any kind as *specialists of apparent
life.* He says they become objects for the rest of us to *identify with
in order to compensate for the fragmented productive specializations that
{we} actually live.*

Look at the idol, see yourself in the idol, and maybe at a certain point seeing someone be that way becomes feeling that way,
and feeling that way means we don't have to think about what
it feels like to be ourselves, spin-cycling through ordinariness.
What changes in that tried-and-true equation when the idol
is ordinary, or at least possesses no obvious skill set other than
that *apparent life,* simply living away, with the added narrative
purpose and external reward of our gaze? I don't know—maybe

nothing. Maybe reality strips stardom down to its simplest mechanism: who is seen living and who isn't. I mean, yeah, that's exactly what it does. That's the point. So in that case DeBord's idea should hold true—it doesn't matter whom you're looking at; as long as you spend your energy seeing the pageantry of their life, you don't have to see yourself.

This isn't a cheerful thought. I've never voiced it when we're together on the couch, watching Ramona or any of the others who fill the same role on a given night. But I am thinking it often in those moments, so really I *am* seeing myself. Even if I want to hide from that sight, it's unavoidable.

David Foster Wallace once called television *a river of images,* and I like that idea—the constancy, the movement. I see myself on the surface of the river, somewhere in the ripples of everyone else's repeated stabs at apparent life. In the ripples, I am blurred, fleeting, and they, too, are blurred, fleeting, even as they're working so hard to be vivid.

Another metaphor to try on: the British scholar Kristyn Gorton explored how, on television, *these emotions of self-becoming become contagious.* I especially like the bluntness of her framing—TV emotion as a sickness. What better way to describe this *apparent life* than as a chronic condition of self-becoming, all done in front of me, as I feel all the symptoms? Watching makes me feel the worry that seems to underpin all the actions of all the people I watch, even as they say the opposite thing: I worry that I am not enough.

Here's what *The New York Times* said about the premiere of *The Jersey Shore:*

> *When in the perhaps not-so-distant future scholars try to figure out just how a great culture fell so far, so fast, they*

won't have to look too hard. They can just pop in a DVD
or download this happy train wreck or others like it, sloppy
slivers of American reality, and it will be right there in
front of their eyes.

No more dire a promise than that of a future absent our formerly great culture. And the key to this absence is the fact that
the unworthy, the untalented, the unanointed have been allowed
to star. Gym managers, bartenders, wedding DJs—all a bit dumb
and dissatisfied and striving in a run-down party pad in South
Jersey. We didn't miss an episode of that show. We picked the
ones we felt to be heroes, and then the villains, and then those
we weren't sure about, and we watched to make up our minds.

I remember how and where we watched the premiere. It was
in a grimy, gray-carpeted Iowa apartment, with meth heads and
undergrads as neighbors, the week after we moved halfway across
the country. The last tenant had been an old man evicted for
unpaid rent, and he'd pissed everywhere before the leasing company forced him out. The carpet smelled like both carpet cleaner
and piss. I lay supine, nursing the ankle I'd sprained falling off
the back of a U-Haul, and we seethed at each other for the fact
that we were both in this place. We finished the last dregs of the
coke we'd brought on our move, and this became the first time
I'd ever smoked pot with a sense of need. We paid six hundred
dollars for rent, more than a hundred for a good cable package.

I remember the way we laughed at *The Jersey Shore,* when
Snooki got too drunk the first day, threatened to leave, fell down,
and ended up staying due to immobility. I remember that you
loved Sammi Sweetheart's tagline, the first thing she said on-
screen: *I'm the sweetest bitch you'll ever meet.* And of course I loved
The Situation, and the way he was always on-screen looking at
himself as though rediscovering the image, the anxious joy he
found in touching the mountainous swell of his biceps, the stare-

down he gave to every reflective surface. I was sort of infatuated with him, to the point that I defended his most indefensible behavior, and I said many stoned, earnest things that I think I still believe about his magnetism, the power of his unmitigated ridiculousness, so looming but also so helpless.

Looking back, it's easy to point out our desperate escapism, but it was a particular version of that urge, and I remember it with more fondness than I'd expect. We escaped, desperately, into a show about other peoples' desperate escapism. These stars did not want to be themselves; they wanted to be stars. *Stars* might be too acute a word for their ambitions, but I can't think of another one, and I'm not sure they'd be able to either. They went about becoming stars by showing the embarrassing small-ness of their current existence, hoping that it would be inflated by the attention. And as we paid attention, I could feel them inflate in real time—does that make sense? They seemed to feel so deserving of something better, even more than we did, but then they also seemed like they didn't believe that. They lacked. Openly, messily, even strategically, they lacked. And so we watched and felt something more than bland idol worship, something less than empathy.

The first blizzard of the fall came quickly, and we trudged to the gas station, bought all the beer we could carry. We fin-ished it that same night as we watched, and passed out on each other, semiwittingly emulating the *sloppy slivers* who ran from their own *fragmented productive specializations* and turned them into something superficial, elevating their real lives and drag-ging down stardom until they met in a fault line of everything I did and did not want my life to be.

We're no strangers to the desire to feel exceptional. No one is, I know that. But we, particularly I, seem to feel the weight of this desire especially. Even now, see, there it is—my need to deem myself more illustrative than others of this basic human condition.

We've been doing this thing lately where we say, "That's so *me.*" We say it the way your garden-variety narcissist, the unself-aware kind, might, tilting our heads to one shoulder and adopting intonations somewhere between Valley girl and music snob. It's a critique of that way people so casually yet forcefully define themselves in the middle of conversations, claiming a pattern of behavior as identifiably their own—saying the mean thing that everyone else is thinking? That's so me. Assholes. We're saying those people are a particular kind of asshole. The only problem is that usually these impressions grow out of moments in which we have exhibited this behavior and are scrambling to stake a claim on being the kind of person who notices and self-corrects wittily.

It is important to emphasize this quality. It is very *us.*

It's exhausting to be, and be loudly; let's agree upon that. So many ways we can say something, so many ways it can be interpreted, so many ways it can be disseminated. How many versions of the questions we ask each other come back to this: Did I do it right? Did I say it right?

In all the easy hand-wringing about the narcissism of our generation, I think what's being specifically maligned is the need to *voice* the self, not just obsess about it. It's the prevalence of the self-introduction, that command: see me, and when you see me, see this.

I was raised on people telling the story of who they are. Growing up, I always admired the people who said it best, with the most force, force I assumed I could never muster. So I was one of those predictable ten-year-old white boys aping Biggie lyrics for the way he started a song and announced exactly how he was to be seen: *When I die, fuck it, I wanna go to hell / Cause I'm a piece of shit, it ain't hard to fucking tell.*

The two pillars of American entertainment perfected during my lifetime have been hip-hop and reality TV, and I don't think it's coincidental that the two rely upon a similar force of personality more than any musical or narrative forms before them. In song, or in scene, they so often begin with a throat clearing and a proclamation. I'm talking about exposition as mantra; what's more seductive than that?

My whole life as a storyteller, story consumer, has been dominated by shows in which scenes of dramatic action pull back into a private moment with the actor in a room alone, confronting the action, outlining their motives, laying out patterns and trademarks within their own character, the form of the Shakespearean soliloquy taken and repeated on demand. They refuse to just be character; they are first-person narration. I think again of NeNe Leakes saying, *If you just ask anybody about me,* pssh, *NeNe, she's* real *fun.*

And I love that about NeNe—it's like she's attempting a monopoly on the idea of fun, like if others try to horn in on her fun territory it runs the risk of diminishing her.

When I was a kid, in my head, I would contextualize the things I said, as though I were quoting myself on the page. So I'd tell a joke, and after it, silently, I'd add: *he said wryly, a knowing smirk on his face.* Or when my grandmother died and I told my father I was sorry for him: *he said softly, wanting only to let the older man know he was there.*

It was a bit much, and certainly revealed the beginnings of an adverb passion that hasn't ebbed. I used to think this tic was a sign that I was born to be a writer, but that's not it. It was more symptomatic of a sensibility than a skill set.

You're the first person I ever admitted this habit to. The reveal was meant to be a conscious offer of intimacy. It was early on in the relationship, and I remember I was worried about seeming autistic but also kind of hopeful that I'd seem like an autistic genius, or at least an enigma. I ended up seeming neither, but it was a repeatable thrill to sit opposite each other on your bed, speaking the way we used to speak when we had no idea what the other might say next, and finish each sentence with a description of how we said it. Maybe that was when our obsession with each other began, nineteen and momentarily unashamed, allowing the space to reintroduce and reannotate ourselves as we went along.

That instinct has never diminished, even if the scaffolding has fallen away. How can we not say to each other, so many times on any given day, This is who I am? What do we want more from a companion than the promise to enhance the stories of ourselves? To take the stories and believe them and care for them and heighten them, and then reflect them back as a reminder that we've been seen and heard? To confirm that we've been, might continue to be, worth the interest?

My grandfather was not an interesting man. Not in the ways that I've always found interestingness to manifest itself, anyway. I never heard him tell a story, which I have later come to understand is the main responsibility of grandfathers. This was over sixteen years of regularish visits. He polished silver that he'd made many years before (which would have been interesting if he'd ever discussed it), pretended to be unable to hear my grandmother, and looked for excuses to climb ladders.

This changed after his Alzheimer's diagnosis; not right away, but when things were bad enough to land him in a home. He was in a special wing that had heavy doors with code locks to prevent escape. (Side note: If somebody could find a way to market this so that it didn't seem morally reprehensible, the Alzheimer's wing of a nursing home might provide the greatest set for a reality television program ever.) It was electric in there—so many bodies with so many years' worth of material, all of it fractured and swirling, slipping and then rushing back. We visited enough times for patterns to begin to emerge in the stories that the afflicted returned to when given an audience.

One woman, who had lived most of her life in Massachusetts, a housewife and mother of many, had apparently grown up in the South, had been beautiful, and had been involved in high school theater. She inhabited that self, and when we visited, she spoke mostly to me, the only high-school-age boy. She'd try to rush out the door whenever a new visitor opened it, and when the aides restrained her, she would revert to this beautiful, howling Bette Davis accent and cry out that the stage was waiting for her. It was as though she'd somehow managed to choose the self she wanted to end with, the most vivid version of all she'd ever been.

She wasn't the only one; the ward housed champion sprinters and lotharios and scientists on the verge of something unspecific but definitely great. My grandfather, suddenly and without explanation, became impish. One of my uncles sneaked in some wood glue for him (this is, with the very notable exception of me, a family that values manual tinkering), and he stuck a bunch of pennies to the floor in his room.

"Oh look, a penny," he would say to everyone who entered, his face wearing an expression that I'd never seen before. He'd get impatient and laugh before you could even crouch and pretend to try to pick up the penny.

"I always get them with that!" he'd roar. "I invented that gag."

My mother would say to him, "You're *funny*, Dad," and he would respond, forcefully, "I'm *funny*."

These are the only moments I regularly remember about my grandfather, ones during which he was, by all medical and anecdotal accounts, not himself. I still surprise myself with how moved I am when I remember the detail of him working to hold on to and present this little wisp of who he had maybe been.

Of course, I can't ignore his suffering. Or I shouldn't, anyway. This was all happening during a time when he was grasping for any sense of normalcy as he died in opaque terror. He became more interesting to me when I could marvel at the fact that he was steadily coming apart, that every sentient sentence he spoke could be the last he ever managed, and maybe he realized that. Maybe I cared only because of the rushed passion in his jokes and the wrenching cloud on his face when he lost them. Within this worst narrative constraint, he finally wanted to be heard, to be seen—and in such a specific way: the kind of mischief maker who glues a penny to the floor. "Beauty" seems like the wrong word, too gentle, too absolving, but I sat there and saw beauty. I still do. Or whatever it was, I've remembered it.

Near the end of *Regarding the Pain of Others,* Sontag wrote: *To speak of reality becoming spectacle is a breathtaking provincialism. . . . It assumes that everyone is a spectator. It suggests, perversely, unseriously, that there is no real suffering in the world.*

The book is not about Sontag, nor is it about the run-of-the-mill, white-collar, nonviolent suffering that we love, but I do think it's worth noting that this quote came from the last pages of her last writing project, on the precipice of a leukemia death that involved much suffering. *Spectacle* is a grotesquely anti-septic word; I think that's what she was getting at. There's no mess or risk to it. It suggests a lack of proximity to the thing, which keeps the dirt and the blood away, until all that's left is an image that can't ever hurt, an image to call funny or sad or beautiful.

I know that I'm every bit the cocooned, self-satisfied dweeb Sontag critiques, not at all a part of the great majority of this earth who, as she puts it, *do not have the luxury of patronizing reality.* And I do wonder if there's something unavoidably insidious in the luxury of my patronage that allows me to conflate reality and spectacle, while also creating mutually exclusive moralities between the two.

We can lie together watching someone shrieking in agony (usually emotional, though sometimes physical, too) and tell each other how we feel for the pain expressed. Of course we do; that's why we're watching. But I can also turn to you in the middle of someone's real pain, and say, "My God, what a line" or "Jesus, this is *perfect,*" or even mutter, precisely on the nose, "Spectacular." I cannot be thinking of something terrible as real if I so easily call it "perfect," right? I'm calling the spectacle perfect, not the reality. I hope that's what I'm doing. But when I'm next to you, watching, smiling, I never stop to consider the distinction.

I think a lot of the discomfort written into the types of shows we watch, and a lot of the pleasure, comes down to the control that we can convince ourselves the people on-screen have. The particular brand of moral and intellectual vitriol that each show provokes depends on whether the subject seems to want to be seen. In the case of someone like Ramona Singer, the performer is judged. She is the narcissist who profits from her demands to have an audience for her rage and pain, which sets up an unwinnable negotiation—the more empowered she appears to be, the more hated she becomes. In the case of hoarders and addicts and the clearly financially desperate and the morbidly obese, the subjects are seen as too pathetic to be complicit. Their producers, then, are the ones held to blame, out there searching for cheap human clay to mold and eventually squash. Either way, we watchers, while not the chief villains, are at least accessories to the crime.

Sontag wrote about the tradition of war photographers restaging the dead before capturing their deadness, and the simultaneous tradition of this horrifying people even as they devoured the images—*Everyone is a literalist when it comes to photography,* she wrote. Part of the horror stems from the fact that the grievers of the dead or the mutilated, or even just the defeated, might see the images of their tragedy turned into story, into art. The victims (or muses) have no voice or intentionality in this equation. They merely exist as a sight—malleable, tragic, compelling.

So what do we make, then, of that woman addicted to eating cigarette ash on *My Strange Addiction?* Or the man who finds his cat rotting under a pile of his garbage on *Hoarders: Buried Alive?* Or the tweaker at the end of a pretty typical episode of *Intervention,* running from his family, weeping, screaming on a street corner outside the hotel about the way they let his stepfather abuse him and now they suddenly claim to care for him? Or the six-hundred-pound woman trying to explain away her quasi-covert eating of one last cheeseburger in the bedroom of her trailer on *My 600-Pound Life?* We watched them all. We watched some of them twice. Every time we've watched, I have had actual goose bumps; that's how much thrill I've found in these shows, in the way these unexpected stars glance at the camera, the way they try to explain and deflect and rationalize themselves through pain we have seen so many times but cannot know.

In her essay "Imitating Disaster," Susan Lepselter frames the production of *Hoarders* as ruthlessly driving subjects to a very clear identity and meaning—people with a specific psychological flaw, a trauma that explains it all, a sickness that must be cured. But even as they're shoved into pathetic, predictable patterns, Lepselter says these performers transcend (or are made to transcend) their own stories. There is something going on underneath the obvious stated meaning: *I look at reality television hoarding narratives as themselves symptomatic of a public feeling: a feeling of disaster . . . simultaneously encroaching, imminent, and already lived-in disaster.*

Yes, disaster. And yes, simultaneity. To feel something pressing on you, to feel it in your past and see it in your future, to feel it omnipotent—when a sufferer is at her most compelling to me, it's this storm in her words and gestures that holds my attention. And there's the feeling of complicity; that's part of it. The camera is inserted, and by extension we who love what the camera brings us are also inserted into the mess. We are part of what's encroaching. I feel the subjects aware of the way they're trapped, the camera among the debris between them and the doorway. When they're asked to tell their own stories, they speak to us, they look out at us, and maybe they're imagining our bland safety in the home we clean at least semiregularly.

We watch *Hoarders,* like so many other shows, in binge form. That it was made to be watched that way, is almost always aired that way, is not unimportant. In the face of the show, we lose control. The show spills over us, holds us down. The mess of all the episodes, the tragedy of all the freaks—it begins to encroach and another, larger narrative evolves: a narrative of overwhelm.

I say "overwhelm" because I feel it, but I'm still not sure I know exactly what I mean. What overwhelms is hard to handle well enough to express—that's part of the fear, part of the pleasure. It's a wave cresting, perpetually about to crash. I see what I'm trying to get at in Eve Sedgwick's *Touching, Feeling,* as she attempts to diagnose the paranoid ways that people so often read a text, or the world. She writes: *Paranoia seems to require being imitated to be understood and, in turn, seems to understand only by imitation.*

The feeling permeates all; the borders between what is watched and what is experienced were always meant to bleed. It's the fear of what you see in front of you, and the desire to protect yourself from what you see until the intensity of that desire begins to resemble the panic of what you're seeing. When we watch, our glances back and forth are furtive. Our bodies touch, then come apart. One of us is always asking, voice strained, if it's time to get up and do something else. The panic of the subject in front of us begins to contort to resemble our own?

Sometimes—and this I've been too embarrassed to admit even to you—I read the scrolling comment-thread responses to the episodes we watch after we watch them. I say I need to take a shit, and I sit in there with my phone, not shitting but letting the shrieked feelings of a thousand strangers update in real time:

> *Pffft! Call it entertainment?! It's just trash and typical of the modern age we live in.*

> *It's just cheap and nasty television!"*

> *Shouldn't this guy be thinner if all he drinks is those diet drinks. This house appears to be the easiest hoarding clean-up I've ever seen. All you have to do is pick up the bottles. 2–3 hours tops.*

> *One of the daughters seems to be hoarding some sizable items in her sweater. I'd be happy to help her out with those.*

> *For those saying we shouldn't ridicule, remember he CHOSE to invite the cameras in. Last I checked, no one forces someone to do it. People CHOOSE to humiliate themselves with their eyes on fifteen minutes of fame and fortune.*

Like the gawkers at Bedlam in the 18th century . . . haven't progressed much, have we?

You, along with all the other gawkers, just had a gawk.

Actually, Glen, I don't watch TV . . . thanks for sharing your lack of insight!

And this is what's wrong with modern society. Chastising the vulnerable. I'm sick of it!

Why don't the fat, lazy daughters get off their asses to help him? So typical of today's youngsters. . . . I hope their own place is just as messy!

I've never commented. Fine, that's a lie; I used to, but I stopped very quickly. I'm not saying this because I'm proud of that difference between me and the rest. Mostly I'm too afraid of the exposure, which feels unfair: reveling across multiple platforms in others' exposure (even if it's anonymous), withholding my own contributions. I read until you ask me what I'm doing in there. I reemerge into the order of our home, red spots on my knees from my elbows pressing down.

6

{REQUEST FOR AUDITION}:

I'll be short and brief. I am 43 years old. I perform as childrens magician every weekend to make ends meet. I auditioned for a cruise ship in the late 90s as a childrens comedy magician. I was highly considered but I had a government job I was afraid to leave, and I was planning on getting married and having children. I stop chasing my dream. I now have a wife, and pre teen children that can handle me being away for weeks at a time. I am from north Philadelphia. That is the poorest part of Philadelphia. I was raised in and out of the homeless shelters and salvation armies. My friends and family laughed at my weekend job and never supported me. They said "there is no such thing as a black clown or magician." I would love to perform on a cruise ship. . . . To show the world what I can do . . . and keep my dream alive. Thank you in advance. Love in Christ.

—from www.castingcallhub.com

The moment of my life so far during which I felt most fully was when I saw the stretcher leave the ambulance and heard you cry as they wheeled you through the parking lot to the university hospital.

I already knew what had happened—a cop had called me from the scene of the accident to tell me about the crash, how you'd been thrown from your bike when the SUV T-boned you. He told me you were alive and awake, but to hurry. I hadn't felt very deeply when he spoke to me—there was worry, of course, but it was numb, imprecise. Mostly I'd felt the pukey rush that occurs when an event that anyone would agree is a *big* event has happened. I was aware that this was a moment that might change everything, whatever that means, and we'd had very few of those. I thought of how I would sound when I called your mother to tell the story.

What changed was actually seeing you and hearing you. You didn't see me, so you weren't behaving in any way toward how you would want me to see the scene. Your neck was braced to the stretcher, your head facing straight up at the cloudless sky. It was 109 degrees out that day; I remember that's what my car thermometer said. You squinted into a merciless sun. The soles of your feet, bare, were flat on the stretcher's mattress, and your bent knees were swaying back and forth. I couldn't tell if you had no control over them so they swung limply or if you were writhing. The sound you made was horrifying, one I'd never heard, but also had. I associated it instantly in my mind with Nancy Kerrigan, in that ubiquitous clip from our childhood, after one of Harding's husband's goons bashed her knee. And I also thought of that *Survivor* episode, the sound right after the bald man pulled himself out of the flames.

At a certain point in the scream, you actually said *Ow!,* which I thought was amazing, like when little kids cry and the sound is actually *Boo-hoo!* Sometimes the referential moments can be the most emotionally acute. Remember when we took mushrooms in that park in Amsterdam and I started clinging to you and crying when I imagined us rolling around on the grass together like Heath and Jake in *Brokeback?*

I don't mean to make light. Really, I don't. They wouldn't let me see you until you were out of triage, so I stood leaning against the tiny window of the locked door, my balled fists resting so dramatically on the doorframe. I wanted to see my own face because I felt so horrified at the prospect of a world without you, or with a changed you, and I wanted to see what that degree of care might look like on me.

A very young resident came out to placate me in a thick, careful accent, and I pleaded with him. My voice actually broke; I noted that as it happened. "Please," I said. "Please. I love her. I want to see her." He looked at me with a mixture of pity and admiration. I registered his look as one I'd never received. An EMT with a military haircut came over and put his hands on my shoulders. "She's making it, man," he said. "She's gonna be okay."

Over the following weeks you were helpless, and seeing you that way without complication or guilt (you literally could not move yourself, after all), I stepped into the broad-strokes role of the *good man*—faithful, stoic, sturdy. I watched the way people watched us as I wheeled you around a Super-Walmart, trying to find a shower stool, a back scratcher, a bell for you to ring when I was in the other room. I watched the neighbors come to their windows to see the twice-daily show of me holding your weight as you tried to shuffle down to the end of the block and back to test your strength. Your skin was so warm in the heat. Your hair stuck to your cheek, like on nights that felt long past when you were dancing, and I wiped it off.

All of this, in the Midwestern July swelter, felt more than surreal. It felt operatic. Or really, it just *felt* in ways that I'd never lived through. Your pain was physical, inescapable; I made it mine, made it a saga of domesticity and perseverance as you nodded into momentary OxyContin relief.

I still think about the day of the accident, and the weeks after. Mostly, I think about how much it hurt to see you hurt. I remember the look on your face—terrified, puppyish, yet angry enough to remain resolute. I was in awe of you, even just the way you giggled at whatever we happened to be watching, wincing but still allowing yourself to giggle. But that brings me back to the swell of my own emotion, to the awareness of how monumental each little beat in our lives felt then, as I piggybacked off your ache, your steady, stubborn healing.

What I still haven't figured out is what this pleasure in feeling does to what it is that I feel. I return to the memory so often; I let my eyes tear up about it and that feels both bad and good. But if one admires the emotion he feels for someone else, does it mean that he wasn't ever really feeling at all? The third person is deflecting here. What I want to know is this: Can I fear for you and tend to you and love you and our little life together, and also love the show of it, as I play the loop again in my mind, tell the story again to hear the drama?

"Do you think people write off *The Real Housewives* as unserious because they're women?" I ask Brenda Weber, who has written or edited two of the best books I've encountered on reality TV. "Like, the title has 'wives' in it, so—"

She interrupts me: "Yeah, but it doesn't matter. It could be 'The Househusbands of Wherever' and people would still turn up their noses. The form is feminized, no matter who the participants are."

I've been telling her that since I love a particular set of reality shows, I realize that most of my watching is dominated by portrayals of women in prominent roles, a landscape divergent from much of the fawning critical acclaim that, until very recently, was reserved for mad men, or men breaking bad. I am, I should admit, outside my target demographic in my favorite shows, though I find the structure and emotional appeal of most reality programs to be identical in their day-to-day interpersonal emotion, with the chief variant being that men are often operating machines and women are often holding white wine. In telling this to Weber, I should also admit, I am transparently

hoping that some sense of *ally*-ship is leaking out through implication. That it seems apparent that I watch with thoughtful, even
altruistic intent. She is disinterested in this line of conversation.

"Don't limit it to the bodies you see," she says. "It's about the
mechanisms of storytelling that surround the bodies, and the
way that gets coded."

She says that reality TV has bastardized an accepted, masculine
form, the investigative documentary, and polluted it with tropes
that people have seen as feminine for centuries now—soap-opera
story lines; refusals to stop for long-winded characterization; an
ongoingness, as Weber puts it—an obviously serialized quality that shows that, more than resolution or insight, the maker
wants to ensure that the audience has something to return for, an
emotional pitch that promises repeatable crescendo. If a giant,
discursive, *serious* novel about a brooding man's internal struggle
is perched atop our hierarchy of artistic merit, then what could
be a clearer opposite pole than fast-cutting, serialized teledramas
about emotional peaks in the daily lives of women who didn't
even exactly write their own material?

I laugh too quickly and assure Weber, again, that I'm a writer
rejecting such hierarchies, a writer interested in the opposite of
the discursive, serious novel about a brooding man's internal
struggle. This sounds disingenuous the moment I say it—after
all, what is this that I'm trying to write, regardless of what I use
to spur the internal self-seriousness? I fall silent; she doesn't push
me. She just laughs, too, and says, "Fine, good."

But why is the argument over seriousness so important to me?
Is seriousness just one person's particular hang-up, the way fame
is another's? And if the end result can captivate me, what does
the intent matter? If one person says, "Hey, I've got multitudes
over here; you couldn't begin to figure me out even if you tried,"
and another says, "Life is pretty good, and I love the things that
money buys me, but you'll be fucking sorry if you cross me," is

the actual content of either perspective all that different? Each still lies open to the audience to explore, to make visceral with subjectivity. Regardless of the credit the artist wants to take for awakening these emotional responses, isn't that ultimate effect still the barometer for whether a character or a story has any meaning?

We get to talking about *The Biggest Loser,* a show that comes up in Weber's writing about makeover TV, the ubiquitous narrative of forced change—a problem for which someone must be shamed and then, after the shaming, helped to overcome. Unlike many of her peers, Weber often places herself in her work, a participant in the phenomenon on display. She identifies as an "acafan," an academic who can both study and love her subject, which is what I think I'm trying to elevate myself to, as though that will make the loving part of the equation more respectable, more serious.

For Weber, to reduce the effects of these shows into something wholly good or bad, or even fully comprehensible, is to miss the point. They are didactic but also nonsensical, uplifting but also cruel, simultaneously stupid and deeply engaging. They open themselves to visceral subjectivity, a heightened, perplexing dissonance, where cognitive skepticism and emotional submersion can coexist. As Weber writes, these shows are an art form meant to *invite viewers to think and feel complex and often contradictory thoughts and feelings.*

"I know some people, like my cousin, who love a show like *The Biggest Loser* and are moved by it the way I think the show wants you to be moved," she tells me. "Who cry when the people start crying after they get thin. I know other people who watch it to be angry at what's being sold as desirable or even possible, but isn't really. I know people who specifically eat ice cream when they watch. That combativeness gives them satisfaction."

We both laugh again. Then I ask, "What about you?"

She pauses and starts over, wry: "I watch it when I'm exercising."

———

When I binge-diet, I do it without you. I'm sure you've noticed. Twice in my life, after multiyear periods of willful ignorance toward any changes in my appearance, I have broken the ignorance quickly and painfully, and have lost roughly fifty pounds in roughly two months. This is my pattern of transformation: fiftyish pounds, two months, every five years, only in the summer. I don't do steady routine, or (even the word is unappealing) *lifestyle*. I only change at critical mass (pun unintended but apt), and perhaps that's a learned narrative device, or perhaps I just haven't found a way to make contentedness productive.

I convince myself that your gaze is too gentle. Almost all the time I need that gentle gaze, its forgiveness, but then you go away for a while and there I am, and there's a mirror, and there are all the eyes of all the other people, and there are those pictures taken of us and posted online, and I feel like I've been caught.

When I pick you up from the airport after any long absence, these feel like the last moments available in our lives together in which we can register change. I want to see you see me, and ask if it really is me. I want to sense you feeling, How can someone be so different from what they used to be? I want you to yell that as you run to hug me, and have people watch us and smile and clap as though I were in army fatigues and you were my young daughter.

The last time I lost the weight was right after my first book was published. I have never felt less seen than when I was writing that book—peering out at others and describing them, writing their images, alone, in the dark, in total, necessary, effortful obscurity. I ate fries with every meal then. Whenever I stopped to get gas, I'd buy a family-size bag of Combos. I'd go to the diner where you worked at closing time, to write and eat the leftover pie that was going to go stale by morning. I'd catch my reflection in the window, lunging toward the spoon to catch

a falling morsel of crust, then turn quickly back to my manu-
script. When the book got published, I felt the rush of exposure,
however small that exposure may have been. The reminder that
I existed, that I was seen, that I had always wanted so badly to
be seen differently.

The first time I binge-dieted we were still babies, just twenty-
one. I was hung up on feeling that you loved me first out of pity
and availability, then out of habit. You spent summer vacation
in California, getting high and selling handmade dresses at a flea
market with friends. I isolated myself and ate 1,200 calories a
day, reduced-carb English muffins topped with tuna, no mayo,
ziplock bags of celery sticks that I took to work. I grew my hair
out at the same time and fixated on the idea that one day I would
be a pleasingly shirtless man with a samurai topknot. I told you
about each day's caloric sacrifice. On the phone you would say, I
can't wait to see you. What a phrase. It's the only phrase I ever
really wanted to hear—again, we're back to what it's like to feel
worthy of being seen, chasing that.

Another thing I never told you about that summer: I watched
The Biggest Loser alone. And *Celebrity Fit Club.* On my parents'
couch, in the dark, when they were busy with dinner that I'd
yet again skipped, I scrolled their TV and watched each new
contestant step shirtless onto an industrial farm scale to strip,
then see the image of their stripping bodies played back to them,
fresh red stretch marks like lightning cracking a tree trunk, a
reminder that they were broken but still malleable. I munched
my celery sticks and cared very deeply for these people on the
farm scale, and I told myself there was hope, triumph even, in
forced malleability.

The moment in our lives together when I worried most that you
could no longer bring yourself to love me came right after that
first adult crash diet, when we went on vacation with your fam-

ily. It was one of those sprawling, gated resorts where nobody had to hold currency or wear more clothing than absolutely necessary. The whole situation was intimidating for me, so I took solace in my own improved reflection.

Remember how none of my clothes fit? I hadn't had time to get new ones after I shrunk myself down, and also I think I hadn't wanted to because the moment I normalized my new body would be the moment it ceased to be anything worth noticing, and the transformation story would be over. During the early evenings, I'd make a show of saying I had to go to the hotel gym, so then I'd be hurried for dinner—Sorry, just need to wash the sweat off, lost track of time. When I arrived at the table last, loose shirt flapping, I tracked the eyes turning up to me.

You had not spent the summer starving in front of the television; you'd been cultivating a life that resembled happiness—being social, getting stoned, eating tacos, hawking your dresses with your hippie friend at a thrift market, wearing matching long T-shirts that you'd turned into short dresses. You looked tan and beautiful, and comfortable with yourself in a way I didn't understand. You had a new bleached streak in your hair.

My sudden commitment to a flagellant type of change had created a rift, hard to exactly describe but very acutely felt. Looking back, I think the tension was a small version of the one that makes reality television so frightening to consider for some: when a particular set of ideals is introduced as regular or desirable or even morally superior, it's so hard not to internalize that certainty. I was certain that I had improved myself. I was certain, for the first time, of the value in the ever-reach for self-improvement, punishment given an aspirational name.

Your parents were certain, for the first time, that I was worthy, and at dinner the last night, they laid compliments and questions at my feet—When did you know it was time to change? Where did you find the discipline? Does it feel different now when you move around? My answers were, I'm sure, insufferable. I don't want to try to remember the specifics of them.

I do remember the final question, the move in the story that was, looking back, inevitable. I remember the way your father said it: Do you think my daughter could—well—could learn something from this new you? We all turned to look at you and your body, which did not deserve to be made to answer for itself, which I knew and loved more than I knew and loved anything but which had been spotlighted in a new way, or maybe that spotlight was always there waiting for a moment in which it might feel less reprehensible.

Look at what you can do, your mother said, and I remember how you looked at me after she said it, the fury on your face quickly losing out to a plea for me to be furious on your behalf.

What I said was something like this: You can do it, babe. It's not anything to be mad about. I'm here to support you.

Then I sat back, already smug in my support.

How could this not have been a learned way of speaking, intuited from all the times I've seen one person, with a pitying, tilted head, tell another how they should change, from the voice that *caring* men give to *needing* women who are supposed to openly admit that they need the care? Of course, naming that tradition doesn't absolve the act. Neither does willful obliviousness. What a vicious lie to try to pretend that such a sneering, self-congratulatory tone was born out of care.

My words lingered, heavy, tactile. You left the table.

Later, on an empty beach, there was a bright moon that felt fluorescent, and you wouldn't look at me. I followed you along the sand until rocks blocked your progress. I tried to hug you or hold you or something. You still wouldn't look, and I hadn't considered, until that moment, what a night would feel like without the promise of your eyes on me, which even as I write it sounds more self-involved an idea than I want it to be.

I kept saying *Please,* and then finally, *I'm sorry.* Then I vacillated between the two until, though you still wouldn't turn to face me, you spoke.

I don't think you know what a betrayal that was, you told me.

I do know, or at least I think I do, which makes the betrayal worse. I did something that I know you'd never do to me, and when I even try to imagine the possibility of you doing it, I freeze. It was the breach of a really basic contract: I will see you without cruelty; I will help you love yourself at least slightly more.

You walked away again, but you let me catch up and walk next to you, and all I wanted to tell you was a collection of shitty lines about the interaction between your beauty and the moonlight. I didn't say those lines because it seemed like no matter how much I meant them they'd sound like lies, as though the cruel force of one statement had instantly superseded the attempted decency of any others. It had. Back in our room, you fell asleep first and I lay looking at the ceiling, still so as not to wake you. I didn't look at you because to do so felt newly uninvited, and therefore profane.

Up until that moment, I'd allowed myself to see only goodness in the way I looked at you. More than that—an understanding. I reasoned that I'd been made to feel shame in ways similar to ways you'd been made to feel shame, and somehow that meant that I couldn't be cruel. And I still catch myself feeling that way, because I often allow myself to forget that I ever did that to you. And I allow myself to feel less conflicted when we sit down to watch women in shaming situations because I grew up a fat boy and have always thought that the perspective forced upon a fat boy is at least similar to that forced upon a girl. Which I still think is a tiny bit true, but such self-claimed empathy has its limits. I see how quickly I managed to take a brief moment of self-pride and turn it on you, weaponizing it, luxuriating in the role of "well-intentioned" body shamer, the worst kind of *Biggest*

Loser trainer-bully, and why? Because I thought I'd been on the other side of it? Because I was so sure I would be again? That's the opposite of empathy.

Apologies are so easy, so temporary. I'm sorry; I was sorry immediately. I said so. Yes, fine. Explanations are harder; there's an implied ongoingness in explanations—no closure, just a stab at something human and gross that could repeat.

Why? I don't really know. Why? Maybe just because I could.

That answer provides nothing, and still I want it to sound like it has meaning.

Eventually I get around to asking Brenda Weber about reality TV's relationship to memoir. They're two forms that have run nearly parallel through my lifetime, each discussed as *booming* over the past couple of decades, each boom met with a certain amount of cultural hand-wringing about the triumph of greed and voyeurism and self-love over art. Each form relies on the pleasure of a person presenting (and monetizing) the emotional crescendos of their own life. Don't we see (and then dismiss) that gesture as feminized?

"That I don't think I agree with," Weber says. "The autobiography, the public archive—I mean, generally who are the people who think their letters are so important that they must be saved for posterity? That doesn't seem like a stereotypically masculine gesture to you?"

This is true. But it's a particular instinct, I think, when someone who is already famous or powerful or artistically respected saves his every ephemera out of the chest-puffed notion that people will want to know what went into the making of him. It's something else entirely when the only product, the thing that is meant to be worth attention, is the mere self, laid bare, probing forward—instant autobiographical emotion.

In the literary world, there's a paper trail for sneering at this kind of personal immediacy. In *The New York Times Book Review,* all the way back in 1987, William Gass tried to explain what he saw as the fast-eroding merit of literary writing, reading his way through the history of American letters.

As I advanced toward the present, he wrote, *the number of women writers increased, as did the number of fictions in the first person and tales in the present tense.* In a single sentence, the first person present ("Look at me now!") was tied to the perspective of women. In the same essay, Gass railed: *Adolescents consume more of their psyches than sodas, and more local feelings than junk food. . . . Is no indulgence denied them?*

As Laura Miller and Alexander Chee both pointed out decades later, Gass connects the feminine perspective to a lack of craftsmanship and reflection, then a sense of immaturity, all of which reeks of self-indulgence. Then all that is equated with the worst kind of consumption: empty calories. He pines for great literature, an old standard of bravery and curiosity, writing interested in expressing more than *a self as shallow as a saucer.*

This screed came a decade before the memoir boom, but I think it strikes the same derisive tone that would pop up in those critiques: a performed horror at self-indulgence, shallowness. To me, it also reads like a modern stock argument against the Kardashians.

"Are you saying that you think *your* work is dismissed?" Weber asks me. "Is that the issue here?"

I say no, but probably yes. That's part of it. I'm worried that I see my every exploit or perceived hurt, or even the hurt I perpetrated, as important, for the mere reason that it has happened to me. It all feels so monumental—I tell it and I tell it and I tell it. I'm indignant that such an artistic gesture can be seen as lesser. I want to believe that the domestic or day-to-day can have value simply for being shown scrolling by, performed well, intensely.

And I want to think that's a moral stance, a democratic one. But I'm not sure. It's just my part in the scramble for whose story is allowed to hold weight and whose life is seen as frivolous, filler.

Weber argues that ideas of seriousness, artfulness, shouldn't matter; that those are projections of a flawed, biased system of cultural critique. And I think she's right. But it's easy to say that I think she's right. Then it becomes a conversation about *my* taste, what I find in these shows of lives that are often dismissed; a conversation about the transformative power of the writer's consideration, and, in my case, the cliché of the self-serious male writer thinking and brooding and expecting the benefit of the doubt—just the version that claims to eschew seriousness.

At an artist's residency once, a composer complained to me that all residencies were being overrun by the cult of middle-aged-lady memoirists crying about themselves. I said that I wrote a memoir, and he assured me, No, come on, man, you know what I mean, and as much as I felt angry, I felt grateful to be safe from the critique.

In truth I can't conceive of being scrutinized the way so many I admire or claim kinship with are scrutinized. I can say I admire the act of exposure, the act of unrepentant autobiography (I do admire it! More than anything, maybe!), but that admiration, or attempted solidarity, brings so little risk. It's like when I convince myself that we look at our bodies the same way, with the same pressure, as though growing up a fat boy was the same as growing up a girl, just because I recognize the general feeling. What starts as something like appreciation or desired identification begins to blur toward appropriation—again: all rush, no risk.

Remember that NeNe Leakes line I always used to say? It was from early on in the show, the second or third season maybe. It was a throwaway line, or at least it was framed that way. NeNe walked into a restaurant to have lunch with her then-friend Kim, who was waiting with the cameras, and as she strolled into the shot, NeNe waved and called out, *Woooh, it's hot as fish grease out this motherfucker!* Then she guffawed at herself, hugged her friend, sat down, let the scene commence.

I don't know what it is exactly that I enjoyed so much—her volume? The specificity of fish grease, that expertise with types of greases and their heats? The fact that it all came so offhand? It felt like I had caught some sliver of realness in whatever contrivance the producers had set up for the scene. Like she was asserting NeNe, and I had the taste to appreciate it. *I* wasn't seduced by the bickering or the real-estate talk. *I* was there for authenticity, NeNe's voice and style—a glimpse of swaggering, New South black opulence, a world so far away from my own that I wanted to be allowed to see and interpret confidently.

I should admit that this repeated impression comes in a lineage of the many ways that I've obsessed about watching and— first alone, furtive, then with you, safe—parroting versions of blackness.

So many anecdotes: leaning against chain-link at street basketball games, too afraid to play but letting my lips move silently around the shit-talk spoken by players I never spoke to. Or when I made my mother buy me N.W.A.'s *Greatest Hits* and played the album on repeat in my bedroom, scowling in the mirror the way they scowled on the album cover, rapping *every* word, unable to contain a shiver and a grin when I hit *that* word.

It goes back further: she saved my assignments from first grade, when I was learning how to write. Top of the pile, on green construction paper, answering the question, "What would my name be if I could choose it?" I had scrawled: "Jamaal."

I went through a very strange Richard Wright phase as an eleven-year-old, starting with *Black Boy,* then moving on to his short stories. I remember weeping on a bus at one story that ended with an African man who'd been quasi-adopted by a white couple, saying, *Massa, you God,* before murdering the adoptive father, thinking he would, like Christ, return. I didn't understand the humor or subversion of the story (it was, I know now, satire); I saw only beauty, helplessness—a character that I wasn't obligated to understand but that I could admire, fear a little, pity. When I wanted to feel sad, a weightier, more legitimate sadness than what I was already feeling, I said that character's words and let myself cry over them.

You know all these stories because I told you all these stories— they came early, probably right on the heels of the red vacuum cleaner, the methadone clinic next door. It was all part of my origin story, being that predictably shameful kind of white boy, but it couldn't have been that shameful if I told you about it all, replayed the performances for comedic or dramatic effect. You smiled, or we laughed together, or you told me I wasn't as bad as memory suggested. I did the same for you, when the opportunity arose. So much of how I understand closeness is the reveal of what we formerly said and did alone, and then the creeping of a once-solitary language into collective language that is made up of so many voices and phrases and sensibilities that are not our own, that we look at and listen to together.

Remember the way I'd say that NeNe line? The way I'd walk into the room on a summer afternoon, push my hips out to one side, snap my fingers (so uncreative), and then holler my best impression of what a black woman from Atlanta might sound like, which is another way to say my best impression of NeNe?

We still do the same shit, but with a new line: *Fix it, Jesus,* the trademark of NeNe's castmate Phaedra Parks: lawyer, mortician, felon's wife, pastor's daughter, self-proclaimed Southern belle. She says it almost earnestly, but with a grin—whenever anything is wrong or untoward, everyone knows what Phaedra's going to say. You've mulled over using it as a hashtag on Instagram: capture a shot of something literally broken, then #fixitjesus. It's always a funny idea. And I love when you work it into conversation, weary from work, sighing as you take your shoes off and plop down, commenting from the couch that you get these nagging headaches but still can't bring yourself to drink enough water: *Fix it, Jesus.*

I've debated getting you a Phaedra Parks T-shirt as a present: an uncomfortably giant-lipped cartoon rendering of her face with *Fix it, Jesus* written below, but then I think about us walking down the street of our fast-gentrifying neighborhood, you adorned with a cartoon image of a black woman across your breasts, and I hold off. We dance around at the borders of our own self-awareness, grinning to each other about that line we know we shouldn't toe.

It's tempting to see all this as only intimacy, to revel in these ways that we speak and behave that we wouldn't show outside the walls of our little home. We are sharing something, after all. It's harder to acknowledge that this interpersonal sweetness is built on a sort of unrepentant vampirism, a series of little joys extracted from strangers that we mutually appreciate or mutually gawk at—how uncomfortable to consider parsing the difference between those two words. Blackness, queerness, Southernness, Jerseyness, devout religiousness. We love them all, or "love" is the word we put on whatever it is that we really feel because love is participatory and hard to argue with.

We catch the snippets of these identities strategically performed on-screen, and then we try them on for each other. What the performers shout, we take and whisper, and that language becomes part of our story. We glance at each other and smile because we know we shouldn't be doing it, but we're doing it again—our little intimate transgression, a private language that was never ours.

———

The thrill of the confessional form has never faded for me—both my own confession and the witnessing of whatever someone else wants to offer up. Augustine, Montaigne, Rousseau, De Quincey, Whitman, Ginsberg, Plath, Sexton. There's something lively in the confessional voice, so swaggering in its willingness to tell you, even as it's supposed to remain somber and contrite. And for all the blood left on the page, the blood that we read for, there's so much left out, still hidden. It's the incompleteness of the show of confession that is so appealing. The ongoingness. There will never be enough time or space to confess everything; you will never properly atone. It will always be a mode both surrendering and combative. The material is limitless.

But nobody wants to be reliant on his own wrongs, the inevitability of their recurrence and the potency of their retelling. What's a greater tradition among confessional poets than asserting that their work has been mistakenly categorized as confessional? And here's Meghan Daum bristling at the idea of her personal essays being confessional: *I don't confess in my work, because to me that implies that you're dumping all your guilt and sins on the page and asking the reader to forgive you. Confessions are not processed or analyzed; they're told in a moment of desperation.*

Desperation, yes, but the pleasurable kind—like popping a zit when it's grown too big, too painful, then wallowing in the relief of pus. What I'm saying is I don't think she gives enough credit to these moments of desperation. As though desperation is only a lack of control. As though on-your-knees begging is only a last resort, never a style, or a joy, or an invitation, or a negotiation.

Judith Butler addresses the appeal of confession with this barrage: *Is it a deed, a desire, an anxiety, and abiding guilt for which the confessional form serves as a balm?*

A confession can be all of these, all at once, as it shifts and winks, gains momentum. Butler is writing specifically about sexual, bodily confession, but I think that tension permeates across the form, the twin intimate transgressions of the action, then the voicing of it. She writes that the confession becomes its own action, related to the act being confessed but distinct, an experience of its own, an experience of release but also with a new tension: pitiful, powerful, hostile, always incomplete.

Lately I can't stand a narrator who isn't confessing to something. I think that if it doesn't feel, even just for a moment, like a secret joy or burden to unload, then why say it? Desperation is more comfortable than reason, a more inexhaustible resource. Sometimes I let myself think that every action is excusable or interesting or even valuable, as long as you're willing to confess. Let it linger, let it squirm, and it's beautiful. And I know that's not right, but the seduction is real. What is being confessed fades, as the act of confession swallows me. It feels like intimacy, which is the whole point.

Reality TV is the first narrative medium I can think of that isn't merely open to confession but demands it. And the act must be repeatable. The one thing a performer must do is live publicly and comment back on that living with some show of revealing what should be hidden, being moved by it, then repeating the process.

The confession is the most important part of the performance, even (or especially) when the performer feels compelled to resist the act. There are even two distinct types of confession—the OTF (on-the-fly) shot and the formal interview. The formal sets the performer down days later to reflect on what they did; the OTF seeks them out just moments after the action and asks, before the sweat or tears have even dried, What have you done? The answer is always impassioned, always incomplete. Always hedging. Often annoyed. And so the tension continues—how many times can one be forced to see one's self and still not atone for anything?

As reality narratives have matured and solidified, a characterization of that development has been the shortening of every action scene. I've been concentrating on this of late, trying to find a scene where the audience is allowed to linger for more than a minute. Impossible. Instead, a two-second pause passes for a linger; all is compressed, heightened, so a single gesture or glance carries weight. When critics bemoan the *formulaic* nature of reality shows, the surfacey predictability of the narrative movement, I think they're referring to this.

The scissors cutting through the action, and also the glue to the story line, is the confessional scene. The comment is so much more important than the action being commented on. It's become impossible to watch any significant moment of action without stepping out of the action at least once, usually anywhere between two and ten times, to see a character prodded into accounting for her own behavior, hoping the account is sympathetic or at least compelling. Everything they do is just fodder for what they might have to answer for. And so each response is an act of desperation, the desperation of being sat down and told to see yourself, to assess.

There's rarely full contrition. There's self-defense, waffling, deflection, exaggeration. There is, amazingly, the attempt to say that what was filmed didn't really happen. Atonement glints through, fleeting, incomplete. It is confession at its *most* desperate, the strong-armed and endless kind, and as such the confessors all bristle and shrug and snap back. Usually it's these moments that grip us and, in turn, make us the kind of audience members we don't like to see ourselves as.

Just *own* it! we whisper at the TV.

Every fucking time, we say, shaking our heads. Every fucking time, it's the same thing with her.

I remember laughing once as you addressed the person on-screen the way you have so often addressed me when there's nothing left to say: Cut the shit; for once, cut the shit.

———

Ramona Singer (*The Real Housewives of New York,* Season 4): *I'm sorry, I'd like to kick the shit out of her, okay?*

Phaedra Parks (*The Real Housewives of Atlanta,* Season 5): *Me? What did I do wrong? Really. You tell me.*

Teresa Giudice (*The Real Housewives of New Jersey,* Season 2): *There's a saying: Don't throw stones, or whatever.*

Shannon Beador (*The Real Housewives of Orange County,* Season 8): *I'm just here for one reason and one reason only; can we get to my issue?*

The producers' questions are rarely left in, but their implied power is felt in each answer. I imagine them always beginning with, Don't you think . . . ? Or, Isn't it time to . . . ? The invitation, the prodding, is there offscreen, forcing the response.

It's a mistake to think that such moments are simply a reflection of badness or shallowness or, worse, unaware stupidity. Their coarseness, their absolute refusal to perform the kind of humanity that makes me feel good about humanity, is what keeps me watching. Truth shimmers within every one of these semiconfessions, even if the performer is outright lying—truth within their consistency, their concern for self-preservation and self-promotion, their confusion, their anger. We return for so many seasons to see if these moments of reflection lead to better, more sympathetic moments of reflection, and they never do. The glib are glib, the cruel cruel, the angry perpetually waiting to burst. Every word is a justification, a negotiation, a plea to be seen as something better, and most of the time that's the way I feel when I worry that I can't, won't, let myself evolve. Is there ever a moment of reflection that isn't at least a little bit disappointing?

7

{REQUEST FOR AUDITION}:

I feel I would be great for this because of many reasons. I'm a full time student majoring in psychology. I'm very into to the mind, behavior, mental issues, cause and effect. I'm also a club host for a very popular night club; in which I'm so different. I'm a construction worker. Most of all I have major commitment issues in which I'm very aware of in can't change. I have never dated just one female no matter if I was with one for years I still had other girlfriends whom I dated thru out that same year. This cause me a lot of money due to crazy drama; I mean CRAZY DRAMA. From my school to work place but they always stay. O yea I'm a lesbian. My parents are deep in the church which is another issue. My mom hold on wishing and praying I will get delivered. I just feel I got a lot to offer situations some can learn from and be so interested in. It's so many parts of me and my life, crazy part is I realize my issues, understand them, know where they come from and yet i refuse to do something about them. . . . One I'm sure I will but now I jus want to live learn n have so much fun

—from www.castingcallhub.com

From the beginning, there has been controversy about how to think of and what to call the collision of real people and TV-ratings grabs. "Documentary" was originally the catchall term for anything nonscripted on TV, but that grew to annoy some people—why should a term so loaded (and also, producers whined, so boring) be allowed to encompass everything? In 1962 in *Television Quarterly,* Burton Benjamin, the legendary head of CBS News, was already sick of the conversation:

> *Bosley Crowther suggested "Think Films." Jean Benoit-Levy plumped for "Films of Life." The semantic argument exists. Not long ago, a quite prominent documentary producer was complaining to a New York television critic that the label had to be changed. It frightened viewers, inhibited sponsors, and made network executives see red ink. His recommendation: Non-Fiction Programming . . . Other producers have suggested "telementaries," "docudramas," "factdramas" and "actuality dramas with a hard spine." All of these are a bit Orwellian, but understandable in a medium where an hour show is an hour show and an hour-and-a-half show is a spectacular.*

Benjamin went on to say that instead of arguing about what to call the alluring display of lived drama on small screens in millions of homes, networks should think of what these displays could be used for. He advocated for the *"little" film about man himself. It may be said that the issues of our times are too cataclysmic for us to deal with the life of an Eskimo in Canada. We are dealing with war and peace, life and death—with survival. . . . The problems are so large and the people seem so small. But are the people ever small?*

I think that last question of his is still being asked, or at least some spiraling version of it. Over half a century, the people have grown ever larger, in one way—they're famous, they're always present, sometimes they spawn a lasting personal brand. Yet we worry about those blown-up lives becoming smaller in meaning: petty, inconsequential, further from the power of any actual truth. So the question shifts: If we see so many small people turned spectacularly large, do we end up shrinking the value of each individual life? Then the nastier subquestion: Do we maybe *prefer* to see people as small when we watch them, so long as we don't have to think about anything big?

It's hard not to want any piece of art or media that calls itself nonfictional, or even implies it, to be useful. When the power of *nonfictionality* is present, it should be used to promote a good force in the world, or expose an injustice. And if you film or describe an injustice, it should be to make people . . . well, *something.* It should make people something. It should make people feel something, sure, but those feelings should be specifically the kind of feelings that might incite action—anger at what is being done to the subject, anger at what the subject is doing, fear of the danger shown, and then inspiration to change or help another or spread the good word, whatever that particular word is. It's validating to be involved in the potentially useful, even if your only involvement is watching, which isn't really involvement at all.

We watched that movie about the Japanese fishing industry killing dolphins and cried when the activists played the sound of their death shrieks, told us we were listening to murder. We watched that string of factory-farm documentaries on Netflix and then you stopped eating meat, and then I admired that so I did, too, and now we're those people that mention how smart pigs are at dinner parties. We watched the coverage of the Ferguson protests for hours, then went to our local protests, then returned to the coverage for more. Whenever one of us looked antsy, the other would say, "We could switch the channel now," but always the antsy-looking one would answer with real gravitas: "No, no, we *must* keep watching," and I'd carry on monologuing about the terrorism of the state.

I'm not trying to be glib here, just honest. Or maybe not even honest, just open—an unburdening, another little confession.

In their book, *Shooting People: Adventures in Reality TV,* Sam Brenton and Reuben Cohen trace the documentary traditions leading up to the form. They start with John Grierson, the man who first used the word "documentary" in 1926 (when describing Robert Flaherty's work), who himself heralded an age of serious forays into the serious issues of the time, and whose own soundman said that his chosen term "smelt of dust and boredom." These were propaganda films, celebrating labor: *Song of Ceylon,* bankrolled by a tea company, showing the noble lives of Sri Lankan tea growers as they adjusted to industrial modernity while also holding on to valuable traditions; *Night Mail,* funded by the British postal service, showing the hardworking patriots who transported a nation's letters. Grierson described these first documentary techniques as *the creative treatment of actuality,* and he peddled that trade in the service of a particular kind of morality: sponsored jingoism.

Next was cinema verité, which found a different angle of moral responsibility within the act of filming stories about real people. Vérité was messageless—no somber narration over carefully selected shots to tell the viewer where her sympathies should lie. As Brenton and Cohen put it, the move marked *the abandonment of argument.* Or at least claimed to. Because, of course, that's an impossibility—the camera argues simply by what it chooses to see, the editing argues by what it deems expendable. Instead, the form took up a new, silent argument: What you are seeing is pure truth, the accurate everything of another life; we are letting you make up your own mind.

Finally, there came moral responsibility to oneself, a generation of nineties filmmakers who claimed that the only truth that mattered was the personal connection: Michael Moore telling us about the auto industry, but really telling us that he grew up in Flint, Michigan. Or Tracey Emin challenging giant patriarchal institutions by very specifically chronicling her sex life. The claim to truth was replaced with the claim to authenticity. The person had *lived* the story they told, and there was no greater purity than that of the first-person address.

It's either heartening or the opposite to think that the conversation about reality shows picks up, in some way or another, all the threads that have been around since the beginning of filmed actuality. Maybe it's the perfect coevolution of these traditions into one beast. Maybe it's the mutant child of every bad instinct—beholden to the messages of financial interests, claiming truth speciously, stopping to pray at every slapdash church of the self.

The term *abandonment of argument* keeps sticking out to me, the implied purity of it, how you can choose to see it as the closest thing to truth or the ultimate lie. The shows we love are, if anything, *about* the act of argumentation, in that the subjects of the shows are all actively arguing with one another. And even just by their sheer presence on-screen, they're arguing that they deserve screen time, as well as making more specific arguments about and through their own lives—Wealth is desirable! Being fat is dangerous! I really love Jesus! Looking good can lead to feeling good! True love is real!

But I don't think those add up to arguments in any grander sense. They're not trying to convince us of anything, other than to hold still, to come back for more. So the abandonment of argument here is more the abandonment of purpose. This is antiaspirational watching. Sometimes, as we watch, I feel hopeless. Sometimes turned on. Sometimes weepy, sometimes benevolent, sometimes cruel. Sometimes I feel like the most honest version of myself, festering, which brings its own strange sense of accomplishment. With no argument, we're left to our own worst devices.

———

A couple of years ago a study was shared around the literary Internet, where I feel compelled to spend much of my non-TV-related time. The headline: "Reading Literary Fiction Improves Empathy." The study split subjects into sample reading groups: some got nonfiction, some got "popular" fiction, some got literary fiction, and some read nothing at all. Then the researchers asked questions that somehow tested the readers' abilities to understand the thoughts and emotions of others. Apparently, only those who read literary novels got better at understanding perspectives outside their own. Literary fiction, the study reasoned, paid more attention than other genres to the inner workings of the mind, requiring the readers to imagine themselves in those thoughts on the page for a sustained period of time, encouraging nuance, curiosity, care.

Of course, I have a lot invested in quibbling with these findings. I'm pretty confident that they are, at least in some way, bullshit—such studies exist only to stock tenure files and provide ammunition for Facebook fights, another manufactured battleground on which people can weaponize the claim of who gets to be a good person. But I'm also a bit nervous that I don't fully understand empathy, or that it's tempting to willfully misunderstand it.

I like feeling emotions, and often I'm tempted to equate the mere act of feeling with empathy. I think again of the pity with which I misread Richard Wright—the warm swell of connectivity I felt when crying at the pain of characters that I made no real attempt to understand, even as they moved me. Which isn't to say that the feelings were insincere—I loved those books; I *was* moved, but then what else? What knowledge of anything beyond my own inflamed emotion?

I'm not trying to imply that Wright isn't literary fiction, only that I didn't seem capable of reading him for those qualities. That's part of the deal, I think; not just the creator's intent to reveal the whispered intricacies of human psychology but the interpreter's willingness to look for them. Perhaps that's the better question, or at least the tougher one to confront—not what the material is providing us but how hard we're willing to try to understand, how content we are to stay at the surface of another life and wallow in the emotion it can provide. It's much easier to feel than to understand. It's also easy to equate feeling with understanding, and that leads to satisfaction, and what feels better than satisfaction?

I remember watching *Cops* with my uncle Chris. Chris was a heroin addict, and for much of my childhood he lived, off and on, in my grandparents' basement on the couch. During the day, he would tell his mother he was going to Dunkin' Donuts or to meet a guy about a potential IT job. I'd watch his van pull out, and then four or five hours later he'd return with shuffling feet and huge pupils. He'd head back to the basement, where I slept on a mattress at the foot of his couch when we visited. It was usually a Friday or Saturday, so *Cops* was on prime time, and Chris had gotten to the point where he could name various officers and discuss at length the merits of their personalities before their names even appeared on-screen and they reintroduced themselves to the cameras in their squad cars.

He watched to laugh at the criminals. When they ran, he laughed and pointed at the screen; when they invariably got caught, thrown to the ground screaming or crying or both, he would sit back satisfied and chuckle the chuckle of someone whose expectations were limited and had just been met. I didn't particularly like Chris, so I watched to hate the cops, and then watching became about anger for both of us, the distinct satisfaction of being *certain* that some man on-screen was a bad man who deserved whatever humiliation he got.

One of the last times I slept in that basement, *Cops* wasn't on, but Fox News was playing clips of the first U.S. air raids on

Afghanistan. I think it was night-vision shots from the perspective of the bombers. Most of what we saw on-screen were flashes of light coming from below, and we could hear voices explaining, rather gleefully, that the old Soviet antiaircraft guns that the Afghan fighters on the ground were using couldn't reach the height of a modern jet.

"Look at those fucking *losers*," Chris said. "Look at those fucking cavemen. Shooting at airplanes they can't even hit."

He was older at this point, maybe sober but physically falling apart—swollen ankles, a distended belly like an infomercial child's, a dying man's face. He was quieter and gentler than I'd ever known him, ruefully self-deprecating, just beaten, really, but he was still vicious and clear-eyed as he watched.

The conceit that there were real people being filmed—real cops shoving nightsticks into the smalls of the backs of real crack-addicted petty thieves, or real fresh-faced American fighter boys winning shadow-war victories—seemed to allow him to feel *less,* to engage in *less* reflection. This was a man who nodded out in the back of his van until mall security rapped on the window. Who must have, at points in his life, felt as neutered and rageful and doomed as any makeshift soldier shooting defunct missiles up into the sky. Yet when he watched criminals get beaten for public amusement, young men dying defenselessly in a war that technically hadn't begun, he couldn't feel, or didn't want to feel, anything approximating connection. He seemed to feel only righteous joy.

Sometimes this is my worry for me, for us. That we see real lives, framed just so, and are invited to assess their merits, and that assessment becomes a way to perform our own morality, to double down on how we like to feel. We're the opposite kind of watchers from Chris—we're doe-eyed bleeding hearts, not callous believers in bootstrap myths—but we still watch to judge. Saying *Awww* isn't that different from saying *Ewww.*

In front of *Dance Moms,* when Kendall tumbles midsolo and

her mother clucks and averts her eyes in the crowd, I say, "Awww, Jesus Christ, these poor kids."

In front of *My Big Fat Fabulous Life,* when Whitney is called Shamu by a bunch of shitkicker dudes in a parking lot: "Awww, *nobody* should have to hear that."

Then you grin at me, and maybe rub your fingertips on my scalp. Maybe we hold hands there on the couch, and what a lovely feeling that is, briefly: soft skin like we just remembered it was there, fingers intertwined easily—not routine but definitely accustomed. We discuss our own aversion to cruelty, our own ability to care, say that's the quality that makes us who we are, and the screen flickers neon, and the music plays us into the next commercial break.

8

Hey our name is _____ and _____ im 23 and he's 26 we've been going through a lot we argue way too much and we just want to be successful in life its just that me and are really struggling and want to show the world what we go through and still love each other he's working and im working but we don't live with each other but we want so bad just don't have the money so us being on this show we'll show everyvody what we go through and how we make ends meet with each other so can we please be on this show we would really appreciate this.

—from www.castingcallhub.com

When I was sixteen, I watched *Joe Millionaire* every Thursday. The conceit of the show was that women competed to marry a handsome man who was not actually named Joe, who they were told was a millionaire but was in fact a construction worker. On one of the last episodes, Joe had narrowed it down to two women, and one of the women took him for a walk into the woods around the house set. They were offscreen but miked up, and the shot lingered on a bare, boring tree, with subtitles at the bottom of the screen. There was a final, key sound with a corresponding triumphant subtitle: *(Slurp).*

It's hard to express how thrilling this moment was for me. To not see anything sordid but instead to hear it and read it over the most benign possible background. It felt like encountering the monsters drawn at the edges of an ancient map, the unknowable, beautiful danger that was always waiting just outside the available frame. I longed for what the show was selling—the kind of impropriety that wasn't flaunted but also (obviously) was, a place where secrets were massaged into the realm of the nearly hidden: whispered intentions, covert sucks, sordid mysteries that I'd begun to imagine happening in every dark corner, just out of my grasp.

(Slurp) became the first big moment of moral indignation at not just the reductive, antifeminist premise of such a reality show but the execution of it. The slurper, Sarah, came out after the show premiered and said it never happened. Or that the sound happened, the image happened, but the blending of the two was fiction. The slurp was spliced in from an earlier bit of audio when she was eating some soup in the communal kitchen, or something equally lame. They'd just been talking out there in the woods, kissing a little, whatever—PG-13 stuff. A common noise was mixed into a common situation to produce the desirable effect of scandal. This became its own scandal.

This technique has since been given the rather dramatic title of "Frankenbite"—mad scientists meddling with the order of lives, monsters made, et cetera. It's a term ever ripe for attack. One of the most thorough attacks comes from Jennifer Pozner, in her book, *Reality Bites Back: The Troubling Truth About Guilty Pleasure TV.* Pozner takes on the role of the investigative reporter, probing through the lies. She quotes an anonymous producer from *The Bachelor* saying, "It's misleading to the viewer and unfair to the cast member, but they sign up for this."

The "they sign up for this" part of the quote seems to refer specifically to cast members, but Pozner uses the Frankenbite example to reinforce the fact that viewers are being lied to as well, manipulated into seeing a reality that was never really there and buying into whatever moral judgment is neatly manufactured by that contrivance.

"Though this technique is commonplace," she continues, "most reality show runners want us to believe that, as *Laguna Beach* executive producer Tony DiSanto claims, 'We never make up something that hasn't happened.' Actually, they do."

Yes, they do. Or maybe they do. Maybe it's somewhere in the middle existing on a sliding scale between document and deceit. Either way, what I want to know is who was ever really fooled?

The most irritating thing about telling people that I'm "working on this new project about reality TV" is that the first response it invokes is, without fail, reactionary disbelief.

From a journalist mentor: "Oh, the fake shit?"

From a really condescending Uber driver in LA, taking me to a restaurant where I might spot a favorite star: "You *know* it's all made up, right?"

From a student: "You mean *un*reality TV?"

From my mom: "Isn't that all just a trick or something?"

I don't know if reality producers ever cared whether we believed that nothing was conjured, everything pure. After all, that's an incredibly boring thing to believe, and also rather stupid. I tend not to believe that about the world or the news or the people I love; why would I suddenly be my most naive when faced with the nakedly cynical prospect of seasons of forced intimacy between people who are strangers to me?

The opportunity to be aghast, or to be the asshole at the magic show who tries to solve the trick before the magician even finishes, has to be an enormous part of the desired effect. It's the thrill of simultaneously trusting and questioning, that edge within every interaction in which you are asked to believe; the maybe-narrow, maybe-vast gulf between the person who exists and the character they've made or have been made into, or both. As Brenda Weber points out in her work, there's a space between suspiciousness and belief, a willful participation in the semi-truth, that is far more compelling, far more active, than being lied to.

Every critic who brings up the word "Frankenbite" hurls it onto the page like recently exhumed proof of a long-suspected murder. It's been happening for over a decade. *The Washington Post* uncovered it in 2004, *Slate* after that. Then the *Chicago Tribune.* Then *Time.* On and on. Each article carried a breathless tone toward how we are lied to and what such lies mean for the culture. Nobody cared. Or they did, but not in a way that inspired any change, and so the discovery was left to resurface again, just another layer in the narrative.

The alleged slurper, Sarah, made the rounds on various talk shows and glossy magazine profiles to discuss a number of things—why the fake millionaire was an asshole; recent revelations that she'd previously supported herself as a foot-fetish video performer; her motivations for auditioning for the show and thus gaining a much wider audience than the foot-fetish-video community; and finally her rage at being edited into the kind of character who'd semicovertly suck a dick on TV.

It's all a lie, she told new cameras about what had or hadn't been captured on old ones.

I don't recall any feeling of disappointment at her denials. I had watched a show built on a narrative foundation of cruelty and dishonesty, the implication of sex, and the enormous, destructive power of the things seen as conventionally attractive. I'd watched it *for* these reasons, I think—a world where people approximated Greek mythology, in their perfect bodies, their petty retributions, their seductive impossibility. A world where everyone expressed guilt for what they were doing but still went out and did it. What changed upon knowing that the slurp was inauthentic? And in the context of everything else, how inauthentic was it?

A decade after his show, Joe Millionaire sent a letter to a reporter who'd once written a profile on him when he was still in full show mode and claimed that his *perfect girl* was *blonde, with big boobs, a little waist and a big, thick bubble butt.* He wrote to atone.

First, he said: *Truth is, I never really wanted to be on TV.*

Then, later, came: . . . *the ridiculous thought that I would be on top for a long long time.*

And finally: *The person that my parents raised was better than the one I showed the public when I was introduced to America.*

Even a decade after the action, the confession is a vivid, if predictable, part of the story—the pretense of never wanting attention in the first place, then admitting the opposite; the acknowledgment of a bad character followed quickly by the assertion that the character wasn't the true man at all.

Robert Galinsky makes characters for a living. People come to him as themselves, leave as something a little . . . more. Galinsky invented and still runs the New York City Reality Television School, the first and only of its kind, preparing hopefuls for their cattle calls, like a Lee Strasberg reconceived for twenty-first-century ambitions. When I meet him, he's guarded—the only press coverage he's ever gotten has been brutal. But after I tell him (sincerely) that I find his critics to be pearl clutchers, he becomes animated and jumps right into telling me about one of his best students.

"There was this girl I had come in," he tells me. "She walked with a cane and she had a service dog. I asked her, 'Who are you?' She said, 'I'm the girl who has a prescription pill addiction because I'm mentally ill.' She asked me if that was okay, and I asked her if *she* was okay with it. And she said, 'Oh yeah, it's true. That's what I'm bringing to the table.' And so we went with that."

Galinsky finishes his anecdote with a proud shrug and leans

back into a leather couch. We're in a coffee shop in Alphabet City that seems to serve as his home base. He comes out of experimental theater and improv, speaks in those terms, wears jeans with flip-flops and red sunglasses that are a bit of a personal trademark. The barista kids know he always orders a macchiato.

For a long time he was just an improv coach. He started teaching reality when a Argentinian dog groomer called the number on his website and said he had a month to prepare for an audition for a show that would end up being called *Groomer Has It*. Galinksy lets that name hang out there like I'll recognize it. Remarkably I don't, but no matter. If I'd seen the show, I would have seen Jorge become the star. Out of all the groomers, it was Jorge whom everyone wished good things for. He played the whole damn season from hero position, just like an improv game, the way Galinksy taught him to, and he killed it. He didn't win the show, but he won affection, he proved to be watchable, and after his season, he landed a roll on TLC's *Extreme Poodles*.

"He was never the guy who threw the glass at the wall," Galinksy tells me. "He was the guy who went up to the glass thrower and said, 'Don't do that; why'd you have to do that? What are you feeling that made you do that?'"

Galinsky figured out pretty fast that the same principles he'd always taught improv-ers applied to reality shows—that willingness to constantly stoke the story forward, that in-the-moment fearlessness, sustained commitment above all else. A common misconception among people who deride reality performers, he tells me, is that nobody's interested in the ones who don't get into fights. That they provide no intrigue. The truth is, and any seasoned on-the-fly performer knows this, if you jump into the middle of a fight to break it up, you become a hero. Or you become someone trying to be a hero, and as long as it seems genuine, everyone wants to see someone *try* to be that.

I agree with this, and then we both try to come up with that

F. Scott Fitzgerald quote about heroes, but we can't quite remember it so we go back to TV, and what makes for a great performance of self.

We speak of Rodney King breaking down on *Celebrity Rehab,* Galinksy's favorite of the shows. And the guy from *Taxi.* And the drummer from that grunge band. They were so fucked up, these men. They were so pained, and they had been pained for so long, telling the story of their pain like every day of their lives had been an audition for the moment they could finally be that pained for an audience.

"I don't know if you should exactly call it talent," Galinsky says. "But, yeah, it always helps if they've got some really fucked-up lived material to draw upon."

That's a scab that he can pick at, help turn into the blood that an audience tunes in for. We're back to his pill-addicted, cane-using pupil. I ask Galinsky why she wanted *that* to be who she was on a television show. And did it work?

Galinksy can't remember, but he's pretty sure she hasn't made it onto whatever show it was she wanted to get on. Doesn't matter. Those producers must be insane, he says, and the important thing anyway is that she went into her audition clear-eyed and armored. She would be an active storyteller. *She* would be the one valuing her trauma, valuing it enough to lead with it, as opposed to letting some producer ferret it out and then define her with it.

I ask Galinsky if he's proud of that anecdote. It's a leading question and gets the expected answer. He helped, in his own way and in his own view, to give this woman some combination of the three qualities any teacher wants to provide to their students: authenticity, confidence, power. He tells me he teaches two classes at Riker's Island, and he tries to provide the soon-to-be-paroled with the same qualities as the soon-to-be-on-TV. We sit silent for a moment, and I consider the two neat, though flawed, parallels he's set up: reality performer as prisoner; reality show as the world. Which makes him some combination of shrink, parole officer, and career counselor.

This all smacks of new-agey-self-empowerment in a way that would ordinarily make me uncomfortable. It still does a little, as we sit in the kind of coffee shop that guys like us always sit in, drinking our macchiatos and sneering about shows like *CSI* because they have no *life,* no *guts* to them. Guts, we agree, come from people like Galinsky's pill-addicted, cane-using student. He prodded her to reveal, to a circle of fellow wannabe stars in class, the tagline that she would put on her life and, regardless of its manufacturedness, it worked because it was nakedly pained, because it made you worry for her or *tsk* at her. And this exercise prepared her to repeat that story in an audition, to repeat that story as the official one—recorded, hopefully broadcast and commodified.

"If she wanted to be that brave," Galinksy says—and he leans forward on "brave" like he really means it—"if she wanted to be that brave, then good—she was ready to tell her story."

Brave is a tough word to accept, I think, and bravery a tough concept. The lines between bravery and arrogance or ignorance or stupidity or, worse, desperation—sometimes it's hard to trust that those lines are there. But what else to call such an act? To put a name on yourself that marks you a freak or an asshole or a reclamation project and then to step in front of a blinking red light, open source material for the Frankenbiters to do with what they will.

Maybe I'm using *bravery* to describe what is really the internal calculation of how much attention one wants (or sometimes believes that they need) and how much one is willing to risk to be seen. But I want to be seen, to be known, somehow; I dream of it, and I've never risked anything like that, and so that act of risk makes this woman at least a little extradeserving of whatever it is that she wants. And whatever she wants seems less important in the face of what she'll do in the service of the wanting.

"It's not the car wreck people are looking for," Galinsky says, and I'll admit this sounds a little rehearsed. "It's that moment when the car wreck is inevitable and we're wondering if someone will survive."

So the camera turns on: Crash. And then.

Ask me for a tragedy and I'll point you to Rob Kardashian.

I can't imagine it's easy to be younger brother to Kourtney, Kim, and Khloé, older brother to Kendall and Kylie—each one so forceful and beautiful and impervious to wilting. Even in the earlier days, the happy times, Rob always stayed at the edges of the screen, darting into scenes as a gentle foil or affable peacemaker. He operated as sort of a cipher for vaguely appealing normalness—often doofy and jovial, occasionally pouty, typically vain, always incompetent but sincere.

I say this not to take away from their talent or work or personalities, but there are no *bodies* in the world more elevated or important than the Kardashian bodies. For a decade they've been omnipresent, simultaneously idolized and scrutinized, and constantly in flux. Kim's ass alone is important—it has racial implications and enormous financial ones; it invites both slobbering and vicious whispers; it cannot be seen without an accompanying conversation about its authenticity. Now we talk about her little sister Kylie's body—at seventeen is it appropriate to be fucking a twenty-five-year-old? Is it okay to get those super intense lip injections, even if the injections make those lips as famous as Kim's ass? And of course there's Caitlyn—how public her physical transformation was made, how triumphant the result.

I'm not the first person to argue this, but to say that their success is superficial is a disservice; they elevate superficiality. They are so *good* at it, so committed, so fully and captivatingly bared. So productive. They make no effort to make it look easy. It can become exhausting to tune in to.

Not Rob. Rob is attrition and apathy. Rob is trapped in the way that most compelling characters are trapped, in the way that I often feel trapped. Rob changes in directions that he does not want to change. And all of it is seen.

Let me just admit this right away: I like to Google "Fat Rob Kardashian" to look at the image results. You know this. I think you do it, too. There are many results. If you wanted to (and I think someone should), you could make a collage of these images that runs around all the walls of a giant gallery space—tens of thousands of images with no break in between, many of them almost the same but not quite. It would be as though he were never not viewed, like a flipbook of a life spent flaunting and hiding himself at the exact same time, his eyes always peering out from under a baseball cap to see who is looking, and it's hard to tell whether he's checking to see if he's safely alone or checking to make sure that someone still cares to watch.

Many of the pictures come spliced next to his early shots—the ones where he's shirtless and celebrating something insignificant in a horizon pool, tattoos dotting his muscled side abs like gum splotches on a cobblestone street. And then. There is narrative just in this juxtaposition, a tragedy because, look, he used to be one way, and look, now he's another and, look, it's still happening, and we get to watch him face it. I love to watch him face it.

I think Rob and I are the same age; that must have something to do with it. He has been on television as himself for the exact span of time that I have loved you, and I have so badly wanted you to see me as the narrow, nubile, carefree kind of beautiful that he used to be. He used to cavort in his shots; that's the best word for it. We used to watch him just sort of hang around the family mansion—twenty-three and still living at home, eating a banana or drinking a beer, winking at the camera in a way that read less obnoxiously cool, more endearingly incompetent. He always seemed a bit adrift, a bit bored, and I took comfort in seeing somebody enact this condition successfully, one that I felt but could never accurately convey.

He seemed not performatively ecstatic, just happy enough, happy in a way that is unnoticeable unless someone is really watching, and of course we were always watching, and there was pleasure in seeing him exist as the least remarkable person in the room. Now when we watch him, we see the way he tries to hide his enlarged self, see his family speak about him in whispers, with cruel worry. We talk about how long ago it was that Rob cavorted, and it always feels at least a little bit profound to point out the way time passes, how ominous that can be.

We were still living in Iowa the first time Rob broke down in a scene that had been clearly orchestrated for a breakdown— family therapy, held in what looked to be a vintage-furniture showroom, complete with ornate velvet couches and fur blankets draped over midcentury chairs. Rob had on a black baseball cap, as would become the norm (presumably to hide the creeping baldness), and an oversize black hoodie to hide everything else. He grew increasingly upset at accusations flying his way. He began to tear up, as the therapist coaxed him—*You look sad; am I misreading you?*—then fled to the bathroom. His mother and two of his sisters, immaculate in dress and posture, stayed on the couch, stoic. Another sister and the therapist, and I would guess two or three cameras, followed him. The bathroom wasn't huge, so he was trapped, and the cameras were tight on him.

The shot stayed mostly on him in profile, newly expanding torso heaving, the lightly stubbled beginnings of a double chin accordioning as he cried. He held a hand towel over his face, and there was that drama of watching someone so closely as they show you how little they want to be watched.

All I care about is, like, saying yes to my mom and making her happy, he said, trapped in there. He looked up. *And doing whatever my sisters want to make them happy. And when it comes to the easiest things, they just—they don't, they won't help me.*

Here he buried his head back in the towel and squeaky-cried.

The therapist's bony hand was on his ample shoulder. She was kneading him, and her enormous pewter bracelet shone in the lighting. In an OTF cutaway to his mother and sisters sitting without him, his mother, stone-faced, said: *I like it when he's vulnerable because I think he needs to break those walls down. He's so angry.* Watching it, I was struck by how much she genuinely seemed to think that she was caring for him and also how much she was consciously writing him into this sad, angry man-boy, handing him over to the viewers as such.

Of course, the next shot was back to Rob, trying to articulate that there are so many things that he wants to *do,* successes that he should have, that dress-sock company that showed such promise, and if his father was alive, his father might understand a little better. The therapist brushed that away, called it a *top-layer issue,* told him that he had spent too much time running from his feelings, from his very *self.*

You're one of those steam kettles, Robert, she said. *You know, sitting on the stove on the fire. You're so full of feeling.*

Then, on cue, he boiled, the squeaking louder, the wheezing breaths more frequent, burying his face again. I realized that the editors had never fully cut out the transition music, just lowered it, so there was a thumping, somber hip-hop beat carrying through the moment, like we were in an old ship's furnace, and the panic and the inevitability were all heightened that much more.

I've got you, the therapist said, which again toed a line between caring, commanding, and threatening. *Come on, let me see your face.*

Rob obliged, moved the towel, and face exposed, camera creeping even closer, said: *Nothing matters. Nothing's gonna change.*

There was one perfect beat extra, and then a cut.

The first time I talk to B, he's on a job somewhere in Canada. He can't give me specifics about the gig because of a standard nondisclosure agreement. I don't know the name or the network, only that the producers watched B-roll of another show, a trip to a ski town, and they saw the mountains and the cute bars downtown and said, I wonder what life is like in that kind of place. And so a makeshift apparatus sprang up—casting calls for would-be stars, makeup teams, camera crews, the whole squad. Then, finally, a bunch of editors like B.

There's something of a gold-rush element to it all. B calls reality the Wild West, and the metaphor seems to fit: a bunch of start-up, nonunion shops descending for a few months on locales that may hold some value, drilling, dredging, then look-ing again for that elusive thing somewhere else. B is based in New York and mostly works there, but he had just walked off a job when the call came to head north. The previous job was just too much. He would cut the same scene with the same shitty material over and over again, and the head producer would tell him it wasn't right, even though there was nothing he could do. He can't just magically make *anybody* interesting. And they were up against it timewise, and of course he's the last line of defense, so he's the guy working twenty-four hours straight knowing full well he doesn't get any scaled pay for overtime. Maybe when he was younger that would have been acceptable (on his first job, for example, he turned out a show in thirty days of postproduction, without a single day off) but he's been doing this too long, and he's too good to get treated like an interchangeable part.

"When the material sucks, the editor gets blamed," he tells

me. "That's just a fact. And sometimes, when I'm angry—and believe me, editors are usually angry—I just want to scream, 'I *make* you!'"

The problem, as B sees it—well, there are a lot of problems as B sees it, but the main one is that the focus isn't on *quality* lives, it's on how quickly a narrative can be turned around. And a lot of people on these shows, they think they can just be themselves and stay away from anything flashy, as though merely existing is adequate. B is enough of a reality veteran to know that is very rarely the case. And often producers don't seem to push their muses for the best they've got.

We tune in to see the characters, B tells me. You need to hone that. You need to stay faithful to this thing that you have made compelling, but the producers don't bother.

"These are your *actors*!" he says. "Direct them! Give them a fucking voice! Help them tell their fucking story!"

In the end it falls to him and the other overworked laptop jockeys given five, six weeks to make a story out of a collection of slapdash situations, hours of dead air between people who are content, in the most insulting sense of the word, to *be.* It's B, hunched at a desk in a bare room in a month-to-month office, sifting through and trying to find the thread to follow, the thing that, when extracted and shined up and displayed, can make a person transcend into watchability.

When I tell B that, overall, you and I always seem to like Bravo shows best, he isn't surprised. He says that viewers like us think we like the stories, but what we're really responding to is character, and underneath that what we're *really* responding to is style.

It's hard to get a Bravo gig as an editor because you need to be able to create within their strict style parameters. They take that shit seriously, as they should. They give out a list of rules if you're lucky enough to get a gig. I ask him if I could see a copy, but somewhere in that list of rules is a pretty strict nondisclosure-of-the-rule-document rule. I manage to cobble together some vague examples instead:

For a restaurant scene, we should see at least one of the main subjects order their food and at least one main subject take a bite in the midst of dialogue.

For any argument, there should be at least a few seconds of chatter immediately before and after the explosion. You should never show the explosion without some kind of tepid lead-in and a breather at the end.

It's all part of moment building, he says. If you watch a show that feels flat or inhuman, that's probably because the moments aren't built; the crescendo of the scene seems to just arise out of no curated foundation.

I think of NeNe in her very first episode, the way she changed from a side of potatoes to crab cakes because of the look Gregg gave her. I mention this to him, and he says, "Exactly. You've got to let NeNe breathe on-screen." Let her be NeNe ordering, NeNe changing her mind.

NeNe is an example of someone who gives you so much— all NeNe really does is give, whether it's volume or emotion or humor, an opinion for every situation, a constant simmer always eager to reach a boil. NeNe gives so much that she can cease to make coherent sense—that's not just her, that's anybody. Think of any person observed, trying to tell a story, or many stories, that don't really begin or end. How could that be coherent? B assigns the meaning.

"My calling card is the way I work with music," he says. "I use the beats of the music to punctuate the stories they're telling. If you're watching and you pay attention and you feel like the action is grooving really well to the song in the background, then you might be watching my work."

Sometimes I think it's not even what NeNe's saying but the cadence of it, like she's a melody line and the beat is there in the backing track, and then she delivers her put-down and a good editor sets that right on a crescendo, then adds that pause to let it breathe, then a reaction shot of the person she's just insulted, then goes back to NeNe, who doesn't even have to say anything, just gestures, and the editor cuts out the music right then, and everything is perfect.

B has never met any of the performers whose lives he edits, and he's never been on set, but he calls the scenes *my scenes* and admits that sometimes he thinks of every shot of every show as another page in a book that he's writing about people and the way they are.

"Am I disappointing you?" he asks, with a hard laugh. "Everybody loves beef and everybody knows that cows die for beef, but nobody wants to know *how* the cows are killed."

I try to answer him honestly. "I don't think I really care how the cow is killed," I say.

He says, "Figures," and we both laugh.

He has to return to work—he was supposed to be back in New York a week ago, but the Canada project is turning into a real shit show and they've extended his contract to try to find something worth salvaging. I return to an *Atlanta* rerun, waiting for you to come home from rehearsal so that we can catch the new episode together.

The rerun shows NeNe at a party with the rest of the housewives. She's wearing a flowing, pristine white pantsuit and arguing with a once friend, current enemy, about a future event she's planning. The volume and emotion have been building, along with the music and the mounting anticipation for an inevitable NeNe crescendo.

She delivers. She raises herself up, tells her frenemy that she doesn't even think about her, and then says, *You know what, when I have my event, I'm gonna be thinking about how fabulous NeNe's event's gonna BE.* She leaves a pause between *gonna* and *be,* and she snaps her fingers down in front of her foe's face. The song hits its own crescendo when she snaps, the drums dropping back in, subtle yet forceful. Then another almost imperceptible beat, and then NeNe turns to strut away.

The scene continues for a little while, but it's all clearly outro, winding down, letting us bask in the moment NeNe has provided: perfect.

There's something vital in the space between spontaneity and authenticity—that's what I want to get at here. There's a progression. It's what makes NeNe tower and Rob Kardashian whimper and jiggle so compellingly. It's not quite spontaneous, or rather what I mean is it's honed spontaneity. It's what B and his kind are busy building, always another job taking what might be the blandest spontaneous utterances and massaging them into something structured enough to feel authentic.

Barthes once wrote that the accurate transcription of what is spontaneously said rings false. In its lack of stylizing, the result seems like *an excess of style.* There's something rigid, inhuman about the process of attempting to express something totally unvarnished, when that unvarnished moment is already gone. Somehow that style, which is the absence of style, is the most jarring.

Barthes was writing about how a voice only seemed true to him when filtered through the artifice of turning it into something else, a new text born from what was once there. This is beyond style-as-substance; it's style-as-self. And I don't know if a star like NeNe sees her substantive style when she watches a scene back, like Barthes reading his work. And it does feel a bit ridiculous to apply the philosophy of a French semiotician who looked upon TV watching as a *doomed* and *tamed* practice to our reality-show obsessions. But I do, and that idea heightens the pleasure—the person on-screen not merely transcribed but *made* by a whole team of people who cut and shift and add a little pulsing soundtrack until a vivid, presentable personality emerges.

The moment Barthes became text, he became free of the responsibility to represent the constricting coherence of himself. He could instead become a sensibility, an idea, a feeling. I know the appeal of that desire. I've felt that imagined freedom, and maybe that's what I'm after now—disappearing into the text until I'm nothing but a recognizable vapor, and within that construction I think I can see myself better, from a distance. I can convince myself that I'm no longer yoked to my actuality. It's seductive. I much prefer to see myself when I think I'm not really there.

Now I'm thinking of a moment when we were both younger and very horny but also very sad, living in New York City and trying, as one does, to convince ourselves that we were somehow different from all the people who looked like us and lived in the same place we did, doing the same things and feeling the same way. We were fighting on Fourth Avenue as our friends pulled away in cabs to go to a nightclub that you didn't want to go to.

I remember you pouting under a streetlight, leaning your arm on one of those bins full of free newspapers. I love the way you pout. You pout fully and unabashedly, bottom lip out like a shelf, cheeks flushing red the way angry peoples' cheeks are described in shitty novels.

I remember you hissing, "You should have fucking *left* with them; I didn't *want* you to stay with me."

You said it like there was a period between each word, and this felt performed, as though you were thinking about the implied punctuation the same way I was. I was so angry at you;

also, so aroused by the intensity of the moment, how much we could hate each other, how we could, however briefly, become *that* couple that we so often watched on late-night subway rides. Drunks passed us and slowed their stumbling walks to look and listen. What did they think of us?

We had to wait a while for a cab because a lot of cabs didn't want to go out to where we were living, the side of Prospect Park farthest from Manhattan. When we finally got one, we refused to look at each other. I watched the driver's eyes on us in the rearview mirror. I thought about how many pairs of people he saw in the backseat, framed in the small square cut out of the plastic divider, and then I thought of *Taxicab Confessions* and all the people I'd seen framed that way.

We didn't speak, so I began to plan what I would say to you. I began to plan how I would explode. I'd never exploded before, or it didn't feel like it, anyway; I hadn't with the full, towering rage that I thought I was capable of. Back in our apartment, I sat on our bed on the sixth floor, top floor, windows open, and you sat straddling the windowsill so you could blow smoke out over the fire escape.

You were talking about how you didn't want to be made to feel bad for not wanting to do the same stupid shit that we always did, with the same people, at the same bars, like we were doing these things just because they felt like *something,* at least, and I always assumed that the alternative was nothing. This was a very good point and very well articulated, but I remember not wanting to think about the content and instead focusing on the volume of my response.

"Fuck you for saying that," I said.

I said it very quietly, in a manner that I felt could be accurately described as a seethe. I was building the moment, and you helped when you said, "*Excuse* me?"

You put your cigarette out and stood up and moved toward me, starting to say something else. I remember so clearly springing off the bed and moving to loom over you, a foot away maybe. I could see our reflections in the window.

I screamed, "Just shut the fuck up! Just give me a fucking break! I'm so *tired*!"

There was a rhythm to the way I screamed it. When I said *tired,* I punched my right fist into my left hand, and it sounded like a good punch. You gasped, like really gasped, when my hand drove down in front of your face into my palm. You began to cry, your crying, like your pouting, so perfectly on-the-nose of how the action is supposed to look and sound. You were frightened of me. I felt stoned. I felt not-me, or at least such an exaggerated performance of a me that I'd never been that none of it was real, even though it was real and it was me in the reflection in our bedroom window. It was a scene; we were making a scene in every possible definition of the phrase. I would watch that scene. I'd been watching it. But in the silence that followed, the comedown, it began to feel too much, too long, unnatural, over. There was a beat, then a shift. I began to apologize, quivery—a new cadence, a lowered volume.

After I stopped apologizing and you stopped crying and then I stopped crying, we went in the living room and watched *The Hills.* Do you remember that part? The main girl, Lauren, was on a date with that college baseball player from back in Laguna who ended up in rehab, I think on *Celebrity Rehab,* actually.

They weren't speaking much (God, they so rarely said anything at dinner). She just sipped and he just gulped, and she poked at her food. At some point, I think Lauren indicated she was frustrated, as always, and as always he said something like, "What do you want me to do?" Their eyes met briefly, and hers were pleading and his were vicious. The show cut to them in bed, still clothed, his hair still cragged with gel. They looked at each other, then away, their bodies tense but perfectly compatible as she fit into the bulk of his torso.

For us, then, on the couch, I don't think there was any

moment of reconciliation, just a fade into sleepiness—our bodies slackened, moving toward each other, our eyes beginning to shut; a scene that had run its course, with the screen flickering in the background, familiar. In the morning I made eggs. It was a lovely morning, slow and hungover, from that time when hangovers weren't physically incapacitating so they could verge into romantic. Routine was weighted with lingering notes of the previous drama. It was like we watched ourselves reemerge, doing the crossword and taking turns refusing to let the other give up. I said I was sorry again, you said you knew that; you taunted me gently when you got clues I didn't know—hands on shoulders, hands on knees, a walk to Prospect Park as church ladies smiled at the sight of us.

On the Kardashian shows, for a long time, Rob has been mostly an absence, though a fraught one.

His mother says: *Maybe I spoiled him and that's why he's like this, but he's my* son.

His sister says: *I'm not saying he's not in pain, I'm just saying he could learn to take a little responsibility. He could* do *something about it.*

His other sister says: *I showed up at the condo to take him to the gym with me, and he doesn't even fucking come out. Like, I'm an adult. I've got things to do.*

Where is Rob? What is he doing? What is he *eating*? Is the room dark? Has he painted all the mirrors black? Will he be okay? Can anybody save him?

I'm not going to pretend I don't sometimes ask, "Am I as fat as Rob Kardashian?" I ask so that you'll say no. There was a time when I asked and you said no, but the honest answer would have been: "It's a toss-up, depending on the angle." I still like that the great tribulation of his story line is as petty as mine, but that on-screen it can seem seismic, and that seismicity feels like an accurate reflection of the way I experience it. Still he returns, and you and I watch him with a gleeful memory of all the times he looked like he wanted to escape.

Last season Rob apparently didn't want to be on the show at all, but there he was. He appeared only sporadically, but he was there, sitting silent on the couch as the rest of the family continued at their normal volume. We smiled at each other—Of course he's back!

I remember one scene when Kourtney, Khloé, and Scott were arguing playfully on the couch next to him about something that didn't matter. They were giggling and tugging on one another, and then Kourtney, the littlest, was draped across the rest of them, her sister slapping her ass, camera focused on her exposed thong. Their self-satisfaction was extragratuitous but also extra-appealing next to Rob, who, as usual, embodied the way I have so often felt: perfectly still, aware of every inch of space he took up on that piece of furniture.

"It ain't over till the fat lady sings!" Scott yelled.

"Khloé, start singing," Kourtney said, and everyone laughed in that exact way that people laugh when there's nothing of them in the punch line. And then there was Rob at the edge of the shot. Rob leaning away but letting his eyes turn back to his sisters, as though waiting for one of them to notice, hiding, exposed.

I thought of Rob when we got our engagement photos. Why, I'm not sure—maybe the anxious pleasure of having to pose myself; maybe a weird feeling of satisfaction, like I'd progressed past him, this world-famous multimillionaire I'd never met. First I tried to protest our getting the photos at all, but they came complimentary with our wedding package, you said, and the photographer pointed out that they presented a chance for us to begin to tell the story, *our* story.

I watched you lay my outfits on the bed. I booked a last-minute salon appointment just for a beard trim—I wanted to be a *bearded* man, not an unshaven one; you smiled and said you understood perfectly what that meant. Then you stood in front of the TV in your underwear, holding potential dresses over your body, one in each hand, back and forth, asking me to decide, with *Say Yes to the Dress* playing on the screen behind you. I told you that you were beautiful, effortlessly. I emphasized the effortlessness because it felt kind to do so, but that was condescending and not the point. We *were* going to put in a lot of effort. And it was going to be effort made to appear seamless, effort designed to show us as we would like everyone to believe we are when no one is looking.

I flipped pancakes in one picture. We read on the couch together in another. You read Plath and I read Foster Wallace, two writers who offed themselves, of course, which meant that we were winking at the whole situation, a very important aspect of *us* to show. We asked the photographer to make sure he got the book covers in focus, and he didn't understand why, and we giggled—typical; no one gets it.

We walked around the neighborhood we'd just moved to, held hands on the stoops of brightly painted old Victorians, kissed in front of coarse brick walls covered with graffiti messages that weren't meant for us. We stopped at the coffee shop that we always stopped at, and as neighbors ate their hangover scones they watched the photographer crouch to the ground for new angles, stalk in slow circles around our outdoor table while we pretended to talk to each other. The dog weaved between our legs and looked at the camera when we told her to.

We ended up with a zip drive of 460 photographs, a two-hour narrative in which we moved between staring deeply at each other and playfully at the camera. You put the best seventy-eight shots into a Facebook album titled, "Hey, it came with the package," which I thought was a nice, diffusing touch.

We'd scrolled through together to pare down the material. No. No. No. No. You look good but I look old. I have murderer eyes in this one; do my eyes always look like that? Jesus, is that really my *face*? This one is okay.

We read all the comments people made on all the photos, and when they began to dwindle after a few days, the throbbing disappointment settled in. It's too easy to say we'd first felt validation, so we were disappointed when the validation went away. More that every image held so many implications, every overproduced scene a narrative of implied change, forward momentum toward a life that might be enviable, that appeared permanent. The kitchen where I made banana pancakes was nicer than any kitchen we'd ever had. And we looked good, newly wrinkling in a not-yet-weathered way. And we were dog owners, which meant we were successfully keeping something alive. And the way we held each other on the couch in that one picture, so different from Rob Kardashian on his mother's couch, tense and alone—our comfort together, staged and captured, the care displayed back to us. How nice to be loved the way that love looked, to be the people that those people there in the photos appeared to be.

9

I grew up an athlete playing all sports. when I graduated high school I missed competing so I played softball golf and pool I took to pool cuz it it was all year round and fairly cheap to play. I practiced my heart out and in 2010 I won the Pennsylvania state championships took 2nd 2011 I moved into semi pro but I was then hit with a devorce my life changed dramaticly I ended up traveling for work climbing towers for AT&T I did that for 3 years shooting pool very little but now I'm back in Pennsylvania and my dream is to return to playing championship pool and playing in the pro circuit thank you

—from www.castingcallhub.com

The second season of *My Big Fat Fabulous Life* was starting last night, so there was a marathon of the first season to bring us up to speed. It was unnecessary, but we watched anyway.

I'll admit that I was skeptical when you started watching *MBFFL*. I pretend to distrust feel-good realities, and I do get bored with their constant victories, but something about this show captivated me almost instantly—its star, who *owned* the predictable narrative parameters in which she worked, who seemed a near virtuoso at inhabiting herself.

Whitney Thore is morbidly (though I suppose she'd quibble with this adverb) obese, due (at least in part) to a weird gland thing called polycystic ovarian syndrome. The disease is the engine for the show. She would not have a show if she hadn't gained 200 pounds one year in college, and if she wasn't now fluctuating between 375 and 400 pounds, and if she hadn't posted a wildly successful YouTube video of herself dancing-while-obese. Either the name of her disease or her exact weight is brought up every episode. During her confessionals, the invisible producer feels very present, and I cannot help but imagine a steady prodding—Remind them what's wrong with you after the commercial break. For a new viewer, give them a number to work with. Call yourself fat; show them you're okay with it.

That's really the whole dramatic tension of the show: Can she love herself and try to change herself all at once? She faces the camera, over and over, and speaks directly to the ways that her body is perfectly lovable; she moves with cheerful, unrestrained grace, yet the show leads with "big, fat" before ever throwing in "fabulous," and when we watch, there's always the tension of whether we might see any crack in her cheerful facade. Every smile seems to be an act of will, not because it seems hard or unnatural for Whitney to be happy, but because she steers that emotion safely through the constant public reminder of shame and danger. The cliffhanger at the end of season 1 was: Will Whitney get diabetes? The whole last episode draws out the sustained story of that concern, carrying us into season 2.

The show is intentionally unremarkable in almost all aspects beyond the one malignant physical detail. I suppose that's in the service of normalizing, or near-normalizing, creating that sense that she's totally regular, except . . . Whitney is thirty-one, still trying to figure stuff out. She's saving money living with her parents in Greensboro, North Carolina, which seems both small and big, a perfectly adequate place to live. Her parents are good people who love her. Her friends are good people, and one, a guy named Buddy, could maybe be more than a friend. Whitney's still trying to navigate the implications of that relationship. We lean closer to each other whenever we get to watch them flirt.

Scenes and episodes tend to run together in my mind: Buddy goes shopping with Whitney; they banter. Whitney talks to her parents about moving out; they will miss her, and they worry for her. She is grateful for them. At Starbucks, Whitney forgoes a Frappuccino and has only an iced decaf, while her friends get what they usually get. They acknowledge her willpower and she says she's trying, and then one friend says when he gets hungry waiting for his food at a restaurant he'll just eat a sugar packet.

The rest of them say he's sick.

They all seem to like one another and their lives; well enough, anyway.

In season 2, Whitney is right back at the doctor; the ever-present threat is highlighted again. As she stands on an industrial scale, the background music gets louder. *Oh Lord!* she says. In a confessional shot, she explains to the audience, patiently yet emotively, that when you weigh what she weighs, you can gain twenty pounds and have no idea until the scale shows the number. She conveys this as truly terrifying. We go back to watching her stand, frozen, finally not smiling.

I am wracked as we watch her. I feel my own body, feel it spilling over my teaching slacks in ways that bother me most when I'm sitting down watching TV. This is not to say that I'm seeking to relate or that I'm capable of understanding her situation, only that when the camera is closing in on her and she's explaining what she's feeling, trying to hold herself tall and proud, trying to keep smiling, it provides me with the recognizable sensation of a spring coiling tighter and tighter, and the cheesy music build and the gratuitous shot of the scale screen as it reads *weighing* don't make the moment any less potent.

She is coiled in feeling on-screen, and that is allowing me to feel—she's done her job well. And you are next to me. We are looking at her, not each other, sharing the act of parallel feeling, which means that we're not really sharing any of ourselves, but mere proximity begins to seem like a gift, like a risk, as we keep staring at her, hoping together for a small, temporary triumph.

In the end we discover along with Whitney that she has lost three pounds. She dances in celebration—trademark! The lights in the office are nasty, invasive fluorescents. In the next scene, Whitney's doctor is telling her that despite the weight loss, her blood tests are still edging toward diabetic. No dancing; she's back to fighting away tears. Not much has changed—brief relief is followed by renewed terror.

Her parents are worried and kind again; she embraces them. Her friends are fun and supportive again. She resteels herself. By the end of the episode, she rides a bike for the first time in years. *Come at me!* she screams to the world, between jagged breaths. *What now?!*

She unleashes her full lovability, a nonirritating bubbliness that is an innate gift, a relentless charm that makes her inspirationally fat where others are depressingly so, even to those like me who convince themselves it's somehow more intellectual to resist inspiration.

There I am on the couch, crying. There you are next to me, crying. We glance over at each other's tears, like always.

"I love her," you say.

"I want to be her," you say.

I don't know if you mean it, and you don't elaborate, but we're ready for more.

Robert Galinsky looks stern, proud even, when he tells me it's his job to empower naive aspirants to stand strong in the hellscape of exposure.

The producers are all fucking monsters, he tells me. Every one of them. And everybody knows it. They're looking for commodities, and the performer is looking to commodify herself while still retaining some dignity. Everything you say can be snatched up and ruined. That's the game (*every* show is a game, is another point he emphasizes): try to make it through unruined.

"I am armoring soldiers to battle for their very selves," he tells me, and when I react with a smirk, he says, "Seriously."

"Show me a reality-television producer and I'll show you a beast," he says. "They are looking to annihilate peoples' spirits and exploit their pain."

He continues with the battle metaphor and gives specific examples of the wars entered on-screen. A young blonde woman with great tits comes to him, proud of those tits, certain those tits deserve some attention. To Galinsky, she is naive when she walks into his studio. She prizes only attention, doesn't think about the implications of what gratuitous tit shots can end up doing in the hands of the wrong producer. She doesn't think about the fact that she's giving herself over to an apparatus that doesn't exactly work respectfully with those who have tits.

Be aware, Galinsky tells fame-hungry young women like that. Be aware of who lurks on the other side of the camera, of what you will be asked to give over just for a chance to be seen.

He tells me plenty of his students leave having paid him for the experience of renouncing their desire to be on these shows. That can be its own kind of success. Or they soldier on in the lust for exposure, with at least slightly clearer eyes. I'm not going to go so far as to say there's a nobility in that, but there is, at least, a hard honesty.

We start talking about the alternative prospect of a hypothetical (or, really, composite) young woman trying to become an actress in the traditional sense. Would those casting calls be somehow less demeaning, the elusive roles less pigeonholing, the corporate interests less evil? The only difference, Galinsky says, would be the lack of friction in the interaction, a slick distance born from embodying a named fiction. And the words, if she happened to land a speaking part, would be written for her— she would read them as a character and make them real enough for an audience to believe as that type of character she was meant to portray, and that's all. There's safety in playing fictional characters, the assumption of artistic intentions and ethical decency that can cover up what is often unethical and shitty art. Nobody's looking to find the worst in it.

When Galinsky announced that he was training hopefuls in the finer points of reality, a lot of former friends lined up to call him a sellout. These were actors and directors, practitioners of an art form, and he had once been part of that noble endeavor, but he chose instead to become an active participant in the ruination of modern culture. You're training the people who will be the death of us *actors,* they told him. The people who want to steal our screen time without putting in any of the effort, who are in it for the wrong reasons.

Galinsky thinks that often what is anointed acting is just faking. And those people who shit on him, he tells me quietly, have a pretty romantic view of the industry of fakers. Faking is just as nasty—demeaning roles filled by hungry bodies, offered up for consumption—but nobody thinks about the nastiness, and that makes it static, numbed, self-satisfied. Don't act like the fakers are doing something more than the people entering battle with their real names, Galinsky says. Don't act like he's the bad guy for meeting his students at their ambitions, and showing them how much it will hurt, asking them if they want to do it anyway.

When you broke your back in the bike accident, I was working on the unload crew at a Kohl's. Three days a week, before sunrise, I'd climb into the truck and face the boxes that reached from floor to ceiling, wall to wall, all the way back. The boxes were full of content branded by famous or semifamous people. We needed to have the unloading complete before the doors opened to customers, so we worked fast, floodlights trained on us in the bowels of the trucks.

Randy, the shift manager, who took his job as seriously as all shift managers seem to, would read out the number of items supposedly packed into each delivery. "Sixteen-twelve today, guys," he'd say, like that meant something to us. We would race with one another to see which team could toss the most merchandise out of the truck and sort it down the conveyor belts the fastest.

The heaviest boxes were cookware: stacks of authentic Rachael Ray Dutch ovens and Bobby Flay grill sets, each with a tag saying something like, "You've seen Bobby use this!" Jimmy Buffett's Margaritaville margarita blenders.

Lots of space was taken up with bedroom sets: the Jennifer Lopez LA Nights collection. And reasonably priced formal wear: Marc Anthony's Slim-Fit evening-out ensemble.

Of them all, the biggest product producer was Lauren Conrad, LC from *The Hills* (when she was a young, rich suburban girl interning and going to fashion school in LA) and, before that, from *Laguna Beach* (when she was a young, rich suburban girl who aspired to someday work in fashion but more pressingly aspired to have Stephen see her as more than a friend).

I moved a lot of LC merch. Some days Randy would say, "Jesus Jones, how much shit is this chick making? Who the hell is she anyways?" The two college bros on the crew were the only ones who admitted to know besides me, and they claimed never to have seen her work; they just were generally aware of popular culture through their girlfriends and could confirm that Lauren Conrad was a fucking smokeshow. Once, in the break room, when the truck was finally empty, I tried to explain her. She's this girl who grew up rich in California. She was on a show about her and her friends in high school. Then she was on a show about living in LA and interning. She's generically sweet but clearly more tenacious than her demeanor and packaging would suggest, which is why I think she held people's attention for so long. She has a penchant for dating fuckups.

Randy made a disgusted sound and said, "I'm giving myself a hernia lugging *her* shit around?"

There were laughs, followed by the grudging acknowledgment that at least she was making herself some money.

The LC collection covered everything—skinny jeans, maxidresses, lightweight overcoats, boyfriend sweaters. It was all nice enough and sold well as a compromise for high school girls and their conservative mothers. For this fact Conrad was, and is, considered a reality-TV success story—she made it out. She no longer has to parade herself and instead has used her self-parades to set up a platform for her actual career, the thing she always aspired to. She did it thoroughly: a full, ploddingly executed transition.

All I can say is that it made me really sad to hoist boxes with "Lauren Conrad" and "Made in China" stamped on the side; even sadder to X-acto those boxes open to find neat stacks of lilac polyester-blend long-sleeved Ts, each shrouded in rippling, membrane-thin plastic. Every time, I thought, This is it? All those shows—the self-deprecating hangover coffees, the friendship-ending blowouts, the Saturday-night perseverance, the crushingly conversationless dinners with alcoholic Jason— tossed aside for a steady, well-planned empire of cheap stitching, safe styling, an eighteen-to-eighty-five-dollar price point?

I loved watching her live, which really means I loved watching her want. Even as I knew that she would never not make it, that she had a *Vogue* internship that was being filmed (her bosses were merely extras on *her* show), I watched to see her in a manufactured state of in-betweenness that always seemed to poke at the in-betweenness of our lives as we watched her, not recognizable, exactly, just a vague parallel, still potent. I remembered every detail of how she behaved in so many little moments: when she turned down a summer internship in Paris to stay in Laguna with fucking Jason. When she fought at that club with

Heidi, and then the next day Heidi tried to make amends but
Lauren held strong and said, *Sometimes you have to forgive and forget,
and right now I just want to forgive you and forget you.* When she
fought with another friend and wept a single, perfect, black-
mascara tear. When she finally made it to Paris and, after duti-
fully holding a clipboard at a *Teen Vogue* gala, got picked up on
a cobblestone street by a grungy, gorgeous suitor identified only
as "Mattias: Guitarist," swinging her legs over the back of his
scooter while saying, *There isn't any ladylike way to do this.* It
was weird and forced and sweet and preposterously stylized and
banal, and it just existed, or it seemed enough like it did.

She was—she made—a recurring drama, something intentionally hovering between bland and bizarre, and when I came
home from work, we watched pirated reruns of her drama in bed,
as you lay stiff in the back brace. We were nostalgic—for her, for
our former selves who watched her originally. She was all over
our memories. We reminisced together: what a show she'd made
out of something like her life. Now she was making *things.*

"If you asked my graduate students," Mark Andrejevic says to
me, "they'd tell you that art doesn't exist objectively. That taste
doesn't exist objectively. Or talent. They'd say it's all a social
construct of class. That it's meaningless. That's where we're at
now. But I don't know about that; I think that's kind of boring."

He teaches in California now and writes mostly about government surveillance. He hasn't written about reality television
in a decade, since he was one of the first to try to analyze the
fault lines of self-expression and self-monetization. This was, he's
quick to point out, before social media. He saw reality TV doing
the work that, very soon, Twitter and Facebook and Instagram
and Snapchat would take over. The earliest shows that fascinated
him were entirely about surveillance—the illicit thrill of cam-

eras rolling at all times, in one house or on one deserted beach. His fear then was that all this material would be available on-screen and that everybody would feel compelled to show everything all at once.

"But social media became what we worried the reality show would be," he says.

What he doesn't fully understand is why, then, reality TV still exists. If people are eagerly and often professionally giving up some selective version of their own realness in real time online, then we don't need to reach to television for the constant murmur of surveilled lives. Access is already complete, so what appeal is left for the shows to provide?

I tell him that I've begun to follow my favorite reality stars across various platforms—Phaedra's Instagram feed, The Situation's Facebook page full of inspirational sayings and videos of bikinied women falling down, Ramona's exclamatory on-brand tweets. The list is very long. I thought this would give me the final, ecstatic rush of access, but instead it's almost always enormously disappointing. I find their constant selves to be either far too overt in what they're selling or boring in their repetition, or just sloppily composed. I continue to monitor them only for the enormous distance I feel between their digital blathering and the performances on their respective shows. It enhances the shows, makes it somehow fuller to watch for whatever ineffable quality has been isolated on-screen, in episode form. It's like how I love *Inside the Actor's Studio* because of how stupid the movie stars seem in interviews, which heightens the mysterious genius present in their work.

When I tell this to Andrejevic, he chuckles.

"So what's your taste, then?" he asks me. "What makes these shows better, or even just good?"

I think this is the thing I'm trying to figure out. Can I isolate some particular beauty in what I see, or am I just used to the medium, or is what I love the fact that we watch together, so watching can become interaction, which can become autobiographical?

Kant said: *When a man puts a thing on a pedestal and calls it beautiful, he demands the same delight from others.*

Andrejevic brings up that line because he says that what I'm doing is demanding the kind of universal agreement that aesthetics cannot provide. He's right; we can both hear the demand creeping into my voice. But here's the catch: for a form to be allowed to be beautiful in any way, to have the potential for art, there needs to be room to make an aesthetic argument. Within that argument there's the crucial assumption that the form has beauty if executed well. We can talk all day about whether or not *The Corrections* is any good and, not despite that argument but *through* it, the novel remains a beautiful form. Legitimacy is born when critics point to beautiful versions of something and shitty ones, too, trying to differentiate. That hasn't happened for reality television; maybe it never will.

The differentiations made between reality shows linger at the level of money and demographics—different target audiences, or different ratings that shows manage to pull in, or particularly destructive worldviews that shows might be peddling. *The New York Times* even released a map to trace what shows are popular in what parts of the United States. This ran on the politics blog, the shows removed from any artistic aims or successes, relegated to the role of *prolife voter* or *Second Amendment warrior*—windows through which to track and then feed people's basest pathologies. The assumption remains that whatever a reality show is about and whoever it's made for, its ambitions are low and its results cynical. It's judged for what are accepted to be uniformly bad intentions. The conversation resists the aesthetic, lingering in questions of ethics.

"I think it's a leftover Puritan thing," Andrejevic says. "We're uncomfortable with someone having something for nothing. We can't see these people as definably better at a particular thing and therefore more deserving. We fixate on that."

The screen still deifies, but it can seem inherently suspect to think of someone not actually godlike being allowed to transcend. It throws off an internalized sense of order. If we look and say, Hey, that could be me, it only naturally develops into Hey, that could be me and instead it's this shameless asshole who's no better than me, and is probably worse. It's an updated version of looking at a Pollock painting and saying a six-year-old could do it, except way more people want to be famous than want to be a painter.

In her *GQ* profile of Kim Kardashian, Katy Weaver writes that Kim is living the American Dream and then perfectly addresses what she assumes will be backlash against that notion: *If you bristle at the designation, remember: Someone who lives the American Dream is not, strictly speaking, an American hero.*

That's the tension the audience is forced to reckon with—to want what they have up there on-screen, while feeling the need to assure ourselves that we don't like who they are or how they go about getting what they have.

Andrejevic points out that people have always loved a behind-the-scenes backstory of what made someone famous or special.

"Now I guess we just eliminated the backstory," he says.

I think it's more that the backstory has been streamlined into one basic story, which has become the only story: the hunger for more. If the question is, Why do you get attention? the answer is, Because I want it so fucking badly.

When I think of my failures—and this is not something I tell Andrejevic—it's very important for me to separate talent from effort. I tell myself it's not a lack of talent that holds me back, that always has, it's that I'm not willing to try in the cloying, clinging ways that others try. This is bullshit, yes, but still I say it. You've heard me say it, falling asleep in bed to my whispers about these straw men and their cloying, their clinging.

It's calming to see talent as divine, ambition the opposite. Talent transcends any petty condition, remains pure; ambition is always vacuous, eventually implodes. This is, of course, untrue—talent and ambition are inseparable because we wouldn't know about one without the other. It's easy to look at a reality star as only ambition (and a very narrow kind of ambition at that), which then must drown out any chance at talent or even sincerity, to see Kim Kardashian as obviously gaudy and gross while Jon Hamm is obviously a genius, focused on the integrity of his gift, one channel up the dial (ignoring those endless Mercedes commercials he's doing). It never seems like a spectrum; instead it's just two poles and a lot of shame in between, and you know how quickly I can get wrapped up in shame.

But I want to tell you how bad I want it. Whatever it is that's required to be seen, I want that. Above all, maybe. I put so much effort into obscuring that desire because of the risk in voicing it, how easy it is to fail at a stated ambition, and how voracious that ambition feels whenever I do acknowledge it. That felt like a purge just to write down; it's already tempting to delete.

The scariest thing about ambition is that it's hard to understand or explain. That I can say I value privacy, small and quiet intimacy, some notion of integrity, and that makes sense and I mean it, but then there's the ubiquitous broadcast, the search to give intimacy away.

There are these moments, the images that are our every day, ours together and alone: how it feels to take turns rubbing fingertips on the soft skin of the inside of a forearm. The clumsy grope for tissues after sex, with the red flush still on your cheeks, grinning at each other while we dab. Silent morning walks when we aren't exactly fighting, but one of us is unhappy, and then the rush of relief, like finally exhaling, when the silence breaks and we can say, What's the matter? Can you tell me? At the bar, after one of your plays, when we try to find language together for what you managed to convey. In these moments there is safety and joy—a gift; enough. But then look at what I'm willing to do: display me and us and our little common, hysterical shames, write about the fighting and the fucking (Jesus, I'm doing it again) in the hopes that someone might look. What is this but a fire sale on our lives—All items must go!—to try to get a glimmer of attention?

I was thinking about talent and ambition and shame, and the spaces between them, while watching the season 7 finale of *The Real Housewives of Atlanta*. There was one scene that you said was the greatest piece of TV you'd ever witnessed, and I think I might agree: Kenya Moore's screening party for the pilot of her self-funded, autobiographical sitcom, *Life Twirls On*.

The title is a reference to Kenya's habit of twirling for the cameras whenever she wears a fancy dress, while screaming, "Twirl!" In fact, everything about *Life Twirls On* is a reference to what Kenya does in the role she's already been playing for years. All the major themes are there: Kenya's inability to keep a man (one which many a fellow housewife has commented on quite cruelly); her love of her gay best friend; her outsize, combustible personality.

From what we're allowed to see of *Life Twirls On,* which Kenya wrote, directed, and stars in, it appeared to be an abject failure. The *Real Housewives* episode built around it, though, was amazing.

Kenya invites the other women to a rented McMansion. We get a shot of each one opening the door to the surprise sight of a rent-a-butler holding a silver tray. From the wings, two cater-waiters throw rice. A spindly harpist plays next to Kenya's stairwell; an opera singer sings arias, ribbon dancers perform. When the whole group has arrived, there's a wonderfully awkward shot of everyone clustered in an almost entirely empty foyer, each dressed like she's attending an Oscar party. They are complimenting one another's outfits and gossiping, when suddenly Kenya is introduced. She enters the shot, at the top of those stairs that all McMansions seem to have, made to look grand in a historical way, despite their newness. Kenya yells, *Hello, ladies!* She is wearing a full-on wedding dress, plus veil.

Everyone stares up at her, confused, laughing, clapping, because what else is one really supposed to do in that situation? Cut to a perfect Phaedra Parks confessional quote: *I'm all for a grand entrance, but one that makes* sense.

Then back to Kenya, a famously single woman in a very expensive wedding dress, twirling in her trademark fashion, simultaneously unhinged and in perfect control, flaunting all that is supposed to make her insecure. The harpist plays. She descends, her train shimmering behind her, dominating the scene. She jumps a broom that has been placed on a red carpet on the floor.

By the end of the episode the women sit in Kenya's basement home theater, providing the absolutely singular visual of couture dresses sinking into oversize red auditorium seats, under dim lighting. Then we watch them watch Kenya playing herself, wearing the same wedding dress in both shows, one show trite and formulaic (the fictional pilot), the other (the one in which she watches the fictional pilot) decidedly not. The other women clap for Kenya and say *good job* about her performance on-screen, even though they all know it wasn't any good, and even though it's the exact same performance she's been beautifully putting on alongside them for the better part of a decade and is in fact putting on at that moment.

When we watched, I didn't intellectualize the layering of her behavior. I mostly felt giddy and overwhelmed. We kept smiling at each other, like, *What the fuck?* Since then, I've been trying to think of what exactly the scene was doing that was so electric. I think it's that Kenya made explicit to us, those who have watched and judged her for so long, the question of whether we were watching her fail or succeed. Whether we were laughing with her or (along with her producers, maybe) at her. Or both. And also whether that self-awareness matters.

Our own commitment to self-awareness, after all, has reached the point where we often reference that quality and then make fun of ourselves for the very referencing. It's exhausting. And Kenya's whole thing, whatever it is, seems exhausting. She is forever *on,* which is, I'm sure, a very difficult quality for her to sustain and also for others to be around, but she's committed to it. She's the preemptive embodiment of anything that anyone could think to ridicule her for—dramatic, overspending, self-involved, child-hungry, single. As a fiction, she'd be stale and offensive. She knows that. She shows that to us, and she is spectacular throughout this process of revelation. It doesn't make her acting or writing any less horrible, but it might make those skills unnecessary. She makes us wonder if there can be brilliance in a performance that reveals how unbrilliant a person would be as anything other than herself.

After we watched her, we tried to articulate to each other how we felt. We talked about the strange liberation in the act of naming your own gestures or putting an exact visual on themes that you embody. Twirling, physically, and then saying "Twirl!"

"How Duchamp-y," I said, and you made the jerk-off motion with your hand.

"Asshole!" I yelled, and pointed at you.

"*Pretentious* asshole!" you said, and pointed at me, beginning to laugh.

"Did you really mean that?" I said, the anxiety of an audience already closing in.

10

{REQUEST FOR AUDITION}:

Hi my name is _____.

I am 32 years old. I am currently starting my own business that will consist of female barbers at a barbershop. I'm tired of working in regular barber shops where men dismiss women barbers. I want to create a place where men can go with female barbers. It will be called "The Barberistas" A Barbershop Salon. I plan on having a bunch of independent powerful women, together, having a ton of fun on this journey. I start construction on my Barbershop in two months and my opening day will be January 1, 2016 happy new year to me and hopefully you want to watch me on my journey and broadcast me to the world. Follow me @_____

—from www.castingcallhub.com

The other day you asked me what I was so disappointed about. The desired answer, I realize now, was, Babe, I am the opposite of disappointed. What I said was something really vague and obnoxious, like, I think that's just a logical way of being.

The honest (or maybe I just mean vulnerable again) answer would have been that it's an issue of narrative. Nothing is happening; that's what I'm trying to say. I don't mean to refuse to acknowledge the luxury of stillness and quiet, to deny static pleasure. That's not what I'm trying to do. The Edison bulbs are glowing warmly and my phone is not ringing with obligations and it's still warm enough to sit on the deck and eat grilled asparagus and make little jokes about smelly piss that aren't meant to be laughed at, just acknowledged as a thing. I'm not sure how it's possible to be content and exhausted and bored all at once, but that's the feeling I would want to explain if I could. Sometimes I contort my face to approximate rage or pain or shock. I do it in the mirror: This is my he-said-*what?* face. This is my nobody-better-fuck-with-my-check face. This is my sudden-death-indescribable-grief face. And on and on like that—so many ways to feel, to be.

And how easy it is, my love, to get drowned out.

And what if the kind of noise you make is less important than the fact that you're making it?

And, look, my friends have money jobs and I know that's actively not the life I sought out, but it doesn't mean I don't *want* it now that I see it existing for others.

And how do people go on so many vacations, not even just moneywise but also in terms of motivation to move? Are we uncurious? What are we missing that we don't know we're missing?

And what's-her-name, that woman from college, she's a corporate lawyer and training for a marathon, and she and her husband just closed on a Park Slope condo and everyone seems so *happy* about how well things are going for her, instead of envious, like me.

And look at all these announcements and denouncements, all this material, all this silent noise, and I used to really like Matt Damon, no, you know what, I still like Matt Damon, but he keeps saying these maybe-racist things and everyone's noticing, and there are memes now, and I feel like I want to defend him but that's somehow dangerous and also I don't even know him, he'll be just fine without me, and look at all the suffering in this world and what are we doing about it, yeah, we're vegetarians now but honestly that didn't even get the social traction I thought it would because I don't think people realize how much

I *loved* hamburgers, like it was way harder for me to quit hamburgers than your average new veg, and you tell me to stop looking, just look at you, but then I look at you and you're looking at that Instagram feed of senior dogs who need adoption and the thought of loving an animal that's just going to die in two years makes me so hysterically sad even though I don't love it yet, and I watched this show that was ostensibly about retired football players but was really about happiness, and this psychologist listed the three main determining factors for a happy life—community, a sense of value to world, and I forget the third one—and I had *none* of them, and 51 people wished me happy birthday this year and you know how many did last year, it was 127, and that's an enormous drop-off, especially considering I read an article saying that twenty-nine is both the social peak of a person's life and the beginning of their most fertile professional years, and I know I'm not supposed to take pop social science to heart, but fuck, it has to be kind of true.

And what if the moments to focus on have already come and gone, and I've forgotten them?

And what if you're disappointed, and that's what I'm too frightened to ask?

I don't particularly want to know NeNe Leakes offscreen, but I like to imagine her, though I only imagine her watching herself do the things that I've seen her do on-screen. I have a friend who saw her once at the airport, catching an early flight out of Atlanta, stopped at Starbucks for a latte. He loves her, so he went up to her, and he admits that maybe he looked a bit too eager or slobbery, but she put her hand right in his face and said, "No. No. It is too early for this." Which is her right, I know, but it's still a little disappointing.

I mostly imagine her on the couch that I've seen in her house,

or maybe it's an image borrowed from a dozen other shows—
one of those long, stiff couches, with gold-painted wood trim
and off-white cushions. Her legs are crossed in stylishly washed-
out jeans. She's wearing sandals. Her toenails are reddish-orange,
freshly painted. Her arms are stretched out over the couch. Her
hair is from that blonde bob phase she tried for a while, which
generally read Marilyn Monroe but occasionally skewed more
Hillary Clinton. She is on an enormous TV that she is looking
at. She's watching all her reaction shots:

NeNe's eye roll, so sustained and vicious. She tilts her head
down toward her collarbone while her eyes roll up, the tug
between these poles emphasizing the emotion.

NeNe's withering scorn, the way she will speak of someone
like they are immaterial, just an idea that God got wrong, and
the way she'll move her hands as though she's ushering this distraction out of her shot or as though she's a conductor silencing
an orchestra.

NeNe's laugh, the genuine one, how it booms. Or maybe it's
not genuine, because who knows, but she seems to love laughing
when she is laughing, and the way the sound carries as she tosses
her head back and everyone else is looking at her, overwhelmed
by the sound.

NeNe's near-apologies, when her voice gets quiet and she sus-
tains her gaze, like she's letting you know she feels for someone,
can feel for someone, even as her words dance around any potential blame.

NeNe, when her mother is brought up on a reunion episode,
the way she is fidgeting, legs crossed, eyes down, until she finally
stands, her voice breaking as she whispers that she won't talk
about it, and then the other women flock to her, hold her, and
her head is above the rest of them, arms leaning on their shoulders as she exits the set, still whispering, whimpering; instantly
sympathetic.

I see her see each moment the way I have seen them—over and over, tweaked just slightly but enough to remain potent. She sees each one spectacular and near self-parody; each one intimate, even with the lights glaring and the makeup, the whole apparatus.

A life. I wonder if she sees a life. I hope she does.

When you go to work and I'm not teaching, I watch you through the living-room window, holding a book or my computer, or sometimes the dog because I know you like it when I make her wave good-bye. As soon as I see the car drive away, I turn on the TV. I enjoy that this is an illicit experience, something to hide even from you, like the tackier types of porn, the kind set in a van, or drinking alone. Or, for me specifically, the way I'd always eat a Häagen-Dazs bar when my parents went out on date night, then push my hand through coffee grounds and banana peels to hide the wrapper at the bottom of the trash. I was hungrier because there was nobody there to see me and shame me, except me. It's all the same idea: watching people together is interactive; watching people alone is compulsive.

In 2007, *The Journal of Broadcasting and Electronic Media* published a report titled "An Exploratory Study of Reality Appeal: Uses and Gratifications of Reality TV Shows." It's the most recent study of its kind that I could turn up, yet it's still woefully out of date. It's hard for data to predict the trajectory of a fad; a fad is temporary and elusive until the moment it becomes old hat, when it no longer seems worth the effort to try to explain it.

Anyway, the researchers wanted to know why a person watches, and the primary response was disappointing: *the most salient motives for watching reality TV were habitual time pass.* Those last three words are, even in their clinical tone, pretty vicious.

The researchers were expecting to find a confirmation of

the hypothesis that there was a powerful appeal for an audience watching shows about "regular" people, and thus being allowed to fantasize realistically(ish) that they had the ability to be a part of the show, as Andrejevic and others predicted. They acknowledged surprise when neither voyeurism nor fantasy were chief motivations. They were present, yes, but secondary. The main sensation was that of time passing imperceptibly, and the genre was most popular among those lacking in *social interaction,* hoping to find some background *companionship* as the time passed. To feel this satisfaction, viewers needed to view *the meticulously edited and frequently preplanned content of reality interaction as realistic.*

The researchers didn't make a distinction between belief and acceptance, though, which is a crucial one. I don't have to believe that the material looks like life, unadulterated, but I do enjoy accepting that it all happened, is happening, will continue to happen, even if that is technically impossible. These are lives of some sort, and they stay available to me. I like to think of flying a helicopter all by myself, over an ocean dotted with a thousand little islands, and on every island is a group of people holding signs and waving up to me, banging coconut shells for my attention, shouting, We're here, we're here! And if they're reaching up to me, then I'm there too. That confirmation feels necessary, sometimes.

When I'm alone, I watch strangers dropped naked into the jungle trying to help one another "survive." I watch men in buckled loafers and tailored suits negotiate the prices of luxury town houses. I watch formerly Amish twentysomethings stumble, newly drunk, around Atlantic City during their first bachelor party. I watch giant, blond Dog Chapman hunt meth heads out on bond, catching them in the alleys of Hawaiian trailer parks and forcing them to pray. I watch a teenage Alaskan fisher-boy try to grapple with starting at the bottom rung of the crab-boat ecosystem. I watch the wives of athletes drink in the afternoon on a deck in San Diego, passing the time like I am passing the time.

The material runs together through the form—the speed of each scene, the confessional asides, and the cliffhangers that promise a drama that never fully materializes, only lingers until there can be the swell of the next cliffhanger: Will he be crushed by a poorly stacked crab cage when the squall hits? Will the fleeing meth head have a gun? Will she get pregnant, and will that make him pay attention? Will he close on the condo now that the offer is all cash?

Will they win? Will they survive? Will I ever see them again?

The essayist Olivia Laing writes: *Loneliness centers on the act of being seen.*

She locates loneliness in the tension of so deeply wanting to be noticed and so deeply fearing exposure. And yes, I know that feeling—everyone must know that feeling—but what about the act of seeing? Laing writes about the seduction of the screen as a *protective membrane,* but I don't feel the promise of safety as I watch, just the promise that, when I want to, I will always have something to see. Someone to see. Masses of those someones, contained and postproduced, instantly timeless, unable to look back at me. Hundreds of people who were there and are already gone, and who I can assume are clamoring to return. Who offer up so much and expect no reciprocation beyond my watching. I can't tell if their constancy makes me feel more alone or less alone; I'm only certain that when I am lonely, they will be there.

I'm generalizing here, conflating a lot of different shows into one pixelated loop of existence keeping my eyes open. The industry would disagree. With longevity has come specialization, a plethora of target demographics, each with its own sweet spot to aim for. Reality even has its own awards, presented by RealScreen, an organization that "sets the definitive global market for the business of unscripted and non-fiction entertainment."

Within that global market, RealScreen has identified and solidified a staggering amount of subgenres. The awards offer prizes for, among other categories, Competition: Game, Competition: Lifestyle, Competition: Shiny Floor Game Show; Lifestyle: Food, Lifestyle: Well-Being, Lifestyle: Home; Nonfiction: Arts and Culture, Nonfiction: Environmental Programming, Nonfiction: Social Issues/Current Affairs; Reality: Docuformat, Reality: Docureality, Reality: Docusoap.

Scroll down on the website; the list is endless.

Each category has an explanation, but the distinctions often feel thin, particularly when nominated shows seem like they could fit into ten different categories. The only discernible difference between *Docusoap* and *Docureality,* for instance, seems to be that the ones called soaps are about women's lives and all the nonsoaps are the same exact show, except about men, often men who support themselves through some sort of interaction with large machinery, and cater to an audience of men who might not want to think that they enjoy anything with "soap" in the title.

Some of the *Lifestyle* shows have competition in them; sometimes *Arts and Culture* bleeds into *Current Affairs,* and sometimes those are competitions, too, each with definite soap-opera elements. It's confusing.

Robert Galinsky would say they're all game shows—whether the game is to win a prize or outlast the competition or simply comport yourself sympathetically, each performer is playing at something rigged and has an enormous amount to lose.

Brenda Weber would say they all borrow from the structure of soaps—so many dramas packed into twenty- or forty-minute chunks; always the explosion, then the cliffhanger for another explosion.

John Jeremiah Sullivan, writing for *GQ,* says they're all about all of us: *This is us, bros. This is our nation. A people of savage sentimentality, weeping and lifting weights.*

Perhaps my favorite conflating description comes from Kelefa Sanneh, in *The New Yorker: Reality shows have a tendency to blur into a single orgy of joy and disappointment and recrimination.*

I agree with all of this—that the shows are all games; they're all soaps; they're all full of American grotesquery, joyful and disappointing, the mincemeat of emotion and vanity crammed each time into a slightly new conceptual patty. Part of me wants to say that I don't care what the differences are, that what matters is the constancy and the reliable volume of it all, but that kind of sidetracks me from the notion that these shows can be good or bad, transcendent or unworthy, and instead suggests a mountain of indistinguishable shit; literally: human waste.

I will say this: We used to love the competition shows. Remember? There was something invigorating about that particular premise—to want to be the best chef, the best designer. Now we've grown tired of a winner in every episode or season, of a theoretically objective set of criteria to organize the emotions of success and failure. Now we seek the drama of people attempting only to live dramatically and by any means necessary, whether it's through the isolation of a bizarre detail (My strange addiction is chewing on used diapers!), or an entire way of being (I'm from Beverly Hills! I'm obese! I'm a polygamist! I used to be Amish!). These are people with nothing to win but more screen time, more seasons, maybe a spin-off—our continued participation in their lives.

Split them into whatever demographic you like—Male 18–24; Female 35–50; Redneck Comedy; Urban Drama—the point is they're there, and maybe they're pretty good at being there. They want to stay, or maybe they need to stay, or maybe they think they do but really they need to get the fuck out of there. Either way, their faces capture that strain and hold our attention, and when you're not with me, they hold my attention. Such a variety of difference becomes diffuse familiarity, constant companionship, until it feels like when you're a kid and you doze off in the back of the car, and then you wake up to the same voices you fell asleep to, and you're a little bit frightened but also soothed.

What frightens me sometimes is how fast an emotion can settle in and block everything else out. Now I look back and read a rant about loneliness, as though loneliness is the only thing felt worth expressing, but really it's just that when I feel it, there's no feeling louder and therefore no feeling easier to express.

What I want to express, too, is what it feels like to drive together, free from the couch, on a highway, for any distance in any direction—cross-country moves, or visits to my parents, or just the long weekend getaway drive that still seems like a novelty.

When I drive, you tell me how I'm doing it wrong, and I say, "I *got* it."

"*Do* you?" you ask.

When I turn to glare at you, you're waiting for it, smiling.

"Come on," you say, and when I still pout you say it again. You point out that it's ridiculous that I can be offended about being instructed at something that I admit that I'm bad at, and I point out that you aren't exactly open to my tennis advice, and you remind me of the one time we swam a race against each other and by the time I wheezed my way to the finish, you were sitting at the edge of the pool with a smile very similar to your driving-critique smile. Eventually if you hold a smile it's contagious.

We stop for pretzels. I get a Snapple and chug it, and you say we'll have to stop again for me to pee, and twenty to forty minutes later you're proved right.

When we drive, we look out at all the people in all the cars passing and we ask each other, Who *are* they? Where are they *going*? If we look at them while they're looking at us, we say, What the fuck are *they* looking at? And laugh. Fuck you, we say to ourselves, at them. Hey, fuck you, guy, do you know who you're looking at?

In motion, between destinations, talk turns from speculation about passing cars to speculation about ourselves: What if we exited at the next town and that was where we lived—what would we *do* there? How did we end up where we are, and were we aware of it as it happened? What's next? Maybe nothing new, just a continuation, and wouldn't that actually be pretty okay? Where would you be right now if you had the choice? Quick, before you can think about it.

We can never think of anything instinctive, and it's a looming, thrilling sensation to remember that we could be anywhere with anyone, but we are in the precise place where we are, with each other.

Invariably, I say, "I mean, Seattle is cool," and then you say, "Jesus Christ, you visited *once*."

Invariably, you doze off, and in the silence I return to loneliness, but not in a way that hurts. You wake up when I pull into another rest stop for another piss. Outside the car we stretch together and watch other people pile out of their cars to stretch together. I ask you to do a whispered impression of what their voices might sound like. I like to walk into the gas station convenience store laughing together and see if I can catch that image on the security cameras. That never loses its surprise pleasure— the two of us there, moving through the Quik Stop, surveilled, laughing.

Why tell a composite story of a drive? To remind myself that it continues to exist and of the pleasure in it? Or to remind myself of pleasure, in general, when I feel myself falling down the rabbit hole of loud loneliness? Pleasure and loneliness can exist side by side, in the same life, the same moment. It feels important to remind myself of that, because of how easy it is to express the mournful, the frightened, the lonely, and how easy it is to fail at expressing happiness as you live it, and that failure feels lonely, too.

So many cars on a highway, and in one of those cars there we are, and all the other cars keep passing. Maybe they see us and maybe they don't, and we drive on. What an inexhaustible, lonely pleasure it is to ask each other to speculate on where they might be going.

11

{REQUEST FOR AUDITION}:

Hola!

My name is _____, but most of my friends and family call me _____ or _____ . . . you can call me whatever you want, as long as I can keep your attention until the end of this email. I am turning 21 on July 30th of this year . . . thank God. It's been a long time coming. I am currently living in Nashotah, Wisconsin on a tiny little lake called Moose Lake. I know, how original. I say "currently living" because I moved back home just a little while ago from New York City, where I was attending the Fashion Institute of Technology (FIT) studying Advertising and Marketing Communications. While I was out there going to "school" I discovered standup comedy. And, the rest is history. Long story short, I ended up dropping out of school, which you know, went great because both of my parents are teachers, to become a standup comedian . . . or at least attempt to become a successful comedian. If you can't tell already, I'm super sarcastic and very self deprecating, but in a good and funny way. Not like a self-pitty party way, I can't handle people like that. I absolutely live to do standup. I've never felt more happy in my life than when I'm on stage bringing down the house. I think what people think is so funny about me is more of my attitude towards things, rather than my actual material. I'm no Queen B or Blake Lively, but I'm defiantly not the ugliest girl to ever walk this planet and I also think it shocks people, again in a good and funny way, when a decently good looking girl talks on stage about taking a dump. I don't want to sound like every other girl that's applied or is going to apply for this show, and how they are perfect for the roll and how they just want to be a famous actress or model, etc. Basically, they just want to be famous. Now don't get me wrong, that would be great. But, I want to actually have a career, and make something of my life, not just a one time quick fling of five seconds of fame. Not trying to toot my own horn, but I know I have the right personality for this show.

—from www.castingcallhub.com

When we were first getting into *The Real Housewives of Beverly Hills,* the husband of one of the show's stars, who had seemed to be a real asshole (like potentially abusive) on-screen, hung himself. The following season his widow was back, shocked yet resilient, weepy but still game.

At the height of *The Real Housewives of New Jersey* (your favorite), Teresa went to jail for the mail, wire, and bank fraud that had funded the lifestyle she so proudly flaunted for the cameras. Her special return-home episode airs next month.

In the middle of our *Here Comes Honey Boo Boo* obsession, Honey Boo Boo's mother's boyfriend got arrested for "rape, child molestation, aggravated child molestation and aggravated sexual assault battery" against Honey Boo Boo's sister. The show got canceled, but Honey Boo Boo did appear in a special obesity episode of *The Doctors,* and now her mother is on *Marriage Boot Camp.*

After we watched the first three seasons of *19 Kids and Counting,* the scandal broke about the oldest of the nineteen molesting his sisters and avoiding prosecution by being sent to some backwards-ass Christian labor camp. Jim Bob, the patriarch, vowed that they'd be back soon, putting complete confidence in God's plan.

I'm not really sure what to do with all this; I'm just getting a list going. The obvious question to bring up here is: Are we complicit? *We* meaning you and me, but also, in that awful think-piecey way, standing in for *the culture.*

Sure. I suppose we are complicit. The attention given to socio-paths, and the public pain that results from the potent mixture of attention and sociopathy, only exists because there are reliable consumers who enjoy the cocktail. And then we wait for more of the same, so more of the same is provided.

The argument goes that the more reality television there is, the more saturated we become with hysterical *realness,* the less enamored we can be by the small, sincere moments that make up a common life, and so the people who make it onto reality shows are only those psychotic enough to cause a scene. Producers, and by extension viewers, are fueling the psychosis by highlight-ing it, elevating it, while simultaneously opening every action to scrutiny, trapping the lunatics in a cycle of self-exploitation until the crack is exposed. Or maybe the shows forced a crack in people that wasn't there before. Either way, the end result is the same. These are not good people, it is pointed out. Some are destructively, irreversibly bad.

I don't think we watch just for the chance to bask in badness, or that we can be entertained only by people who are particularly fucked up, either in a dangerous amount of pain or capable of causing it (though isn't that most people?). We never actually see the nastiest stuff on-screen, after all; we only read about it in articles that scream, Look what they don't show you! But I will say this: every time I read aloud from the Internet about one of these scandals or outright horrors, we look at each other unsur-prised. Like we saw something simmering underneath what made it to air. Like we're almost proud of that. And it does, in those brief moments, feel like we should stop looking, if we've gotten to the point where the worst revelation is simply a met expectation. Just because they're still willing to show us doesn't mean that we must oblige them.

The repentant conversation is always so serious, so predictable, but also so flimsy. It becomes its own pleasure, that gesture of repentance, but it doesn't make the original pleasure go away, it only reminds us of it. If these people still exist, fodder for us to debate about whether to watch, then the story isn't over, right? It's hard not to feel that we deserve some narrative satisfaction.

I've been thinking about that episode of *Intervention* we watched, with the homeless meth head who bolts from his intervention group during the climactic confrontation scene. He's out on the street, eyes feral, looking for someplace dark or at least empty. His sister chases after him, and the camera stalks the scene, closing in as he recoils, then lashes out. *"Let me go!"* he screams. Then there's a shove, and the shot seems to wobble, so it feels like he's shoving all of us. Then he takes off.

The show continues on without him, which is remarkable. It's a show *about* intervening on him, yet when he breaks its confines, the focus moves back to the interveners he fled from, discussing what they'll do if he ever reaches out. He's gone, but the story is the same. He was never really there. So little of his life was filmed—just a week or so of him serving as a tour guide through his own trauma, flirting with the camera with every illicit detail, every wry, self-effacing addict's joke. Then he pushed us away, and there we were on the couch, rejected but still leaning in, and it was impossible not to think about how many places he could be that weren't on camera, how treacherous every little corner of the world can be.

I used to pretend to hate it when you watched *Intervention*. "That's my limit," I'd say. "I don't want to watch a snuff film."

"So fucking high and mighty," you'd say.

"Why do I need to see somebody dying?" I'd ask.

You'd shrug and say, "You never see them *die*."

You were right about that, and you were right that I would end up liking the show—the way each subject is asked to explain, and then explanation becomes ecstatic performance until the moment they want the performance to stop, which is the crescendo. The cameras stand closer on *Intervention* than on most shows. The addicts and their preemptively grieving relatives lean closer, look more directly into the camera, so the claustrophobia feels mutual. It's like everyone involved wants some kind of record that they tried, that they felt *bad* about it all, so bad.

But why should we feel the right to watch, and to feel bad for these people we watch, as though we care beyond the pleasure of watching? I still ask you this sometimes, while making no effort to change the channel. It's an extrapotent question for me because of my own family circumstances—I have loved a person like that, offscreen. That's part of who I am, how you know me. That should dilute the appeal, right? There's nothing exotic or exhilarating about seeing a recognizable tragedy play out all over again, with strangers. Then it's just an unflattering mirror, or confirmation of an unavoidable script—the loved ones performing their resilient love, as if to prove that it still exists; the infirm performing their illness because they are so good at that, so willing, then pretending they don't want to tell the story anymore, growing louder as they realize it's too late to stop.

I'm dodging the question. I don't have an answer yet.

In her essay "Sublime, Revised," Leslie Jamison writes about the endlessness of *Intervention*. She says: *For the regular viewer, the once-in-a-lifetime intervention happens every Monday night at nine. The unrepeatable is repeated. Every week is a relapse.*

Relapse: Yes, maybe that's what we're feeling in front of *Intervention* (and so many other shows, too). It's a word that refuses to allow intrigue to die. A new tragedy is guaranteed, and that makes each individual tragedy a little easier to stomach. We watch to see someone try to change his mind when we know from viewing experience that it's probably too late. If it's not too late for that someone, it might be for the next one, and we can be sure that there will always be a next one.

Some of MTV's *Teen Moms* are beginning to rebel. The original form no longer holds them. For one thing, they're no longer teen moms, overwhelmed by every bit of their surprise situations. They are public women in their twenties now, capable if scarred, who have been famous for the entirety of their adult lives. They've lived through custody battles, car crashes, failed marriages, successful marriages, memoir contracts, memoir flops, magazine stories about their buprenorphine addictions, brief-yet-lucrative porn careers, a sex-toy line.

They are still going. Some have left the show and returned, but they return new, steeled, openly tired and irritated, unwilling to relinquish control. They're used to the camera now and, as a result, sometimes rivetingly annoyed with it. The scope of the show has expanded to incorporate these new savvy selves. The producers sometimes appear on-screen, a part of the narrative, pleading with the moms, coaxing them, reasoning with them.

Farrah has returned for the new season. Rumors were that she'd been cut because of the sex tape that she'd tried to sell as something candid-then-leaked, even though the production value is crystalline and her partner is a porn star. She's back because she needs to be and the show needs her to be—a teen mom is, still, the role she performs best, so she has returned to it.

Her reluctance is vivid. She prizes her celebrity and attempts to achieve divadom, despite the fact that she's back where she always was, in a nondescript, middle-American suburban home, with her mother still nagging at her and her daughter still playing in the background, so native to being filmed that she can, for long stretches of time, seem oblivious.

In her return episode, after a couple of minutes of negotiation, two producers stand outside complaining about her to
each other, then enter the home and bring the viewers with
them:

Farrah, one says, *I hear you're having some issues with this.*

There she is waiting: so bored, so disdainful, eating pizza at the
kitchen counter, the family Christmas tree lit up behind her: *Why
do we have to do an entrance?* she snaps. *Why can't we just be real?*

When a producer condescendingly explains the need to have
some continuity for her fans, she interrupts: *Whatever, we all
agree, it's weird that I wasn't a part of it; now I'm a part of it. The end.*

She's insulting the producers for their formula, which gives
them pause, then more exasperation. She's unrelenting. They try
to butter her up, and the dripping effort of their words about
her importance to the show (*It just didn't feel right not having you*)
coats the shot. Farrah eyes the camera and then, almost instantly,
contorts her face into crying.

You guys just, like, make me more fucking mad, she says.

She storms out of the shot, leaving her daughter to focus on
in the absence, a sweet, at-ease child who has been decorating
cookies but stops and tells the producers matter-of-factly, *I'm just
gonna go see my mom and make sure she's all right.*

Another camera picks Farrah up after she storms away, and
she chooses not to rebel against or acknowledge this camera. She
is maybe still crying, though rather impassively at this point, in
an empty room. Her daughter finds her and hugs her knees.
She reaches down to hug her daughter back, and her hair falls,
obscuring her face. She says, *I needed a hug. I love you. I'm sorry
Mommy got upset.* She hoists her daughter up, that familiar pose,
and she's ready to get on with the show.

I can feel the restraint, or at least I imagine it, of the person behind the camera, because there is no more pushing forward. There is no longer a need to goad Farrah into her entrance.

Instead, Farrah has found the entrance she wants, and everyone—
Farrah, her daughter, the cameraperson, the editors and producers who settled on this footage—has agreed that it's the right
image to hold.

It felt right to us as viewers, too. It was quiet in a way that
implies sincerity, and the child felt uncoached, and the love
between mother and daughter, the show's appreciation of that
capacity for authentic love amidst turmoil, felt important, near-
inspirational.

Jesus, it happened fast. There we were on the couch, duti-
fully smiling and nodding and *buying* it. Fifteen seconds before,
maybe less, we'd been gawking at Farrah's plastic surgery and the
icy apathy that seemed to have taken her over. We were sneering
at the producers cramming into her kitchen to poke the bear.
The show had to reveal a set of collaborators working diligently
to find something substantive within what had become painful
and stale. But then, at the right time, when it needed to happen,
everything turned genuine. We were so ready to accept the turn,
as they knew we would be.

Are we saps, my love? Maybe the better question is: What
are we looking for? Why, at the right times, of course, are we so
willing to believe? Especially when we see the stars saying that
they hate their own show, that it's all bullshit, before they turn
to more appealing emotions. What got me was the way Farrah
leaned down to hug her daughter, and the unfudgeable fact that
children are just very small people who ape their parents' gestures in miniature. No matter how forced the action is, and even
when it's under protest, no matter how furious the players in
the drama are, no matter how exhausted the conceit, bodies will
always behave that way.

I'll tell you what I thought when Farrah cried and reached
down to hug her daughter, in her staged home, once again
invaded by producers demanding her to be likable or at least

amenable when she didn't want to be. I thought of the fact that you want a child, and I do, too. And that we've worked up to that desire together, and now it's still tenuous and terrifying, but increasingly potent. And that I hope it's a girl. And that I can see you—crying, since you're a crier—reaching down to hold a small version of yourself who is reaching up and wondering what's wrong. I want to see you that way.

Like Farrah from *Teen Mom*. Well, not exactly, but you know what I mean.

Bill Nichols, the legendary documentary critic, had this to say when asked about the value of reality television:

> *The very intensity of feelings, emotion, sensation, involve-ment that reality TV produces is also discharged harmlessly within its dramatic envelope of banality. The historic ref-erent, the magnitudes that exceed the text, the narratives that speak of conduct in the world, of face-to-face encoun-ters, bodily risk and ethical engagement ground themselves harmlessly in circuits devoted to an endless flux of the very sensations they run to ground.*

Basically, fluff. But worse than fluff; it's taking what could actually be substantive and channeling it into this echo chamber of only emotion, with no context and no progress. That can be a stupidly harmless process, or that can be dangerous.

Though I find Nichols both cranky and melodramatic, I do kind of enjoy the way he refers to emotion like it's a precious commodity, like it's a fucking truffle. It is only valuable because it's rare and hard-earned, that tiny, beautiful thing exhumed from miles of otherwise unimportant dirt. Serious emotion, captured in earnest—that's valuable to a narrative. But if everyone's just emoting all the time, if every bit of captured footage is a tantrum or accusation or tearful reconciliation, then the value is gone.

Beverley Skeggs and Helen Wood call bullshit on this being the one way to see valuable reality, a deeply gendered definition embodied by the swashbuckling war reporter, risking life and limb for an exclusive shot of another man's blood and anguish. To Skeggs and Wood, if people are going to refer to reality shows as soap operas, then the shows should be examined according to the appeals of that form. They look to soap-opera scholarship and borrow the term *emotional realism*—when every interpersonal drama is heightened and broadcast, the sheer volume of that drama is what strikes recognition in the viewer as something akin to what they feel as they live, and in that recognition the viewer can find tension, maybe even a critique of the culture that makes them feel that way.

If there is a kind of realism to be found in the swell of interpersonal emotional crescendo, then that relationship is heightened when all the emotion comes unscripted(ish), when melodrama is smashed together with *a tension over the unknowable: How will people react in a certain situation? What will happen when X meets Y?* That's how Skeggs and Wood put it.

What will she possibly do next? What is he capable of?

The viewer watches knowing that the emotion will be heightened, but not knowing how each real person will behave within these confines—formula and spontaneity combine and maybe combust, and then there's an inevitable rush as each takes their turn displaying the broadest, brightest strokes of what it means to lust, to envy, to rejoice, to aspire.

Skeggs and Wood reference the term *compulsory individuality*—the need to make, then remake yourself, to display that self and constantly perform or defend its worth. The need to linger and swirl in your own distinct emotion, until it reinforces that all you've got is you, the spectacle.

On the night of the 2016 Iowa Caucuses, I was on assignment, trying to self-style as a serious reality-TV journalist. I went bar-hopping with a group of producers while covering the industry's largest annual convention—some wannabe, some established; lifestyle focused, travel focused, *personality* focused. Any bar we went to, on every screen there was Donald Trump in a dead heat for the lead, and though the TVs were mostly muted, even the closed captioning managed to express breathlessness, incredulousness, fear, glee.

We stopped and watched every time.

Can you believe it? I asked every time. The guy from *The Apprentice?*

Every time, the answer was like this: Can I believe it? Of course I can believe it. This is what they want.

They meaning everyone, I guess. The ultimate audience.

These producers were not happy or gloating, not really sad either, certainly not afraid. They spoke the way I imagine soldiers speak to one another, or bail bondsmen, or sex workers; they spoke as though there was a world of civilians out there—rubes, naïfs—and then there was them, the ones who had seen the thing up close.

The most successful producer in the group had this tic where he responded to every reach for commiseration from his counterparts with "My heart would go out to you if I had a heart." Every time he said this phrase, it was met with laughter and a rush to join in his sentiment, a performed jadedness toward the human capacity for the trashy or the grotesque.

The cool guy, the heartless one, pointed at Trump on the screen and began to explain him, and then the others rushed in with their own explanations. They all sounded like every other explanation that people were beginning to offer, said with that same desire to show that if you can point to how the trick is performed then you are not one of the ones who is caught up in the feeling:

We've jacked up emotion so high that regular talking is boring.

People don't want to think, so all you have to do is offer something easier and louder.

People watch rich people because they want to be rich. People watch arrogant people because they would love to be that way. People watch stupid people because it makes them feel less stupid.

And then: Remember old Scorsese flicks, back when you could make something with a message? [What message? Never addressed.]

And then: Remember Edward R. Murrow? [No one was old enough to remember, but most claimed to like that preachy George Clooney movie about him.]

The way these producers framed it, intellect and emotion were rendered entirely divergent—intellect was what a person should aspire to; emotion was the thing that the lazy settle for to avoid thinking. Every one of these emotion-purveyors said they wished for a world that was better than the shit they professionally put into it, but you know what, the world is the fucking world. They discussed their own projects, the lives they wanted to commodify, with a strange mixture of pride, exhaustion, and scorn.

Cool guy, heartless guy told me I should write a book about reality stars of yore, the ones who knew nothing and were discarded by culture, husks of what they had once presented themselves to be. It would be grotesque, but it would be captivating; he would've pitched it as a show if licensing wouldn't have been such a hassle. We imagined these discarded stars as a group: just as willing as ever, maybe more so. People don't think about the damage, they just want to hear the shouts and see the squirming; everyone agreed upon that.

There was an undercurrent to the conversation, of course, that was about complicity, particularly as reminder clips ran across the screen, little teaser morsels of everything Trump said or Tweeted, whom he had mocked, how he had lied. It all looked familiar— a closed-circuit loop of mania. As we watched, there were whistles and sharp inhalations. There were rueful headshakes, the mixing timbres of semiforced laughter. What a shitshow, it was marveled. What a pageant. What a sham. What a spectacle.

In my hotel room, I watched CNN for a while, and it was still loud and panicked and gleeful. I changed the channel, and it was the same. I felt tired and sad and anxious and guilty. I tried to identify each emotion as it came, as though that knowledge might dull how it felt.

I want to be a smart writer, but I don't know that I am. My thoughts don't clarify themselves on the page, not at all; in fact, they fade and distort. Sometimes I think I can feel them leaking, though I'm not sure out of where or into what. On the page, the *I* conjures only emotion, the loud kind. I'm not a great feeler away from the page; you know that. But here I am on a laptop in a vegan café just *emoting* all over the place, until it feels like the only thing worth doing is emoting. Everything that is supposed to feel private, or even hard to voice, feels the opposite, and I return again to the hysterical well.

The mechanism is turning numb into noisy. The mechanism is saying the worst thing, the grossest, the thing that makes me feel bared, even though I'm not bared because I'm not really there, which is why it feels so good to feel in the first place.

When I watch you watching, I think that you assume the best in these people. Not that you believe they're all great and deserving of our love and absolution, and I don't mean to say that you're not a critical thinker, but you choose to take them pretty much at their word—that's part of the pleasure. When I watch, I'm thinking: Way to get angry! Way to be sad! Way to scream! Way to menace!

There's plenty of male arrogance to that, for sure—as though every action is acted for the opportunity to receive my appraisal. But I think it also has to do with the different ways that the shows allow us to find emotional pleasure. I have my own assumptions that I choose to believe. It's important to me to believe that there is value in self-exaggeration once the red light turns on. Like every *off* moment has been muted and unremarkable for a reason, because there is an immutable self, waiting to be unleashed. I imagine it like a howl. They're howling. I howl. Howl like our dog in the yard, when the neighbor's pit bulls are out on the other side of the fence, and she wants them to hear because she knows they can't get at her.

We sit on the deck together and watch the dog howling, and laugh at her until the sound gets really high pitched and annoying. Then, sometimes, I scream at her, and you tell me to relax. Or you ask me what I'm feeling, because I probably wouldn't be screaming at a very small dog causing no harm if I weren't caught up in feelings about something else. And I can't think of anything to say that makes sense or sounds real, as though I've sapped myself of the resource of emotion and also coherence.

"Nothing," I say, and you don't believe me.

12

{REQUEST FOR AUDITION}:

Okay so my name Is _____. In my opinion, I'm a person who doesn't like to be In drama. It's weird that I'm always surrounded by It though. I literally have the craziest, most loud, but real family. None of them have filters, and are not shy. We know a lot of people and are extremely outgoing. We just say what ever Is on our minds. They could have the whole world laughing If people seen how they acted. There's also soooooooooo much drama, and arguing between my family. I have a huge family so something juicy Is always going on. Though we do not all live together we always manage to be around each other. That's probably why there Is so much excitement. I could honestly right a novel on my family and our everyday lives

—from www.castingcallhub.com

I should talk about Jax Taylor because he's the one we talk about the most lately. He's our newest shared favorite. He's the worst one, or he's the best, depending on what you're looking for in a person on television.

Jax is a bartender at a fancy restaurant in LA called Sur. Jax models, too. He's older now than he'd like to be and than the modeling industry prefers (thirty-fucking-six!), but he used to work a lot. He was the lead on a bunch of campaigns, face and body. He'll show you—look, that's him in a Gucci sunglasses ad, and the poster is still up in the Gucci store where he's shopping for sunglasses right now. He loves to work out—look, there's a montage of him and the boys doing pull-ups on a jungle gym somewhere. He also fucks a lot because, again, he's supergood-looking and works out daily, and also because he likes to feel good about himself. Other people are expendable in the service of his feeling good.

That's it, really. Jax's show is called *Vanderpump Rules.* It's about him and his coworkers—servers who are models and actresses, busboys who are EDM DJs, other bartenders who front pop-rock bands. They all party together, and retake their headshots, and have cigarettes in the alley behind the restaurant, fighting over who gets to take the six-top of high rollers and also who has actual worth, like a future. Who is *just* a server or a bartender, and who is more. They are often vicious and duplicitous, usually horny, though their horniness bleeds into their opportunism, and they always eventually forgive one another. They were not rich before filming, nor were they famous, nor did they overcome anything, nor do they do anything particularly dangerous or weird—they were hot and wanted stardom.

And now they have it, kind of. But really it's like a strange purgatory on the way to stardom. The show has been on for five seasons (as one producer told me, if you make it past three seasons in this game you're an outright hit), but in each new season Jax is still back behind the bar, V-neck plunging low, getting narced on to the manager for going way past his allotment of shift drinks. Whole episodes still hinge, at least partly, on the tension of trying to get someone to cover him while he goes on a boys' trip, even though he's so clearly run out of goodwill among his coworkers.

The entire scenario is nuts—he gets paid for the show and paid for club appearances, paid to wear a certain brand of sneaker. I follow his Instagram, which is all him lounging in comped suites at Hawaiian resorts or getting special detailing on his new

Dodge Charger. He's an investor in another restaurant now, a similar upscale-type thing but a little farther out in Ventura. He mentions that fact whenever he can in any location outside the show; outside the show, he's proud.

On-screen Jax behaves without pride. We have seen him brawling over the girlfriend he mercilessly cheated on in a parking lot in Vegas (pausing, first, to take off his shirt before throwing a punch). We have seen him lie about an affair with his best friend's girlfriend for ten episodes, only to quietly and remorselessly come clean, describing the way they were sitting on the couch drunk and he was falling asleep when she started to go down on him. We've seen him take a punch to the face at a club over that story. We've seen him display a horrendous tattoo he got to win back the woman who left him. We've seen him sit with a drunken glare, real dead eyes, while being called a monster and an asshole, seen him sneer at that and shrug, go back to his drink. We've seen him filming a fitness app, flubbing the simplest of lines, his buddies laughing at him from behind the camera.

He doesn't often seek to defend or explain himself—he simply behaves wildly, foolishly, captivatingly, and then confesses. He looks happy when confessing. Fulfilled. Like he knows the narrative value of confession and knows he's good at it. Like he's been saving it up. Then he sets about the task of reloading salacious material for the next unburdening.

I decided I loved him at the end of season 1, when he goes to see a therapist for what is, we are told, the first time in his life. He's in a black button-up, chest exposed, as always, the muscle line between his pecs a deep groove. He's trimmed his stubble so it's still present but clean—that's his best look. His eyes really pop, shimmering greenish-blue diamonds that he holds wide open as the camera holds him in focus, until it feels like we're sitting right at his knee, leaning in.

The therapist nods gravely when the camera turns to her, and Jax monologizes. He's from Michigan, he tells us. He went to community college, but he dropped out. He always quits everything early. He always feels like he's never enough.

He used to be a regular guy, regular screw-up. Really. Now there's this rock-star lifestyle . . . he trails off, which implies what? Internal strife? Honesty? He looks down at his feet, then up, then back to the therapist. He modeled in New York, Miami, Europe; he did *well* out there. He thought LA would be the same, but it's not. Nothing is ever enough in LA. People aren't impressed with him. He wants to be impressive. So he lies. He says he graduated college when he didn't, because he's ashamed. More pregnant silence.

He speaks again, pauses, then laughs at what he's about to say. He says, Let's start with my name. My real name isn't even Jax. He opens his eyes extrawide and says, None of this is *real.* Like he just blew everyone's mind.

He looks maybe really pained. He talks about women, about going on rampages where he fucks anyone, how he can't stop lying to the women he fucks, and to anyone else in his life, about how the lies are getting tiring and confusing, the partying, too, the lifestyle. He says he's trying to go back to the person that he used to be, the one we've never seen and never will, the regular dude who dropped out of community college somewhere in Michigan in the nineties, a time and place that seem inconceivable in this context.

He's a liar and a fraud, someone who wants attention of any kind at any cost because it makes him feel good, and that's all he is, and he's owning up to it, like the story is over, like he has learned, like he will change. The therapist (who, we will later discover, is Henry Winkler's wife and is starting production on her own show about being shrink to the stars) looks pleased. This is the good stuff.

By season 2, Jax is back in for another session, admitting that he lied about some stuff in the first one. He talks about his inability to stay faithful, calls himself ashamed. Again, the therapist looks pleased. She suggests that Jax may be a sex addict, and he pulls his head back and grins. He asks, There is such a thing? Later, he says, Wow, that does sound like me. He seems genuinely excited to have been diagnosed. It's another thing that can be his thing—hot, nihilistic, and now sex-addicted! Next episode he's back at the bar, flirting back at a boozy brunch, whipping off his shirt.

He makes a show of saying he was once really there, and it's enough to make all the continued emptiness even more intriguing. Nothing changes after the therapy session. Of course it doesn't; if it did he'd be out of a job. He behaves as he has always behaved: craters and confesses, cries sometimes, then reemerges, emboldened, ready. Now when the group fights, they have extra ammo to sling at him—are we really going to believe the self-confessed liar? Who gives a shit about what the sex addict thinks? He smiles. He nods. He shrugs. He continues.

Last month, I flew to LA to interview Jax for a magazine profile. This felt, to me, like the pinnacle of my journalistic career, but nobody I told about the gig seemed willing to match my excitement, except for you. I crashed with friends who laughed when I told them why I was in town. I think they thought I was looking to do a takedown: head to the tackiest part of LA, find the tackiest person there, and start shredding all the surface-level bullshit. I tried to project seriousness when I told them that I wanted to shred nothing. A probe, maybe, was more what I was after. A punctum. This was a man who bared himself well, and what an opportunity to witness the baring up close, one-on-one, which would have to provide a second layer of intimacy, a still-uncovered self.

Jax canceled twice, which I was happy to consider part of the story, an authentically Jaxian way to behave. Finally I was supposed to watch him work out, but he showed up too hungover, and told his PR flack that he'd rather just go to Denny's. So we did—I sat with Jax Taylor at a Denny's and asked him to explain himself anew.

He spoke for hours. He was funny, a nice combination of chest-thumpy and self-deprecating as he slumped in his chair. He spoke of his past—dropping out of college, the pressures of being a misfit in conservative suburban Michigan, a vague stint in the navy. He spoke of his father, a good man, wanting to make him proud. He spoke of being a simple guy at heart, a guy who never wanted everything that he has now, who wanted to raise children someday in a small, quiet place near a beach, maybe work as a fireman. He spoke of his urges, how easy it was to give in, how he wanted to not give in.

He felt raw, and this pleased me. He felt nostalgic in a way that didn't seem empty. When he left me, he was going to hang out with the people he hangs out with on the show—"It's all true, dude," he told me. "We really spend our whole lives with each other. It works because it's authentic."

He said that word a lot.

He shook my hand and called me bro, and said it was an honor that I wanted to hear him out. Then he put on his leather jacket that I've seen on TV and hopped into his Dodge Charger that I've seen on Instagram, and drove away.

I called you so happy. You asked what we talked about, and I said, *"Everything."* Come home and debrief, you told me, and on the plane I anticipated our conversation. Back home, I tried to write something that would express the *everything* he'd given me. We rewatched episodes together, so that I might do a sort of annotation, filling in around what was shown on-screen.

What I discovered was that pretty much every revelation he'd talked himself toward over hash browns was a thing that he'd already said on the show. Sometimes the phrasing was the exact same, and the cadence was the same, the mischievous side-eye as he revealed a giddy embarrassment. The way he managed to project the feeling that the revelations were hard to come by, that he was only just stumbling upon some truth about himself. Most of it was part of the backstory he'd provided the therapist in season 1, in my favorite scene—a guy with no substance willing to tell the story of his emptiness until the story became the substance. Somehow I hadn't noticed the retreading during the interview. Or maybe I had chosen to ignore it. Maybe I'd loved it when he told me because it was all so familiar, as though I could sing along to myself.

I was left with nothing to write beyond a regurgitation of the shit he'd already worked and reworked, just set in the Sunset Boulevard Denny's this time. There was no realization to be had. There was no forward momentum to be found. I thought back to Bill Nichols's claims of the *dramatic envelope of banality,* every emotion channeled into the same insular bullshit—no broadening, no deepening. I felt tricked, trapped in the envelope. I was mad at Jax for a while. And I was mad at myself, for my inability to coax more from him, or something like that. I don't know.

Looking back, the anger seems pointless and misplaced, born from a leftover instinct to minimize the kind of pleasure he so reliably provides. What else did I want from him, other than to be a hungover hardbody at a Denny's, mumbling his way through the things he'd done wrong, cycling between exhaustion, contrition, and pride? The surface he provided was the surface that worked. I got wrapped up all over again in the way he tells the story of himself. The way he makes you contend with the surface and the desire for something beneath it, and then you dig and it's the same thing, and then you ask him for more.

He seemed like he meant it all. When I published the article and read my words about what he told me, I wanted to watch him again. We did.

C produces reality shows. She's been doing it for five years now, an unexpected life that has taken her through freaky medical procedurals made of mostly reconstructed scenes; megahit homages to the trappings of monogamy; longer, more *docuseries* deep dives into the "real" world of a particular community. She goes where the work is. She's good at her job, and there are so many shows, so there is always work if she wants it.

You can make a kind of amazing life out of this if you can hack it, she tells me. And she genuinely likes it. She cares about the people she's filming—some more than others, sure, but she still texts with them, gets invited to birthdays celebrated in their real lives, long after the cameras stop rolling. Plus the money: for anyone planning a life of creativity, the money you can find out in the boondocks of what might be considered creative work is beyond what you've been taught to hope for.

I ask her what jobs have been her favorites, and she tells me that it's always the ones where she has some time. She likes the shows where she really gets to *be* with them, her people. She refers to all subjects as hers, a phrasing that I've noticed across the board from those in her line of work. But when you only have a person for an episode at a time, what do you really have of them? The job can sometimes feel like pressure-filled cocktail-party chat from behind a camera, enough to sketch out the parameters of someone's occupation and hobbies, some likable-ish details to fill a twenty-two-minute narrative arc. When you have someone's story for a season or more, you can dig.

Mostly, she tells me, her job is trying to make people genuine. C and I are at a diner in Brooklyn eating eggs. It's her first day off in a while.

Her job is like this, she tells me, like what we're doing now, except it's more of a rush because the interview never really begins or ends and a lot of the time is spent getting her person, or many of her people, to say the same thing over again, but better.

Take the main person she was assigned to on her favorite show, one in which she had a full season to sit with and know and prod this person. This person should have been great. They'd made it onto the show for the parameters of their life: hard upbringing, self-taught success story, business owner back in the community where they were brought up hard. But they were not a good *person*—not in that they were cruel or anything, just in that they had an enormous amount of difficulty approximating their own humanity. They didn't want to be interesting; they wanted to be impressive. C came to work every day and fought with this person to be better.

"A lot of what I do is prodding," C says. "I would sit with them for four hours some days, this close, like we are. And the camera was on behind me. I told my camera guy to never turn it off. And they knew that, of course, but when you're talking to somebody for that long, you forget to see the red light."

The two of them would sit there and fight. C would say, "You know I love you, but you're not being *real* with me," and this person would say, "You don't know me at all," and C would say, "Of course I do, and the you I know isn't showing up. Tell me the story again." "Again?" "Again."

This person could cry on command; they leaned on that skill pretty hard. But false crying shows like a bad paint job. C was unimpressed. She would say, "You're doing the pageant thing again. Can you please tell me something that's true? Can you tell that story again like it has *meaning*?"

This person got progressively nastier over the course of the shoots, to the point of interrupting the interviews to say shit like, "You know your ass has been hanging out all day? The whole crew has been talking about it." C would say, "I don't mind who sees my ass," and this person would get imperious and pursed lipped and say, "Suit yourself."

On and on like that, a standoff over what kind of story to tell. Because this person thought they could game the whole system; they thought they could give packaged publicity answers like they were teaching a morning-show host how to make pancakes in a fake kitchen. C knew that nobody would give a shit if there was nothing offered up on-screen that hurt.

"You need to *feel*," C told this person. "I know you've got pain; we talked about the pain. And the stress. Remember, when we were over on the couch there before shooting?"

It came to a head late on a Friday shoot. The postproduction team had told C they needed fill-in material. A week's worth of shooting and there still wasn't enough. The story was supposed to be this person coping with the possibility of failure—a big deadline coming up, a potentially life-changing project that they'd signed on to and then frozen in the face of. C had all this footage of the person sitting, looking out the window in intense thought, stacks of untouched papers, the whole thing. Now she needed them to acknowledge and inhabit the story of how they'd frozen, how they were floundering.

It was all staged—the person sitting by the window of the business after closing, looking out to convey reflectiveness. The crew was still there, impatient. C kept pushing, asking the person to talk about why they were stalling—what were they thinking? Was the pressure mounting? What the hell was going on? Then C says she saw the person's face change, just a little, hard to describe. They looked right at the camera and said, "Well, maybe this doesn't bring up happy memories, you know? Because I was raped as a child. That's right, raped."

I'm looking at C now, trying to figure out if this is a success story. I'm nodding, like maybe this is an example of how one prods successfully.

"It was just a power grab," she says. She takes a sip of coffee. "And, look, I get it, that's weird to hear. I'm not a rape denier, and I know I sound like an asshole saying this, but I've been around a lot of people in this job, and I know why people say what they say, and whatever had happened, in this moment it was just a power grab."

We pause, push food around on our plates. C tries to convey how it feels in a moment like that, when there is the personal interaction between two people who kind of know each other, but then the refusal to commit to something larger, the combativeness and manipulation.

C says, "We were getting close to something genuine and instead of telling us how scared they were of failure, how almost off-the-rails things had become, how overwhelming, all that, they tried to one-up me. So, rape."

The clip never aired. This person lost out on a lot of screen time to people who shouldn't have been nearly as entertaining as her. I ask C if it ended up feeling needlessly horrific to air a rape story, like just too much to bear.

"No, that's not it," she says. "Honestly, if the rape story felt like the right story, if it felt like the real person, it could have worked. But we never got that."

I've been checking our realtor's website for the promotional movie we were supposed to be in, and I think it might be time to admit that we got cut out.

I'd been so excited. My hairdresser (yes, another beard trim) was superimpressed when I told her that we'd been deemed realtor-promo-movie material. She said, "My realtor never even put a picture on the Facebook page of us giving a thumbs-up in front of the house. Not even that."

Then, as she was trimming my neck, she said, "I get it. You guys have, well, you have a look." And that felt so good to hear because, honestly, I had been cautiously optimistic of late about us having a distinct, appealing couple aesthetic. It just feels really nice on the occasions when these hopes can be confirmed.

For the shoot you wore those leather boots with the heels that you can't really walk in, but we were in our own house, so whatever. And the orangey-red lipstick. And the black jeans that cling all the way down to your ankles. You had that rouge on that smells like peach and chalk, the kind your grandmother gets you from Italy, and it's a smell that I've only ever smelled on you. You looked the way I describe you to you, and I felt like I looked the way you always try to describe me to me. I wore that short-sleeved button-up with the diamond pattern, kind of hipstery but in a mall-bought way, which is an accurate and, I like to think, charming dynamic for me. I stayed shirtless until the videographer knocked, to avoid pit stains. You smiled at that and said, "Look at you trying." I really was trying.

They staged us on our little deck, and the red bush with the name we can't remember was blooming. I had my legs crossed, and my right arm around you, and the videographer said, "Perfect, you look like you do this every morning," which we don't but we could, and I'd like to.

I want to say something about those few minutes that doesn't sound trite. Our bodies fit into each other so well, in the home we'd made together, adorned by the artifacts of a life shared for so long. And there was this man in our home, and he had an expensive-looking video camera, and he said, "Whoa, cool place—is it old?" and he was impressed when we said, "Civil War era."

He said, "What do you think your unique needs were as first-time home buyers?"

And then we told him. I interrupted you once but stopped myself, and you said, "We're working on that," which I choose to think read as cute.

He said, "Do you think a home has to represent the people in it?"

We said *"Totally."* We pointed to our home, which I described, pretty hilariously I thought, as the shape that a five-year-old would draw if you asked him to draw a house. It wasn't fancy but it was tasteful; we emphasized that. We liked its snugness, that it was no more than we needed. And the built-in bookshelves, we said. That was a selling point. We're readers. We think a home looks better with books in it. Then it was his turn to say *"Totally,"* from behind the camera. I was happy when he filmed the shelves and ignored the flat screen, which is far more centrally located. "This is great," he told us. "They're gonna love it."

He showed us a quick clip that he'd captured, and there were our bodies, entwined, and there were our voices, a bit more nasal than I'd like but still ours. We both began to do our thing of saying *you* look good, but I look horrible. Our hearts weren't even in that. We looked how I wish we looked, and I trusted the image, if only for a fleeting moment, because this man had recorded it. He said he'd want to know us; he'd want to have a beer on our porch. He said to check the company website and we'd see the final product soon.

I'm looking at the video section of the company website right now, and we aren't there. I see some generic shots of the agents touring an empty house, interviews with people who are not us sitting at a coffee shop by the river. I have an e-mail written up, asking our agent what we did wrong. I don't think I'm going to send it, because what's he going to say? Maybe we came on too strong. Maybe we fell flat. I don't know. It's too easy to second-guess. I refresh the page—a little spike of anticipation that settles back into disappointment.

Another thing I've been doing on my computer lately: Googling "dog death." I guess it's an emotionally preparative measure, because whenever I think of the dog dying, my neck and face get really hot and I feel my breath constricting. I anticipate a moment where I achieve full and perhaps irreversible sadness, which is both terrifying and seductive. I once had a student turn in an essay about his dog dying and it was good, but I'm pretty sure not as good as I made it out to be. There was this paragraph where he described the dog near the end, sitting by the window when light came in, and he reached for this metaphor about divine light, which I'm not doing justice here—it was really lovely. I read it aloud to the class and said, *This* is the level of description that every paragraph should aspire to: Divinity! Death! Dogs! I read it again and thought of the finality of that dog dying, and one student was like, "Are you okay right now?"

On *Shahs of Sunset,* when MJ's dog dies, she holds a wake at her condo. The surprise is that the dog, Pablo, an obese Chihuahua, is still in her freezer because she hasn't been able to deal with letting him go physically. It's a nice bit of vulnerability—we laughed as we watched, but I also caught you tearing up. She pulls him out of the freezer, wrapped in a towel. She holds him to her bosom, as if he were a doll baby in a high school play. She sits, cradles.

On *Million Dollar Listing: Los Angeles,* Madison, the beautiful real-estate agent who pretty much *runs* Malibu, loses his Lab mix, Rex, who had lovely sad-and-dumb eyes and was used to establish how naturally caring Madison is, despite his cutthroat work life. At a gathering on the beach for his dog's friends and their humans, Madison stands and watches, arms folded across his chest, face pleasingly harried. He looks out at the Pacific and speaks slowly, gently: *Rex was . . . Rex was good to me.*

On *The Real Housewives of Atlanta,* Kenya Moore's Teacup Yorkie, Velvet, was attacked by a much larger dog and died from her wounds. We learn this information in a scene of Kenya under self-imposed bed rest, sequestered in the master suite of the McMansion she now lives in alone. She's in full professional makeup, like in any other scene. But she's wearing an oversize brandless gray T-shirt, which, it must be said, appears new enough that it could have been provided specifically for the grief look. The scene begins with Kenya's aunt climbing the stairs to get to her because Kenya cannot bring herself to move. Kenya tells the story and begins weeping. When we first watched the scene, I wasn't sure if there were tears, but when I looked closely there seemed to be, which was a relief in a way I can't really explain. Kenya begins pinching and molding her left eyebrow, ensuring that it keeps its clean, arched shape, even as every part of her face below the eyebrows is contorted. She says, *I had her and I told her not to leave me, and I could see her life just go away.*

After Kenya's dog-tragedy episode, rumors started flying on the reality blogs that you wish I wouldn't read about the death being a hoax—a calculated fabrication to position her as something other than the villain.

What gets more pity than a dead dog? one blog asked. *Please. We see through this, Kenya.*

The comment section got really mean, like extramean, and I had to stop reading. I guess Kenya's friend had put an Instagram photo up of his dog playing with Velvet, with no indication at the time that it was an old photo, as he would later claim. People said that was really suspect. Kenya was asked by TMZ about the rumors, and she called them "evil." She would know from evil, people said. Honestly. Making us think this innocent little animal got mauled so that you can bathe in the soft light of the aggrieved.

I believe Kenya. Or I'm not exactly sure, but I don't want to not believe her. I replay the scene. That poor dog. And poor Kenya, in her California king, gleaming violet pillows walled behind her, eyebrows held in perfect shape, heart shattered.

Did I ever tell you about the time I hit an animal on I-80? It was a possum, I think. It didn't squelch or anything, just thudded. I was still an hour from home, and I had to stop for gas somewhere. When I did, I checked and there was blood splattered up the tires onto the bumper. I knelt and touched the blood with one finger, felt the lingering warmth. There was no one else at the gas station, just yellow lights on empty asphalt and me, alive and alone, and the insides of this thing I had killed. That part never happened, I think, though it's been absorbed into the story. I got gas, but there was no blood. I did hit an animal, though. I did feel bad.

Of course I told you the story; I told everyone I could. I fucking wrote about it. First book; I forget that sometimes. I drove all the whole way home thinking about telling you at the bar, and then you were sad with me and I walked home from the bar thinking about telling it again. I put it into a chapter that was languishing, toothless. I thought, This right here is teeth— a creature that was once real and alive died, how seismic. I felt the seismicity; I touched the blood, or something like that.

Tell me. Tell me again. Tell me better. That's what a producer asks for. What happened? How did it feel? No, really, how did it feel? Be honest. Be yourself. Be more yourself.

M is a midcareer producer at this point. She's bounced around, but she's working steadily on *Black Ink* now. It's a show that I think is just okay, but she informs me that it's the second-highest-rated show on all of VH1. *Black Ink* is about black tattoo artists who, despite the professional and personal dysfunction among them all, are running a successful shop in Harlem. The show draws simultaneously upon two themes that have proved continuously successful: tattoo culture (*Ink, Bad Ink, Best Ink, Epic Ink, LA Ink,* etc.) and black people fighting in a particular shared setting (take your pick).

I ask M if it's a fun show to work on and she says it's crazy. Crazy and exhausting. It requires a lot.

"A producer is always a therapist," she tells me.

"Yeah, but a therapist who's filming," I say.

"Yeah," she says.

"So not really like a therapist," I say.

"No, not really, I guess," she says. "A little. Okay, for me, I can say that I try to be there as a friend."

"But a friend that's filming," I say.

We go on like this for a while.

The only reason M got this particular job is because production needed a shake-up. This is season 5 they're filming, and relationships between the cast and their original field producers were growing combative. Early seasons provide a particular passion, openness and camaraderie stoked by the newness of opportunity. But when that withers and the cast stops trusting, the original dynamic with the original people is screwed. Fresh blood, fresh trust, fresh performance.

M was told it was between her and a black guy to fill one of the new positions, and the question was who would draw what reaction? It came down to implied solidarity versus the what-the-fuck remove of M, a chalky pale stranger who'd spent most of her career working on cooking shows.

M wears her hair in prairie-girl braids to work. Sometimes

she dances poorly for the cast before a big shoot, so they may laugh at her before she looks at them. They call her Lightskin now, which suggests trust. All good things. The give-and-take, the real-life rapport, is needed to foster any material worth watching.

"Sometimes I don't even really have to prod much anymore," M says. "It's just, like, *Boom*. They are so *loud*. And you can't make up baby-mama drama, it's just there, and I'm just like, Sweetie, how does it feel when your baby daddy goes to prison again? And she tells me. Again. Stuff like that."

She smiles, chuckles into her Starbucks. "It's crazy," she says. "I'm, like, a crazy manager. Part of me wants to be like, Honey, don't say that, you don't want that out there, but then it's like, maybe she does? And we *need* that out there for the show."

I ask M if the power dynamic ever feels weird—handling the footage of someone else's self-performance, in general, and particularly being the white person tasked with filming these black stars at their most combustible.

"No, I film everybody the same," she says. "There's no difference. I film people; I don't film color."

I make a joke that doesn't land about a new kind of retro reality show being shot in black-and-white. Then we sit silent for a moment.

I believe her intentions; I hear no malice in her voice. But good intentions, or really a lack of any stated intention, will inevitably be complicated by the all-important question of what makes for good material. That's what we're talking around here—a question that eventually falls at the feet of the viewer and is always preferable to ignore: What do we want out of the dramas of these specific lives?

We're on the Upper West Side, where M lives just twenty blocks or so from where she shoots, across one of New York's most famous racial borders. Tomorrow she'll head back to the set in Harlem, which, despite gentrification, still seems to play nationally as a stand-in for all blackness, to continue the work of providing her viewers with the shoehorned, anthropological-ish drama of a world meant to appear familiar to some, foreign to others, certainly foreign to her, but that doesn't matter because you don't need to understand a place to know how it will play.

The ambient noise of the packed Sunday Starbucks fills in the silence. I push my recorder closer to her on the table.

"Noncontrolled environment," she says. "I know how that goes."

I ask M if she's proud when she sees the show. She tells me she never watches, just gathers. She's heard all the stories; she doesn't need to tune in for extra saturation. Watch too much of this stuff, she says, and you start to worry about the state of the world.

13

{REQUEST FOR AUDITION}:

Hello my name is_____ I have three daughters two of which are twins and one single. My family is full of clowns and characters which is never a dull moment in our home. I myself as the parent make people laugh even when not expected. it is always drama with my girls because people always forget my oldest daughter and own the twins as if she don't exist. anyways on to a day and life of me and my girls we have a motto that everyday we on a diet witch is a saying then by the end of the day I reply we will diet tomorrow lol as the kids say mama we say this every day. I tell them one day we will be rich and can have all the diet food that our heart can offer back to our life all we do is fuss daily because everyone wants to use the others clothes, shoes. make-up etc. . . . I feel as if you use me and my girls you will have a treat to deal with.

—from www.castingcallhub.com

Yesterday I returned from a run and described to you a little girl I ran by who was still in a church dress, with fake-diamond earrings, leaping with joy in the gutter in front of her family home, like a full-on human except much smaller and less encumbered by self-awareness. You asked for an impression and I did it, my weight shaking the house as I tried to convey what had looked like weightlessness. You told me you liked the fact that I noticed and remembered.

Last week a baby rested its head on your shoulder, and hours later you said, I'm gonna cry, before trying to describe the warmth of its cheek, and then you did cry and said, This is so stupid. I told you it wasn't stupid at all and held you.

Sometimes you say, I snap too much, I lose control, and I'll never be able to treat a kid with the patience they need. I tell you that's not true.

Sometimes I say, I worry that I'll take my failures out on a kid, like I don't have the capacity to wish better for them than I wish for myself. You tell me that's not true.

I read an essay by a writer who was raising a terminally ill child and I panicked all day, but I did not show you the essay, which I allowed myself to think was an altruistic gesture.

So many conversations feel like all speculation, which is a new rush, voicing still-unreal selves, but also a new anxiety. During commercials, more and more, we tell each other about the people we want to be in the future, people who seem like composite characters. I run our faces through that insta-aging app, and we laugh and then pretend to cry at the image, which covers nicely any temptation to really cry.

Love is expectation is exhaustion is excitement is fear, is the most common observation to make.

Sometimes you say, Let's be done talking for now, and unmute the lives on-screen, and I don't acknowledge the relief when the volume returns, always a little louder than I expected.

On *The Little Couple,* Bill and Jen went to China to adopt a baby boy. We were waiting for this episode, and it delivered—shots of these white-bread Texans with two distinct types of skeletal dysplasia wandering around the Forbidden City. Then there was a lovely climactic scene of the new family of three on a giant hotel bed in Beijing before flying home. The baby they named Will had just fallen asleep after a day of screaming, and Jen and

Bill stared at each other silently over his soft, breathing body, with a mixture of love and terror. In the following season, they went to India to adopt a baby girl—less fanfare since some of the novelty was gone but still solid TV. Bill sat next to the baby on the way to the airport, and she had giant, coal-black eyes, but she wouldn't look at him no matter how he tried, which would have freaked him out the first time around, but this time he just laughed it off.

Jen wanted to be a mom the natural way, but she's three feet tall and very narrow hipped, so there's a great chance her frame would prevent her from carrying a baby to term. Watching her discuss the painful journey toward motherhood is inspiring, excruciating, wonderful.

We have, while watching her, described Jen as adorable, which is deeply condescending and wrong, particularly because her accomplishments and her resolve are more herculean than anything. But the show depends on the balance between the two—the heartstring-tugging juxtaposition of her admirable-ness and her otherness: There's her squeaky doll voice, and also a personality that seems, well, adorable—self-effacing, goody-goody, relentlessly and sincerely optimistic. But then there's the hugely impressive fact that she is a brilliant neonatologist, though of course we'd be less interested in the scenes of her brilliance if they didn't show her doing rounds in her toddler-size white coat. Unadorable are her hospital scenes as she stoically discusses the rare cancer in her uterus, yet somehow it is still an adorable visual when the camera focuses on a wigmaker measuring the dimensions of her newly shaved head.

Jen seems to be (is?) so thoroughly *good*. We watch her sometimes explicitly for a reminder of the goodness in people. We speak about our own hypothetical future as parents, or more fully realized professionals, or better people in an unspecified way, and we speak to her as the ultimate model. Her goodness feels good to discuss. But there's always the background knowledge that we would not watch her goodness if it didn't come attached to her pained, abnormal body. We would not watch her goodness if it didn't feel, in its wonky scale to the world, like it was saying something about *our* attempted goodness, like if she can achieve such kind, competent humanity at three feet tall, why can't we when the world is built for us?

We feel and we gawk. Or we feel through gawking, which is maybe worse. We feel for Jen and Bill because there they are trying to put together a crib, like parents in a bland commercial, but the bars are so big in their hands, the directions spread out across the floor of their den like a carpet.

In the most recent season, Bill's doctor tells him he needs to exercise more because his knees are bad. Bill groans good-naturedly because that's what he always does, but he acquiesces. What follows is a shot staged to mimic a healthy natural activity: the family walking the dogs. C or M would call this a *life pickup,* a shot that a postproduction team says it needs to fill in whatever life stories are addressed in a particular episode, while reinforcing the theme.

The shot opens on Bill, flanked by his children, asking if they're ready to go. They're on the sidewalk outside their suburban Dallas home. The grass on the lawn is browning. There's a man in the distance working on his car in a driveway, leaning down over an open hood. Bill narrates the beginning of the scene, reminding his children that the doctor said it's important to exercise, important for everyone but for Daddy in particular. There's dirty water in the gutters of the street, and his son, holding one dog's leash, keeps stumbling uncomfortably close to the water.

"Say, watch *out,*" Bill tells his son, and his son mimics him with screechy imprecision.

The dogs, scraggly Chihuahuas, tug ahead, and the children totter behind holding leashes, and then Bill, face slightly pained, lumbers behind them. Behind him appears Jen, who has been picking up the dogs' shit, and is now holding a sagging plastic bag, hurrying to catch up. Everything is moving very slowly but feels very fast. There's a camera in front of the family, rolling away from them as they move. It's low enough to the ground to capture them at waist level, so we can see their knees moving as they walk. This adds to the scale of everything above them—the giant homes and trees, the parked cars. It all looms. It's impossible for me to watch without thinking about the difficulty of capturing this family face-on, and the possibility that someone may have just plopped a camera on a skateboard or something, and that the family has to walk along like it's a normal evening, despite a skateboard camera contraption winking at them, always a few yards ahead.

Nobody in the family, not even the toddlers, gives any physical or facial suggestion that they're aware of the camera, despite the fact that their actions appear so specifically choreographed to move along with a camera suited to their particular circumstances. They've walked a single, short block, and they stop at the corner. They stand in a bunch in front of a blue fire hydrant, and the shot lingers for just a second, emphasizing the contextual enormity of the fire hydrant. They make small talk about the way leashes get tangled with legs. Bill does a funny thing where he pretends the leashes are reins and the dogs reindeer; then his son copies him. Jen laughs.

There's a beat to allow us to soak in the sweetness of it all, but also the sheer exhaustion—a single block conquered by six tiny bodies in a two-minute odyssey. The shit bag looks heavy in Jen's hands. Bill looks sore. The children are tired and distracted, and the odds of them not wandering into the gutters seem to be diminishing quickly. The camera is moving around them. The guy fixing his engine is still visible in the background. What a grueling apparatus this is, yet they bear it with such quiet grace.

A good scene, we decide together. Simple, clean, yet still weighty. We're reveling again in the bland dignity of the completely functional yet specifically challenged. We're reveling in the spectacle of the unspectacular—walking the dogs along a sidewalk next to browning grass, holding a plastic bag full of shit.

Back at the restaurant in Brooklyn, C pushes her hash browns around on her plate and tells me that it's the same thing as when babies are first parked in front of the TV.

When she was breaking into the business, she was at a production company that did a lot of kids' shows, and she got mentored over lunches by this powerhouse kids' TV producer. This was back when *TeleTubbies* was the undisputed king, and the producer told C there's a reason why all the kids shows feature characters that are brightly colored and not quite human but still look like a baby. In the focus groups, you could actually see babies go through the journey to identification. They would point at the screen and say *Baby,* over and over, but at first it was unclear if that meant anything deeper than when a baby points at a car and yells *Car!,* waiting to be praised. At a certain point, though, when the babies began to take on that totally docile, almost boneless posture, fully enraptured by the screen, they started to point at their own chins, the way parents teach them to do, and say, *Baby,* and then back to the screen, *Baby,* and then they'd crawl a little closer.

C mimics this to me over the table, touching her chin, reaching out to mine, saying, *Baby.* We laugh. But, she tells me, that basic idea, babies crawling closer to the screen after touching their own chins, has helped inform the way she sees her own work. She understands that it's the same mechanism. She's trying to make adults crawl a little closer.

"That's all we're doing," she says. "We're seeing a bright image dancing around on a screen. But it's shaped enough like us, it makes sounds that we make, it emotes like us. *Baby.*"

Honey Boo Boo might be coming back to TV! I'm not sure when or exactly the form the new show will take, but Mama June posted to Facebook that the wait is soon going to be over. She thanked us for our support.

Whatever the new show is, it probably won't be on TLC any-more, since TLC issued that statement after the sexual-abuse scandal that their priority was the family's "ongoing comfort and well-being." Some channel, it seems, was brave enough (or unscrupulous enough, or greedy enough) to take the plunge, though. Some channel recognized what the people (That's us! We're the people!) wanted, and it sure as shit wasn't the comfort provided by privacy.

If I had to guess what's going to happen on the first episode of the family's triumphant return, it would involve someone, and probably multiple people, farting. I look forward to this. Not since *Blazing Saddles* has the communal fart joke been so well employed. I assume the producers of the show were thinking of *Blazing Saddles* in some of the earlier fart scenes because they're constructed almost like an homage—bodies spread around in a lumpy circle, near-unbelievably Southern accents competing with the sound of proud, brassy toots.

We love farts. Who doesn't? People fart and it's almost always funny. *Baby,* right? And we love the celebration of fart loving, I suppose because it's still titillating to see someone unembar-rassed by the bodily. Sometimes we provide that opportunity for each other. All the Brussels sprouts gas us up, and we are so at ease that we can lie on the couch after dinner, release, and share a giggle, jog the still-potent memory of the first time you farted in bed, how the progression from your horror to our collective laughter felt like a milestone.

By my count, there are three human behaviors that are still taboo in public—fucking, farting, and eating unabashedly. Honey Boo Boo's family eats and farts (that's most of the show), and when there's even a suggestion of fucking, between Mama June and Sugar Bear, the incongruity seems even more transgressive, so I love it even more.

Remember that scene when Mama June and Sugar Bear get massages for no reason? Such an easy shtick—people like *that* getting *massages?*

Sugar Bear says, *You droolin' on the pillow yet?* Mama June says, *Not yet; I'm droolin' but I'm just tryin' to suck it back in.* Her masseuse stays admirably silent and continues to run her knuckles down Mama June's bare back, forming grooves of freckled flesh. After the massage, Mama June and Sugar Bear stand outside, reflecting on the experience.

I'm a drooler, Mama June says.

That's the truth, Sugar Bear says.

Sugar Bear gives his trademark knowing underbite grin, and Mama June gives her trademark throaty guffaw. Thus ends another minute-long block of the foolproof formula of putting this family into yet another situation foreign to them (nonmobile home buying, wedding planning, dieting) and watching them do exactly what they always do in that new situation. They are the way they are—genuine, pathologically uncouth, stereotypically obese, charming. They are the opposite of calculating and certainly the opposite of sinister, which is part of the appeal. They can't help but be exactly themselves. Which made the dark revelations even darker—the notion that they, the incapable, could cover something up. That in the very same double-wide to which we'd been given access there had once lurked a body not sweetly and noisily bared but instead committing secret atrocities.

I'm ready to not think about it again. I'm excited to watch them again, with you; there's no way around that truth. I want the lights to come back on in the double-wide; I want to see Honey Boo Boo, maybe in the beginnings of some awkward preteen phase by now, opening the door in a too-snug T-shirt, smiling with brand-new neon braces, and farting like she's been holding it in just for us. Mama June and Sugar Bear and all the other daughters will be on the couch behind her, and they will still be the way that they can't help being, with subtitles running on the bottom of the screen to make sure we can penetrate their authentic Appalachian dialogue as they share the joy of a body's gasses.

Cue the montage of all their faces: ample cheeks scrunched as they squeeze, then release, doing what it is that they do so well, that I'm expecting them to do, that will never disappoint.

14

{REQUEST FOR AUDITION}:

Hey, I am eager to play any role!

    Age: 14

    Height: 5′2

    Weight: 125

    Hair: Brown, medium length. (Past collar bone)

    Eyes: Blue

    Body: Fit / Ex Cheerleader

    Sex: Female

    Race: White

    State: GA

    Again, ready to play any part!

—from www.castingcallhub.com

I've seen you in probably thirty plays by now. I've seen you in Shakespeare and Caryl Churchill, and this movement piece in honor of Wole Soyinka, and some grad-student stuff that didn't make any sense. Most recently, I watched your original adaptation of *The Yellow Wallpaper* and was so overwhelmed with fear that I had to decompress in the stairwell after the show. I'd never seen something so visceral. Whenever I am writing adjacent to our lives, you are rehearsing; we return to each other, in front of the television, sink into one another and debrief, or sometimes don't.

I never write about your plays. They're hard even to talk about intelligently—your acting, my writing; these things are our own, the contributions we try to make to the world, to ourselves, away from each other. When I run lines with you, it's like eavesdropping on a stranger's conversation, not just because you're playing a character but because you are this different person engaging with a character, making a character live, and that engagement is so all-encompassing, so impressive and separate from ours.

My favorite performance of yours was the one you did in the failing mall at the edge of town. Your theater company filled an empty storefront with chairs and an ad hoc raised stage, and pulled together a three-week run. You and your friend did *Parallel Lives* because you wanted to do a two-woman show, and how many two-woman shows are there? You controlled every facet of producing the play. You met with the mall manager and convinced him there was nothing to lose in filling one of the empty storefronts with art. You got that weird guy who worked as a money counter at the trucker casino to run the lights. When the sound guy dropped out, you recruited me, and I was proud to perform my small role, cuing the iPod and then, for that one scene, firing blanks from a starter pistol, my ears ringing in the closet backstage.

Your knees were skinned from the movement rehearsals. You were furious at home some nights because you felt off with your performance, and you were losing the accents as you switched among them. It was like there was this finite moment to grasp the perfect show, but it was floating in the air around you and you couldn't close your fist fast enough. God, when you hit it you were good—these perfect gestures, the shrugs and hand waves as you disappeared into a Brooklyn yenta, then a fallen angel. You were so intuitive, so seamlessly concrete. When you and your costar embraced at the end, exhausted, the audience stood up from their folding chairs and clapped, meaning it.

The scene I loved most was just you onstage alone, wordless.

The idea was that you were performing the frantic, grueling task of being a woman waking and preparing for your day. I'd cue up a jittery, violin-heavy classical song on the iPod and then peek out from the wings to see you time your movements to its pace. Your eyes were crazed; you held your neck tight, thick veins running along the edges like tree roots. You used your body as evidence, as a weapon, and you were fearless. It brings me an overwhelming joy whenever I see you that way and also a nagging sadness at how brief the moment is.

You mimed what it is to squeeze into leggings, to pull your eyes tight before applying the liner, to stand in front of a mirror and inspect. It lasted four minutes and twenty-three seconds, exactly as long as the song, and there was a heavy downbeat of completion, a last step that you took on the last note. The audience collectively exhaled, as though the final noise and movement allowed them to release the anxiety that had been mounting as they watched you, and then the money counter dimmed the lights and you exited, triumphant.

When the three-week run was over, we packed all the folding chairs into a friend's pickup before taking them to our garage. We gave the key back to the mall manager. We went to the Mexican restaurant, the only thing open late at the mall besides the movie theater, got syrupy margaritas and gooey quesadillas. As the rest of our little group celebrated, you went quiet.

"I wish more people saw it," you said. "It's over and no one knows."

"That's not what it was about," your costar reminded you.

She was right, of course—it was about expression, a pure kind, the exhaustion of trying to create and sustain a little glimmer of a new universe in one empty room. It was total invention, imagining something new, something alive, into public being.

But the purity didn't make it any less finished, any less small in the moment. You asked me if you were good, if you seemed truly human up there, and I told you of course, the people in that room couldn't take their eyes off you. I told you because it was true.

But it was over, and so you no longer trusted that it happened, that moment when you lost the shackles of yourself and became something that resembled you but went beyond you, in that empty room in the mall, with blankets over the windows to ordain it a theater. There's nothing new about this story, a story that is both of ours, the clash between the work one wants to make and the attention one doesn't receive, the breakdowns, the gentle encouragement that it's worth it. These are the emotions that underpin so much of what we do for each other, always the first eyes on each other's work, reiterating its value until the maker begins to believe. And of course we've had those searching, kind-of-kidding conversations about how much easier our collective life would be without the anxiety of wanting to make things, things that are ours and that resonate—*art,* that's what I'm talking about; why can't I just say it?

I've asked you if you feel any connection to our favorite reality performers when they're at their best. You answered with a hard no. You're an actress, and they're only approximating what you do. As much as you enjoy them, there's still that bristle. They're doing something else, something that just *is,* or not exactly, but it's closer to that than it is to the effort of invention—you would never want to be judged for what they do as an artist, as a person either. You want to be judged for the transformation. I agreed when you said it, that the aim to chase is that transformation, but how can that be true when my work is a retreading of what we've just lived? I've seen you embody and then shed so many new roles, and alongside you I have burrowed deeper into what's there, afraid to shed anything. Certainly, when you ask me to run lines with you, it's a less interautobiographically charged experience than when I read you the beginnings of a scene about jerking off in the shower with your fancy shampoo. You ask, Why *this*? And I answer, Was it not funny? I saw you laugh.

What I don't vocalize is the desperation to believe that if we've lived something, it deserves to be worth something. And I worry that desperation turns into assumption, which begins to strangle any other possibility, stunt any chance for transformation. And look, we've moved our lives across the country and back to support my endeavor. And look at those days when you knelt beside me as I melted down on the living-room carpet, hyperventilating and going on about how nobody would ever give a shit—They will, baby, *shh,* they will, you told me.

You're a better actor than I am a writer—another thing I've never said that's true. And I like to romanticize the way that you do what you do for art's sake, juxtapose it with me tantruming after a poorly attended reading, as though either image contains anything close to the full truth of the experience.

I've been thinking about the first time I ever felt good about something I made. My mother signed me up for an acting class when I was maybe fourteen. My brother had just died, and my TV watching was more worrying when it could be seen as a numbing balm for something real. So I took this class after school and sulked through it. The students were all supposed to pick scenes from plays to perform or write our own material. I did neither, couldn't think of anything to bring to those endeavors. During the public performance that ended the class, I sat backstage with the teacher yelling at me that I had to do *something.* She shoved me onstage last, and as if using muscle memory that I didn't know I had, I began speaking in detail about all the girls who'd rejected me, all the little shames, the boners hidden under classroom desks, and on and on. When people laughed at me, I went into greater detail. The audience kept laughing, also cringed. This was a joy for me—none of my classmates' clumsy, sincere versions of *Fences* or *Who's Afraid of Virginia Woolf?* garnered such a response.

I don't remember many specifics of the performance, only that it was liked. And I know a teenage variety show doesn't mean anything, but lately I can't help but see it as the beginning of a perpetually perpetrated act, the only one I feel equipped to perform or to watch. Here it is again—showing off the flaw to abdicate responsibility for changing it, reveling in the power of the reveal, offering up that static intimacy on repeat.

I will read you this passage, and I think you'll say that you like it, and I'm already anticipating how good that will feel.

Some Real Housewives *taglines:*

Seasons may change, but I never go out of style.

I'm stronger than anything in my way. Holla!

I may not be the sharpest tool in the shed . . . but I'm pretty!

In a town full of phonies, I'm not afraid to be me.

Money is what I have, not who I am.

Whoever said blondes have more fun hasn't met me.

If you think I'm a bitch, then bring it on.

I can hold my own. I'm my own person.

*My husband is the top plastic surgeon in this town, and I'm
his best creation.*

If I were a housewife, my tagline would be: *Say what you want
about me . . . I probably said it first!*

When Kim Kardashian was still engaged to Kris Humphries,
the baritone journeyman basketball player who would be her
husband for fifty-nine days, he tossed her into the ocean in
Tahiti, and one of her diamond earrings fell to the bottom, out
of reach. Kim reacted.

Her greatest strength has always been the way she appears so
comically blank but then can convert that blankness into dispa-
rate and extreme emotions very quickly. It's the implication of
someone who is only affect, as though she's waiting, inert, for an
inciting event to respond to, and then her whole being contorts
to the intensity of that scenario.

Cue the extravagant horseplay-gone-too-far sequence: cavort-
ing joy into frozen worry into exploding sadness into stiffened
rage.

Kim is dressed in what can only be described as a beachy ball
gown, a clinging black dress worn over her bikini, with flesh-
toned racing stripes running along the curvature of her sides.
Kris is in his frat-boy-casual vacation trunks, his torso bare
and muscled. He is hard where she is soft; she curves and he is
straight; when he picks her up she squeals with a combination
of fear and excitement and that makes him give a throaty dude-
chuckle because what does a dude like more than making a chick
feel happy and afraid at the same time?

They're vacationing at a small, private resort built on stilts
over pristine Pacific water. Kris drops Kim from the deck down
into that water. She falls elegantly, lands with only a small splash,

and breaks back through the surface with her hair floating in slick tendrils behind her like Daryl Hannah in *Splash.*

She reaches up to her head, at first to say in this flirty accusatory way that she's going to have a headache. But then as her fingertips touch a bare earlobe, her body seizes, and it becomes clear that we are watching someone's day change significantly. She gasps. She screams that her earring is gone, and then it's as though hearing herself vocalize it finally allows her to believe that the worst has indeed happened. She says, *Oh my God I'm gonna cry,* and then lets herself give in to that action. Her facial features pinch and then turn down, as though the precise mechanism that holds everything in perfect symmetrical order has been physically damaged by the emotional trauma and all physiological equilibrium is lost. She throws her head back into the water. She looks up at Kris and pleads with him, saying just the word *seriously,* letting it hang out there, begging him to believe that she's really hurt. He doesn't seem to believe. She switches from sadness to rage. She splashes at the water. She says *seriously* again, this time with bite. Everything about her face and body, the tone of her voice, is becoming unhinged.

That's seventy-five thousand dollars! she screams. Her face is still contorted for tears, though none seem to be coming. She's justifying the legitimacy of her emotion while experiencing it and also attaching specific monetary value to it, until the justification becomes the emotion, and it's all happening in a matter of seconds, in the postcard waters of an exclusive Tahitian resort where, despite it all, she can't find peace. She climbs out of the water, pulls her dripping hair away from her face, and heaves and gasps as she hurries past the camera, turning around to scream, *I'm not faking!*

The camera tracks her along the maze of decks, until she finds her mother and unloads. Her fists are balled and her body sort of bounces as she howls out her description of the events. Her head shakes furiously when her mother tries to suggest that maybe they can find the earring. *It's in the fucking ocean!* she screams. Her mother holds her as Kim keeps her elbows in to be embrace-able and softens her face just for a moment. She keeps explaining herself, searching for allies. From a distant cabana, her sister calls out, *Kim, there's people that are* dying, and Kim's cheeks flush with more rage, contort for more tears.

The scene became hugely popular, mostly for the ease with which so many people could ridicule it—Kim's embodiment of pure privilege, the perspective that everyone assumes a Beverly Hills girl to have being confirmed and advertised in the creases of her pouting face, as she so sincerely mourns the loss of one tiny bit of opulence while surrounded by so much more of it. We ridiculed it when we first saw it. We couldn't get enough. We compared impressions of this icky self she'd invited us to see—her pout, the constricted warbling of her wails, screaming at each other: *Seventy-five thousand dollars!*

The problem with intimacy is that it can make everything other than the intimate object blurry. A person's face, beautiful or strained or silly, a person's body—in close-up these are power-ful enough to satisfy. Watch for an eye dart, listen for a catch of breath, and it becomes harder to see the scope of what is causing the darting, the catching.

It's a question of what we do with the access to intimacy, where we're meant to look and what we see. And that's always been the question when viewers have been allowed to see a life—ever since the first film of a man sneezing, ever since Robert Flaherty zoomed in from a safe distance with a telephoto lens, ever since seven strangers all met in a loft to stop being polite and start getting real.

The smaller the screen, the closer the face; the scope narrows and it's like you can reach out and punch the face, or wipe the tears off the face. The face is in your home, demanding your reaction. There is a story, the specific story of that face and the emotion it conveys, and you are a witness to it, up close, and that makes you a participant in, a captive to, the emotion.

Beverley Skeggs and Helen Wood describe it like this: *Television can produce a 'beside-ness,' a binding to others as well as a dramatic distancing.*

Our stars are beside us, but they're not with us. So if they're greedy or selfish or cruel, if they lash out or if they lie docile, what does that say about us? Always, it's about us in that space so seminear them and so near each other; always, it's visceral.

Skeggs and Wood conducted interviews with people from all over England who self-identified as watchers of an array of the nation's most popular reality shows: the one where families of different classes switch moms; the one that follows the employees of exclusive vacation resorts; the one where a child psychologist helps parents deal with their terrible kids; the one that allows people who are "stuck in a rut" to "transform" and look ten years younger. They asked a series of questions to understand how each watcher interacted with the shows. The responses were varied, but a clear pattern could be traced in stated emotion, across demographics: sadness, which could be wielded as a judgment or offered up as an attempt at care, and often the two intentions blurred:

> . . . [It's] really . . . sad, you know?

> Well, it's sad. [Laughs] . . . It's sad and it depresses me.

> How sad is that? Her problem is that she has no self-esteem.

> [I] just think you're sad—get a life.

After all these years, I can't get enough of watching you sympathize. You sympathize often and well. I know your cringe; I know the sound that you let escape when a silent cringe is not enough to express just how bad you feel for a stranger. Lately we've been doing this thing where we lean against opposite sides of the long couch and let our legs entwine on the middle cushion, the soles of my feet warm on the swell of your ass. From here we can see each other, and it's just a quick semiturn of the head to go from screen to face, then back.

Sometimes I think the easiest thing in the world is to feel for someone. Take our favorite sociopath on *Million Dollar Listing: Los Angeles*. Josh. He's unabashed old money: selfish, ruthless, his humor often skewing racist in small ways. We don't care for the way he sees the world and behaves in it. But he did, for the show's first four seasons, have a grandmother whom he loved, a mink-draped Holocaust survivor named Edith who died before season 7. She was ninety-something and sick, and she died happily, leaving her Beverly Hills penthouse to her grieving grandson, who certainly didn't need it. The whole thing, as I think about it now, is a bit disgusting: hoarded generational wealth, and the fact that, instead of selling the property and giving the profit away or living in it to at least make use of it, Josh plans to keep it as a shrine to his grandmother and a testament to the fact that he isn't concerned with anybody else's wants or needs.

And yet. One episode ends with a shot of him in the empty penthouse at night, lit by soft yellow bulbs, and his face is puffy and pale under his awful flat-brim hat, and his body is deflated. He sits, so small, on the corner of a massive vintage L-shaped couch, and he whispers, into the empty space around him, *I miss you*, wistful, blinking. Across from me you make a little sound and turn your bottom lip down to show sadness. I see you, you see me see you, then we turn again to the screen.

15

first of all, looking for an energetic people person with the powers of attraction and an uncanny ability to improve the lives of humans around him? . . . I'm your guy. I put the social into a social gathering and have been told for years that there is something special about my presence—its about time I recognize it myself. Smile, you just met your next best friend.

—from www.castingcallhub.com

Back to NeNe. Always back to NeNe. NeNe there; us watching.

Andy Cohen, an executive vice president at Bravo, the man who conceived of the juggernaut housewife framework, speaks of NeNe as though she were art, meaning as though she were unreal. As Raquel Gates emphasizes in her essay "Keepin' It Reality Television," Cohen sees NeNe and her fellow housewives in the tradition that Sontag so famously defended: camp.

Gates quotes an old Cohen interview from *The Advocate:* "'Gays love the shows for the same reason gays love drag queens. They're an exaggerated portrayal of women, what gay guys want women to be in their twisted fantasy lives.'"

I want to pledge allegiance to his celebration of campiness, but I think it's a bit pricklier than that. Sontag began "Notes on Camp" by saying that the topic she was going to attempt to discuss was hard to discuss because *It is not a natural mode of sensibility. . . . Indeed, the essence of camp is its love of the unnatural.*

What does it mean to say, then, that NeNe is unnatural,

spectacularly so, particularly when her role is theoretically a performance of her life as she lives it? It's a claim that only feels complimentary if you can say confidently that you're in on the artifice. We both know how much I love being in on the artifice. But would Andy Cohen's whole thing (and our whole thing as viewers) fall apart if NeNe started walking around calling herself camp? Would that open awareness kill the appeal? Does Cohen see NeNe as the person making the campy thing that we love, or is Cohen the maker and NeNe simply the thing he's anointed as camp, as fantasy, as show? Sontag wrote, *Pure Camp is always naive. Camp which knows itself to be Camp . . . is usually less satisfying.* I find it hard not to cringe when I read this.

Yet amid the discomfort, or maybe because of it, I still love every detail of her performance. I love when NeNe says *Honey.* Or *Child.* To me, it seems like she calls everybody *Honey* or *Child.* This fact in itself is unremarkable. Really, it's a bit on-the-nose, adhering to the kind of stereotype that even the lily-whitest of viewers (us) has access to. Or maybe she's not adhering to any stereotype; maybe she's just talking. I wouldn't know. All I know is that, for me, she has made common words into catchphrases, not through the frequency with which she uses them but through the consistent, recognizable fullness with which she performs them—the commiserating exhaustion with which she says *Child* before catching a friend up on gossip; the way she separates the syllables of *Honey* with such precise intent, like she's savoring the word.

She's saying the things that any viewer of formulaic scripted sitcoms might assume that she says, and she's saying them more consciously, somehow better, than you could ever anticipate anyone saying them. Which could be a compliment or a critique. Either way, I remain a tourist at the performance, with no authority to assess the merits or motivations or authenticity of her behavior, yet that's what the show is inviting me to do every time we sit and watch.

After all these seasons of the same schtick, it's hard not to feel that Cohen is trying to make NeNe's gifts *his,* his for noticing and framing her natural unnaturalness, and doling out a paycheck for it. And I don't like that. How dare he?

It feels good to say we're growing tired of him, his whole jokey-yet-condescending bit, everybody's pal but also everybody's boss. We scoff about him to each other, point out the little seams we find in his nice-guy veneer, as though pointing at him deflects from the fact that we're next down the unsettling line of predictable appropriation—a straight white couple setting aside our Tuesday nights to giggle along to a gay white man's self-proclaimed fantasy of black femininity, still finding joy in the way we parrot lines back to each other in voices that are not our own, all too happy to dub our stolen performances *problematic* as we continue.

It's tempting to reach for more theory here, to try to add some sense of expansiveness and inquiry to this scenario, but honestly that seems like a cop-out for what I'm trying to express. What am I trying to express? A desire to have something authoritative to say about a performance of a life not my own, as though that desire were justification enough?

This is where the gears of the narrative get stuck—same couch, same shows, same thoughts again. I'm in the confessional room, doing my bit about you and my fantasy of you, and us on the couch watching a fantasy of NeNe that's filtered through so much distance and rationalization that it's hard to understand the fantasy.

A Sunday afternoon in Iowa:

We'd been playing tennis—me and you as a doubles team against two friends—on the swampy public courts down by the river. The match was, as I remember it, close and horribly played, a combination that left all participants irritable. We all went back to our house afterward to get drunk on G&Ts, and

I got into some argument about something with one friend, a gay white man, the only person I've ever met who likes to talk about NeNe Leakes more than me. He had, I thought anyway, adopted some of her mannerisms; he consciously, publicly jacked her catchphrases and referenced her sensibility in ways that we only feel comfortable doing alone. And I loved him for the performance, which felt only one step removed from NeNe and therefore made me think and speak about NeNe in ways that didn't make me feel guilty because this person who was at least closer to being a stakeholder in her affect was welcoming me into the conversation.

Anyway. I think we were arguing over a book or a writer or a professor, because those were subjects of importance to us then. He started getting more and more animated about his dislike for whatever the subject was that I didn't dislike, and that got me mad, and then suddenly I heard my own voice fall into a crude impression of his version of a black woman.

"Oh, I'm sorry he ain't *real* enough for you," is what I said. Or something like that. I just remember that I said *"real"* like it was the most important word in the sentence, the only word that mattered, the way NeNe always says it. And I said it with what can only be described as appropriated blackness, and also, confusingly, appropriated gayness. I bobbled my head around on my neck as I said it, that kind of caricature shit.

I remember the way you looked at me, with a little anger, and then the way you looked at him, with a silent gesture toward attempted apology on my behalf. I felt cruel and impotent at the same time.

I said it because I was mad, and I wanted to lash out, and I guess in the moment I thought one way to lash out was to try to attack him for *his* appropriation—a white prep-school kid who was continually assuming the voice of a black woman, as though that were a voice authentic to his own experience. I wanted to hurt him with that, make him feel guilt for the way he took up the character, but the moment I said it, my voice hung out there like the worst kind of talk-radio host, with a combination of arrogance and ignorance, an assumption that from the total safety of a life lived without even a dent in my own privilege I could understand and assume every perspective.

"You can't do that," he said to me. And you nodded. And our other friend nodded. And I know I shouldn't do that. Of course I know it. I like to think I've grown, grown in awareness, anyway, but then there's this action that is the same action, so careless, so dopily, cruelly, predictably unaware.

All I remember feeling at the time was the particular petulance that straight white men feel when anyone suggests that any small corner of the human experience is off-limits to us. A familiar feeling. A familiar spectacle of my worst self, and the quick wallow in regret. A familiar confession to make.

At a certain point the act of confession becomes too self-satisfied. If it's thrilling, rather than painful, to reveal the things that have theoretically always been too tough to reveal, then the idea of pain becomes just another exaggeration to help raise the stakes. And I have to wonder, and you have to wonder about me, if there is any correlation between what experiences somebody is willing to share and how much those experiences mean.

This is beyond commodifying experience; it's commodifying shame.

Of the many condescending descriptors applied to reality-TV stars and producers that I disagree with, the most annoying always involve the word *shameless.* Absolutely nothing could be further from an accurate assessment of the motives at play, both for the makers and the watchers. Shamelessness implies obliviousness, and obliviousness is almost never interesting.

Better to acknowledge that what is happening is the elevation of shame. I don't want to say a *reclamation* because that term
implies a lot of pride and do-goodery, and that's not the sort of
thing I'm talking about. I'm talking about the willingness to
see each ugly memory, each questionable action, each pattern of
worst behavior, each bit of chum fed into the gnashing teeth of a
small and self-interested life, as something to exhibit because at
least the exhibition might make you feel as though you've done
something. I'm talking about getting one over on yourself.

In most conversations I have about reality TV, along with the
main expression of disbelief (the that-didn't-really-happen
kind), there is often a second strand: disbelief at the fact that
anybody would still be willing to participate. Given all we've
seen for decades now—the shame and lies and pain—how could
anyone still want to offer themselves up? But disbelief does not
affect desire. If there has been any dip, it has been in viewership,
not in the people clamoring to be viewed.

At the 2016 RealScreen Summit, more than two thousand
people descend on a Marriott conference center to give panel talks
about the future of nonfiction programming, and to make deals.
It's a trade show for content, the place where ideas and people
are monetized or rejected. Every conference features countless
thousands of projects being pitched, currently in production,
or already picked up but looking for further development fund-
ing. Some are full-length documentaries about topical, terrifying
things—example: *Charlie Hebdo: Three Days of Terror.* Most are
meant to be serialized and are looking for a channel, trying to
entice many seasons' worth of attention.

Skin Tight: An intimate look at twelve subjects recovering
from gastric bypass surgery—one is struggling to train for an
iron-man marathon, one is struggling to reconnect with his
daughters, et cetera.

Santas in the Barn: Ten Santas from across the United States will compete in a raft of Christmas-themed challenges (e.g., chimney climbing, gift wrapping, sleigh building).

Railroad Alaska. Stripped Bare. The Bible Wars. Monsters: When Moms Go Bad. Facing My Accuser. So You Think You Want to Get Married. The Great American Veteran. The Romanians Are Coming. Sex Box. TransFatty Lives. The Real Strippers of Baltimore (hopefully spinning off into further cities). *Rise of the Superstar Vloggers. Natural Born Outlaws. Klondike Trappers. Finding Love. Backstabbers. The Illegal Eater. How to Make Love to My Wife.*

The conference is biannual, nearing two decades of existence. Some of the shows have been pitched over and over for years running. Some people are pitching five or six shows all at once. Masses of attendees wait in lines for their meetings or speed-pitching roundtables, with identical "producer" badges, but the term's meaning becomes diffuse—some are established hit makers; some represent small, fledgling companies from around the world; some represent themselves. Their portfolios are extensive—three ideas that might work for Discovery, a freaky family that might appeal to the Lifetime demographic, something macho about a bike shop that's perfect for the Spike audience.

The logic, one independent producer tells me, is to have so much content that it can't be ignored.

"Content volume," he says. "Stake your claim on as many concepts as you can."

"Content, like people?" I ask him.

He says, "Yeah, so when you meet someone weird, file that away in your brain. Then check back in with them and hope nobody got there first."

I ask producers if anyone says no, when approached about being used by or turned into a show. Almost never. Even if they're hesitant or distrustful or scornful at first, if you make a person feel like someone wants to look at them, listen to them, eventually they come around. Call them, check in, film a test reel of their lives, make it look slick, play it back to them.

At the conference, it seems as though everyone's online bio, and also everyone's in-person elevator pitch, begins with some variation of this: As long as I can remember, I've been a story-teller. As though that instinct can explain or absolve anything.

Somewhere in here I'm telling our story, right? That's at least part of the idea. But look how it has become streamlined. Look at how little life there is—just sporadic emotional plot points— even as I felt I was revealing so much. Look how I focus on the loud bangs and the sulky silences, the fucked-up moments, the occasional bared body, refusing to let you and me be fully real- ized on the page, to be human in any way beyond broad, emotive strokes. I recognize us in those strokes, but also I don't.

At first I was tempted to describe this effect as *unraveling* because I like the drama in that word, but this is the opposite of unraveling. This is tightening—winding the moments we spend together into a neat little cylinder of two people who need each other and love each other and love watching and sometimes hate themselves. That's not right. Or it's partially right. It's right enough, and incomplete enough to have order. It's the thing that happens when the search for having something to say becomes consumed with the desire to say something.

Last week, in the kitchen, after you'd read a draft of this, when you were draining and cutting the tofu and I was massaging the kale, you said that it's like I've been taking notes on our life. Everything that you had assumed to be just us living was, all along, serving double duty. Like you thought you were just pre- paring a nutritious, home-cooked meal since we've been trying to move away from the hidden greases of eating out, but really I was shoving you into the role of the type of yuppie asshole who would make such a life plan. Like we were both a punch line to a lame joke or, worse, like we were a tragedy.

"That's not it," I said. "That's not it at all."

Then we fell silent and cooked the tofu, and then we ate, chewing sounds interrupted by the occasional comment about the marinade being almost perfect, needing more heat.

I loved it as I lived it. I loved every quiet moment; I loved the marinade. And I picture a series of scenes, our mouths biting the curd from a thousand different angles on a thousand different days—the perfect cutaway shot. And our faces change, even as we don't want them to. And we chew. And we chew. And we chew. And we yell. And we fuck. And we say kind things that need to be said. And we look at our bodies. And we look at other bodies. And we look for meaning. And we sit silent again for another thousand moments.

16

I am not normal. I don't want to be normal. I know I am eccentric
and flamboyant at the same time. . . . I want a chance to show the
world the being weird is the new normal!! #Diva

—from www.castingcallhub.com

There was actual debate last night over whether we should watch
the first episode of *Jill and Jessa: Counting On.* We vacillated,
made vague suggestions for alternative activities. Eventually
our conflictedness satisfactorily performed, we both refrained
from changing the channel and settled in for the forced shame
march.

At first thought, it's inconceivable that the Duggar family,
stars of *19 Kids and Counting,* could be back on television mere
months after Josh Duggar's teenage sexual-abuse revelations, followed by the breaking news that he habitually cheated on his
wife in D.C. with escorts who were willing to go on the record
about his particularly rough requests. You chose not to read most
of the coverage of these revelations; I, of course, read it all. I
mean no value judgment in the gulf between our reactions—
there's plenty to squirm about in both.

Either way, we were resigned to watching the family only in
reruns from then on—Jessa and Jill frozen in our memories as
late teens, freshly married, newly pregnant, and excited for a life
of many more pregnancies; the boys all gangly and identical,
their voices cracking during monologues of their faith; the lit-

tlest daughters still angelic and cardboard in the way that all small children are on-screen; the family with endless reasons to host potlucks, a sea of women and girls taking tinfoil off of warming trays, a matching sea of men and boys with their hands shoved in their jeans pockets. It had been a show about the sincere innocence with which they performed and proselytized for their backward utopia, where birth control and public schools and professional women didn't exist but love did. It would end that way.

I wasn't sure if we'd have a hard time watching with the new knowledge of the narrative's underbelly. After all, it's not as though we ever watched because we believed them. They advocated for destructive lunacy, sequestered caveman tribalism. We watched, as much as anything, for the way their carefully selected visuals conveyed to us none of the cheer that the tone of the show so sternly enforced. But also for the way that, despite a backdrop that read to us as bleak, there were moments when some of them, at least, seemed genuinely good. Not in the obvious way that they wanted to look good but in a subtler way, a common way, peeking out from under the spectacle of their belief.

They cared for one another—the siblings more than the parents, who were usually too batshit to resonate much. We liked to watch them shop, en masse, descending on thrift stores in forlorn Arkansas strip malls like celebrity angels, so polite, praising every item in aisles filled with used, modest tops.

Can I just say that it doesn't make any sense to me the way *real* characters, those with birth certificates and bank accounts, who could conceivably (or, fine, often do) stand trial for a crime, inspire less forgiveness and understanding than made-up ones do? I don't know why that's so annoying to me, but it is.

The mechanism of fiction builds off of the emotional power

of the work to find good in figures whose behaviors display so much bad, but we can call the bad *ambiguity*. We watch Tony Soprano walk away from a murder, conflicted, and are asked to focus on the conflict written into his face, the implication that there's more to him than whatever horrible things he has done, and then come to the grander, human-conditiony realization that everyone who has ever lived deserves that generosity, particularly since most haven't, you know, murdered anyone.

Don Draper is a bad father to a depressed daughter, but there are moments when he speaks to her kindly, even if he does so only to nurse his own loneliness, and anyway he was a fatherless child whose own past horrors still lie heavy in his every hungover sigh. He wants to be better than he is. Or at least he has some more depth to him than the surface of his action implies. That's not seen as propaganda; that's seen as the point of art, the joy that can be found in interacting with a life not our own, and perhaps messier. I think that's all realism breaks down to: the approximation of humanness. To look for humanness is to make meaning.

I'm not trying to be obtuse here; I know there's *some* difference between a fictional character and the real people who keep showing up to be made into characters. I know that Don Draper doesn't *really* have a well of wounded backstory to soften his performed edges because he has never existed; he's something a writer thought up after working on *The Sopranos* and seeing how much everyone loves a male protagonist who behaves horribly. He has been made to make us feel, conceived of by a person who is not implicated by the horrible things he decided to make Don do and say. But that only succeeds because, when we watch, we deem him to be a believably human creation—flawed, selfish, threatening, petty, tragic.

Why, then, is it so hard to feel for actual human Jim Bob Duggar? Or I guess not him—he seems like a monster—but at least his daughters, and really all the nonmolesting children who are either blandly obedient or trapped or afraid or believe every nightmarish word of what their father preaches? Maybe they feel all those things at once, to varying degrees, and why shouldn't we consider that? They are humans, flawed, and we don't know what they feel or what they want us to feel, but I like to watch them and wonder.

Maybe I'm being too generous—to them for their unrelenting display of the party line and also to us for being willing spectators. But that's no shallower a reaction than to assume the worst, to assume that there's nothing worth watching for, nothing beyond the most cynical motivations we can so easily read into them.

I think it comes down to this: No matter what these real people are doing, they're doing it to be seen. Alongside any other desires they have, there's that desire, one that fiction never has to acknowledge. Any conflictedness or decency or pain is complicated by the rush to show it. When that desire is visible—its crassness, its desperation—it blocks everything else out. It's the one quality that nobody seems to want to forgive.

One by one the Duggars lined up on their new show to express surprise, then pain, and then hint at something closer to hope. Mostly the episode was a sea of identifiable, nearly identical faces, some looking wracked, others looking exhaustedly blank, each saying phrases like *new normal* with enough rote somberness to suggest that they were to become mantra.

We agreed that Jill looked tired (new baby and all, plus an impending mission trip to what was referred to only as "Central America" and "a dangerous place"). And that Jessa looked as hot as she always looked. And that we had forgotten how interchangeable the sons were as the camera cut from one to the next, creating an optical illusion that even the youngest of them was going bald.

The episode jumped from close-ups on individual faces taking long beats before admitting that, no, nothing is the same anymore, to extended shots of the group behaving as though nothing at all had changed. Case in point: Four daughters walk the aisle of a secondhand store. They're looking for clothes to donate to a Central American orphanage and also for baby-shower presents for Jessa. They bemoan (as cheerfully as one can possibly bemoan) how difficult it is to find gender-neutral toys—Jessa has not revealed the sex of her baby, so they're shopping blind.

Does brown count as gender neutral?

I mean, I guess, but it's brown.

Laughter.

Daughters who used to be tweens, silent in the background, are now strolling next to their other sisters as equals. They all seem to enjoy this dynamic. Time has passed, in a hurry, in many bad directions, but also there's this.

They stop and crowd around a little hat made to look like a football. This football hat, they decide, is perfect. Not one person dissents because, for one thing, the show isn't big on dissent, and for another, any baby of any gender is adorable dressed up as a football. If there's a new son, maybe he'll be a quarterback someday; if there's a daughter, maybe she'll be a quarterback's wife.

Get a little clip bow for it if it's a girl.

Y'all! That is so cute!

Their cheer has turned into something like the last couple of miles of a marathon—they've done it for so long and so unflinchingly that it would be a disservice to their own commitment to stop at this point. Which doesn't make it seem false—not to me, anyway; it just makes it seem earned. The camera lingers long enough to capture the sisters saying *Thank you* so *much* to the store employees before lugging bins of clothing toward the door.

Over the course of the episode, interspersed between the shots of their daily lives, each Duggar faces the camera in formal wear, alone—the daughters in thick, orangey makeup that they would not have worn in the first season, staring straight ahead, sad but steeled. They answer a producer we can't see:

It's not like any of us would have known that my brother was living such a secret life.

People are like, "Y'all ain't perfect?" We never claimed to be perfect.

I kept thinking I'd wake up and things would be how they were.

Some tough days, but as each week goes by I feel healing in this.

The boys don't cry because they're not supposed to. The girls do, quietly.

When we watched them, part of me wanted to tell them all to leave this place, to scream that their new normal probably shouldn't so closely resemble the old one. Maybe they anticipated that skepticism because the episode ends on another church potluck, that thing they do best—female hands pulling tinfoil, blond boys holding footballs, everyone talking about future births and missions and joy, Jim Bob at the mike leading the blessing. They're ready to continue in front of our eyes, and we are already an hour past our original protestations, ready to continue watching. I end up admiring their resilience.

In Brooklyn—Bushwick, of course—I left a bunch of friends watching football at a bar to go to an event at a "center for documentary art," nestled into a perfectly mid-gentrification block, between a boulangerie and a dilapidated bodega.

The place was packed. From what I could tell, the crowd was me, some people who would describe themselves as *video artists,* and a bunch of NYU kids. I was there for a panel discussion about "method acting in documentary," for obvious reasons.

Shonni Enelow, the scholar leading the panel, began the discussion by saying that we who make and critique art should no longer entertain concerns of authenticity. That we shouldn't have come to sit in this room to discuss something as overdiscussed and ultimately regressive as the distinction between *falseness* and *authenticity*. Contemporary culture has already figured out that there is no such thing as authenticity, she said, and maybe that means that nothing is really false.

There was a lot of nodding around me. I felt antsy.

Enelow proposed a new way of assessing honest performance: We must think not about the space between the false and the authentic; we must think in terms of confinement and transformation.

It's not enough, she said, to ask if a performer is achieving something like reality. That goal is stagnant, safe—art does not lie in those words. Falseness, or maybe a better way to put it is lack of true expression, is a cage, and the performer must transform to break free. More nodding.

I thought of Marilyn Monroe and those legendary deep wounds that she brought to every limiting role she was given, how that pain and the way she made it visible was both her realness and her greatest performance, actively pushing against the confinement of her casting. Jacqueline Rose once wrote about the frustrated final film of Monroe's career that her *art is far from exhausted by this moment.* Whatever the conditions around her acting, the limitations imposed by others, her performance burst through, providing something beyond the expectations of her captivity. I can watch Monroe and see that every time; it's an inexhaustible pleasure.

I thought of you, too, and the inexhaustible pleasure of seeing you transform onstage, how that transformation was brief transcendence. It lived outside you, beyond you, beyond what we have together in our lives. I've always focused so much of my love of your performances on the ways you remained yourself throughout them, that current of identifiability, and of course that's part of the power, but it's only the jumping-off point.

When I asked if you felt kinship with our favorite reality performers, what was I really asking? See how they produce human emotion the way you do? As though crying the way you cry, laughing the way you laugh, repeating it, is all that performance is. As though you're always limited, the way I am, by the conditions of being yourself.

If I'd showed up here for validation, for a chance to think of our favorite reality stars as a next evolution of Marilyn and Marlon, that method school where performance *was* self, the word *transformation* ended up doing a beautiful job of highlighting the differences. On our shows, we watch people who perform in gilded shackles, who have sought out confinement and are fighting to stay confined. They say, Look at what I will do to stay here, enscreened. Look at what I will do to my face. Look at what I will admit about my past. Listen to the things I'll say, and if you need me to mean them, I'll mean them.

When a performance is an extended act of being, the way mine so often feels, willingly showing up to repeat the gig of recognizable self, then the performer loses everything if they truly transform. The only narrative completion is death. Or, worse maybe, the narrative ends when people stop paying attention, even as it continues on—the living, the emoting, the calling out, waiting to be discovered intact once again.

I just read an article called "See What Mike 'The Situation' Is Up to After Life on the Jersey Shore." The answer seemed to be that he's grown up a lot and also that he got convicted of tax fraud. On the plus side, the article ended with: *We're interested to see what {he's} up to next!* So there's an argument to be made that the growing up and the tax fraud were worth it.

Most of the time when I'm looking at my computer for too long without looking up and you ask me what I'm doing and I snap the screen shut and say *Nothing* very quickly, I'm Googling myself. Sometimes I read Amazon reviews (I know, I'm sorry), which makes my hands clam up, my pulse quicken. But in the long fallow periods, when reviews have stopped, I can't be so targeted and I search the whole Internet for my name.

This has become worse since a fellow self-Googler (name omitted out of respect) recommended refining my search to specific time periods—Has anybody said anything about me this month? This week? Today? This hour?

This week there was nothing new. There was a podcast I did at a library six months ago, still archived on an ever-scrolling home page. There was my own Twitter bio. There was a website offering a pirated copy of a free PDF download of my first book. This upset me for days. And when you texted me from work, I thought, This is the *only* person who cares to text me. And when I returned from a run to report a brisk four miles and you said, Wow, nice job, I thought, This is the *only* person who knows or cares about my increased lung capacity.

We have winnowed our audience down to be so small. That's what real intimacy is, and that intimacy is the thing that makes me happiest. But the working definition of what intimacy can be has evolved, and intimacy can be a world of people spreading your rumors and staring at your face and saying your name. Individual care, coupled care, can seem so small in the face of that. Even this realization, or admission, is small—how many missives are being sent at this moment saying something along the lines of: Why does nobody know that I've been here? That I'm still here? I feel myself swallowed up in the echo. I yell louder.

Maybe I should be asking what happens when those questions stop or change. Can better questions replace them? What does transformation sound like on the page? Out loud? Or what does contentedness sound like? Or silence?

————

Sometimes the most cherished memories are the ones that frighten me—the ones that feel too tender to broadcast, then too tender to not broadcast.

The last time I watched you like I didn't know you was when we moved into the little white church house in Iowa and you made a new best friend at the diner where you worked. I don't even remember her name anymore, only that it felt more common than she deserved. She was from some tiny town in the cornfields, and she behaved both of that and above it. She was trying on cosmopolitanism, I think, and you were trying on country charm, in our little white house, biking to the diner gig, putting on plays at a 4H barn, and slugging rye at the dive bar around the corner where you shot pool with bemused old drunks.

You fell in love. Or it looked like that. You had long, straight black hair and she had long, straight blonde hair, and you touched each other's hair and talked about never cutting it. I was on the road a lot then, following the baseball team I was writing about, filling my hatchback with notepads of gibberish, the smell of Combos and Red Bull and farts. I was trying on a serious-journalist self, romantic in its own way but ultimately pretty miserable. I would arrive home to you and her sprawling on the little grass patch outside our house, her bike always parked under the dilapidated awning, its basket brimming with bread and local vegetables, goat cheese, the whole farm-to-table genre. I was more jealous than I realized, but more often than not I just liked to watch you.

You did not seem like you. Or you seemed like you were trying harder to be you. You seemed better than the you that my presence allowed for, which was disturbing but also mesmerizing. The two of you spoke of cold mothers and future freedom, and you cupped the bare skin on each other's freckled summer shoulders as you spoke, a constant, silent, necessary validation of the weight of small traumas and the achievability of new adventures.

You put on oversize sunglasses and vintage bathing suits and went to the public pool to smirk at preening lacrosse players cannonballing to hear their girlfriends squeal. She read Russian novels and you read Russian plays; you read passages out loud to each other, or at least you did the one time I joined you, keeping to the shade with my shirt on, due to all the lacrosse players. She looked at me and said, "You should never be embarrassed at a public pool; it's not worth it," and you agreed with her. You smiled at each other, and I watched the rest of the people at the pool looking at the two of you with your oversize sunglasses and vintage bathing suits, something among but apart from everyone else, a shared secret.

You were going to take her to Italy, to your grandmother's home on the Adriatic. You were going to rent one of those tiny Italian convertibles. When I heard you talking, I pictured your hair, long, black and blonde, trailing behind you on a mountain road overlooking the sea, something out of a movie, not a specific one, just the idea of a movie like that. None of it felt real, not what you spoke of, not what you lived. But it was beautiful to see and to imagine, and it seemed necessary to you, a closeness that was more immediate and weighted and performed than ours had become. It was like you were pining for something together, like you were each missing something and the shared missing felt so good, and I couldn't replace whatever it was that you missed and I couldn't make you feel as good as that pining did.

When she stopped coming around, you grieved. When she got that born-again boyfriend, you grieved. When she completed her nurse's assistant degree and you saw her one more time at a coffee shop, tired in her scrubs, with the born-again man rubbing her back and saying they'd be getting married as soon as she accumulated the vacation time, you grieved. I consoled you, rubbed your back.

I was angry that I wasn't enough and also sad for you that

this other relationship was fleeting, so ultimately not enough either. That really nothing is enough for you, for anyone. I had been captivated, next to you yet from a distance. I had wanted to see you in that car by the Adriatic, new. And also, still, there's this memory: a memory of the way you held your body like you weren't thinking about it, stretching across our little patch of grass next to her.

17

In *The New Yorker,* Kelefa Sanneh once wrote that reality TV is *the television of television.* I think that's a nice way to put it—the one thing that remains universally low in a medium that, for the first half century of its existence was *the* face of low culture. Now my university offers lectures called "Game of Thrones and Philosophy." Netflix sitcoms apparently provide a submersion in some valuable critique of the way we live now. And beyond TV: Pop music is written about like revolution. Treacly Super Bowl ads are shared as short films.

This is not a new observation, I know, and I don't mean to be crotchety—this is all a good thing, if sometimes annoyingly self-congratulatory. There's liberation in the freedom of *low* culture from the muck of its implications. But, amid the self-celebrating demolition of cultural hierarchy, there's also a little comfort in the notion that *something* remains less-than, still forcing a consumer to face the worst implications of their tastes, and therefore maybe themselves.

British scholar Annette Hill analyzed survey responses to TV consumption patterns and traced the way reality TV conversations took on the language and habits of addiction. Participants lied about what they watched—surprisingly small percentages of self-avowed TV fans would admit to watching shows whose ratings suggested a runaway hit. And the honest responders often adopted the tone of an addict's confession, a sheepish exploration of the compulsive—*I don't know. I thought it was actually rubbish . . . but I was so hooked.*

Apologetic viewing, Hill called it.

Again, it seems impossible to ignore that the shame is part of the form. After all, we who consume are part of the interaction—it's the people who produce the stars, the stars, and then it's us. Everyone is a little disappointed, a little embarrassed, yet still we return to what is both comfortable and not. We have to see ourselves returning each time, have to ask ourselves why. Have to ask ourselves if there's something better out there to aspire to for those people on display, for us.

In an episode of the latest season of *Sister Wives,* TLC's drama about a clan of likable, progressive-seeming polygamists driven from their Utah homestead to set up camp in a stucco cul-de-sac in suburban Las Vegas, the family holds a meeting. These meetings play a central role in nearly every episode. Some involve just the wives, some the husband and the wives; some include everyone—twenty-some-odd humans of various sizes sprawled across one living-room floor.

In this recent episode, Kody and all four wives sit around one of their dining room tables. They're having a conversation about a family party in honor of Kody's official adoption of Robyn's children from a previous marriage. This is a growing-the-family meeting, the most important kind, but also it's a meeting about food. All families, after all, must eat.

The camera enters the shot like a guest entering the home, lingering over a painted sign in the foyer, with the words *Together We Make a Family* followed by the names of every family member somehow squeezed in. At first husband and wives are seen at a distance. Light fills all the windows so that they're opaque, so that there's no outside. The house appears strangely unlived-in, and this is common—in a show that, as much as anything, is about the constant, crushing, joyful presence of children, when children are absent from a scene there is no evidence of them ever existing. Some recliners and a leather sofa sit empty in the living room. The floors are clean, like they've been prepared for company.

Every spouse has a notepad on the table. Kody is in his usual denim button-up shirt, no undershirt, chest skin winking out. His hair is long, wavy, and blond. It seems like he may color it in service of his boyishness and laid-back dudeness, which is in service of the central drama of the show, the question of how such blandly normal, generally easygoing Americans could partici-pate in such an ancient taboo.

Kody is talking about chicken. He says the wives are mak-ing salads, right, and so he'll take care of the meat—he's going to pick up killer, sauce-dripping wings. He seems pleased with himself. Robyn cuts him off, and the camera turns to her. She says that chicken wings were not at all what they'd talked about.

Kody interrupts and says he hasn't even *ordered* yet, chill out, and Robyn's head pulls back because of how quickly his voice turned nasty. Kody's tensed now, shoulders up a little, fore-arms flexing under his denim. Robyn continues to say that she wants a Sunday-dinner feel, this is a formal thing, a celebration, white tablecloths, nice napkins, and plus they're all trying to be healthier, and how on *earth* would barbeque wings fit into this vision—which, again, she has already articulated to Kody?

Another wife chimes in to say, *No wings, no drumsticks, let's leave it at that.* Then she looks at Kody, grins, and says, *This must be eating you alive inside.* All the wives are grinning now.

Kody looks tired. He says that he's not disagreeing with anybody, he's just trying to help figure this out. *Just ease up,* he says to Robyn, and pushes his palms out over the table in the universal stop sign. Everyone stops, but they're still grinning. The camera scans over all the faces, with the neon sunlight clouding the windows behind them, in the family room of their impossibly clean, nondescript home. My God, how many shows have we seen where people mill around in a house just like theirs? It never looks better, it never looks worse; it never looks lived-in, but that's the only thing it's meant to be: a place where we believe a family might live. And their family is just like all the other families, except not at all like them. And, man, a chicken dinner is hard to organize. And, man, a life of any kind is hard to sustain.

Look, I'll buy all the critiques about the unrepentant superficiality of reality television the moment someone looks like shit in a fictional show. I'm thinking specifically now of *The Leftovers,* which, I get it, is brilliant in a lot of ways, and is about pain and loss and the attempt to believe that you may be a redeemable person even when the universe seems orchestrated to make you believe that you aren't. Heavy stuff. Interior kind of stuff. But all I think about when I watch it is the unacknowledged exterior. I mean, these people look incredible. And it goes beyond genetic fortune—these people are goddamn sculpted, and I never see a scene of any one of them doing that sculpting. They stress-eat a lot, and drink. The only character who exercises jogs a little and stops midjog to smoke. And not to make this all about me, but I've been jogging quite a bit lately and my obliques don't look like his do, and really the only reason I don't smoke anymore, beyond solidarity with your quitting efforts, is because it would slow down my jogging, and this fucking guy casually jogs and smokes his way through the apocalypse and I'm supposed to focus on his *mental* breakdown?

Give me Kim's constant droning on about her baby-weight fears; give me televised body augmentations and the bruised, bandaged after-scenes when a still-drugged star claims to feel more confident already. Give me Jax only drinking hard liquor for the reduced carbs and then forcing himself to face the gym as a near-middle-aged man with a permahangover, living up to the only obligation that he seems to consider important. Give me Kody and the wives at the grocery store, buying chicken in bulk, back home in lumpy sweatshirts, chewing, making small talk about needing a spa day, something indulgent, they deserve it.

They are alive and looked at, willfully, resentfully. It's a constant, high-pitched swell of strings, an unspoken panic that I recognize and believe. What I'm saying is that if the superficial and the interior are diametrically opposed, how come the superficial makes me feel so damn much?

Yesterday, screen muted, I was reading Chris Kraus's *I Love Dick,* and I thought I had an epiphany on this one line of hers: *Bad art makes the viewer much more active. . . . Bad characters invite invention.*

Jesus, how many pages has it taken me to try and fail to say that?

There is so much possibility to be found in broad, surfacey characters; so many details waiting to be filled in. The problem is that I don't have the confidence to call what I love bad and still love it. And I don't know if I think bad is exactly the right word, but I certainly find it hard to own up to the fact that part of what I love is the total absolution from the feeling that what I'm watching might be too sophisticated for *me*.

Kraus writes of being *a lover of a certain kind of bad art, which offers a transparency into the hopes and desires of the person who made it.*

That's the feeling I recognize. That's the feeling of rawness and power—to look at the surface of what someone is presenting and think you can see the naked self behind that construction, the valley between how they want to be interpreted and what they're saying. Either way, the viewer gets to take ownership over how she feels about what she's seeing and why. It's even more of a rush when the performer doesn't demand to be called an artist at all—what greater power than to be the one who projects all the meaning onto the work of a stranger who is so thoroughly, transparently desirous.

Once you looked at me and said, "Do you realize your mouth is moving when you watch? I can't hear anything, but it looks like you're saying something."

I stiffened up and got pouty about it because you laughed, and I suppose that's why you never brought it up again. But in retrospect I like the observation and that you made it. That you see me there in my particularities, unguarded, leaning in, the way I like to think I see you.

18

{REQUEST FOR AUDITION}:

I am very able to be in touch with my emotions and portray many types of characters. It is my dream to be in a romantic film or tv series. I would appreciate the opportunity to show you what i can bring to the table. Please help me accomplish my dreams. Thank you for your time.

—from www.castingcallhub.com

The first time I spoke to Will Autry, he'd just suffered an accident on the job. I asked him, a bit too excited, if *on the job* meant on set. No, he said, and then chuckled. His *job* is working a Norfolk Southern freight train on a route between Atlanta and Macon. His *inspiration* is what happens when the train is parked in Macon and it's other peoples' job to unload the cargo. Will has hours to sit with his notebook and write ideas for reality shows.

Here are some ideas:

Waiting: Following engaged couples who are saving themselves for marriage.

Closure: Each week an injured party confronts the person who injured them. The injurer has the chance to atone. The offenses can range from petty differences to heinous crimes.

America's Greatest Veteran: A show that both honors veterans and has them compete to exemplify valor. Compete, but in a supportive way. Everyone wins, kind of.

Always, he starts with the title, works backward into concept, then theme, then character.

Will has been trying to break into reality ever since somebody saw a feature documentary concept he wrote up and told him that if he wanted a chance at some money, he should try to find a way to make his ideas episodic. This was five or six years ago, when reality still felt wide open.

"It doesn't anymore?" I asked him.

"Not really," he said. "The bubble is bursting. Whenever there's a bubble, it has to burst, right?"

Will isn't the only hopeful writer-producer to tell me this. Just as I'm getting around to writing about reality, the whole thing might be running its course—more than a few people have made this observation. I've heard a lot of nostalgia about the fertile period of the first decade of the twenty-first century, when any concept, no matter how absurd or derivative, had a chance. It began when people loved *Survivor* and *Big Brother* more than anything, and everyone rushed to catch that lightning. By 2005 scripted TV was trying to copy reality formulas, and in 2007, during the hundred days of the writers' strike, reality filled the void with cheap, seductive, endless lives. But now, I mean, just turn on the TV: It's oversaturated with these lives. The market is beginning to constrict.

Will and I end up hanging out at the RealScreen Summit. He's shopping concepts, but it's harder and harder to get meetings with the big-shot networks without an agent. Still, he tries to stay hopeful. He has decided to see the bubble bursting as an opportunity. What has burst, he reasons, is a very narrow definition of what reality is supposed to look like. That means that there will be room for new ideas, new voices.

"I hate to say it," he tells me, "but what you've got now is four or five women drinking together, and then you can expect them to bicker and all that. *That's* what people are sick of. I think the bicker bubble burst."

He laughs and commends himself for thinking of *bicker bubble.*

I can't bring myself to tell him that I don't want the bicker bubble to burst.

For now, Will is stuck with ideas, like most of the other attendees at this conference. So many ideas. He says, "I'll be honest, what got me excited about reality TV was what I think gets a lot of people excited: You look at who is on TV and you're like, man, *that* is watchable? I'm better than *that*."

He uses Honey Boo Boo as an example. What's the *idea* there? Where's the *concept*? He's out at the station in Macon coming up with like three ideas an hour, ways to frame human life—that's a gift that he has that for a long time he hadn't thought to monetize—and apparently it's so easy to get on TV that your whole idea can just be obese people with accents farting and drinking Mountain Dew.

"What makes you better?" I ask him in a tone that I hope reads more curious, less doubtful.

The short answer is resolution. When Will turns on the TV, he wants to see a problem, maybe even a life, resolved. If this is going to be reality, he says, maybe people are ready to see a hopeful reality.

I'm struck by how little I want to see that. If I still find anything satisfactorily real about reality TV, it is its unendingness. Its constant manufacture of conflict and then a brief respite, temporary hope offered up just to keep the gears turning, then a cliffhanger promising that peace (both inner and outer) has not been and will not be achieved.

Leave the drama for fiction, Will says. Make the real resolved.

Other producers fill in the specifics of the bubble burst that Will is struggling with. It's not so much a problem with the concept of *reality,* it's that viewers are tired of the overt construction and overstyling, the obviously sensationalized emotion. A few producers talked about a backlash against shows that wear their contrivance proudly, whose stars are clearly saying things that they didn't think of to say, at least not in the moment that they're captured saying them.

I've heard that *natural* is back in.

The call is out for authenticity, is another slogan.

Industry people are worried that the thrill of the spectacular formula has been beaten dead by its own success—eventually the saturated audience starts getting annoyed at being such an easy mark. People who will say *anything* stop providing a rush, once you understand that saying anything is their whole bit.

Apparently, at a recent RealScreen conference, a veteran bigwig from the old days excoriated the room, focusing on a show about people from Jersey that wasn't *The Jersey Shore* but sought to place that bankable vibe within a slightly altered conceit. It was just one example of a trend. He talked about how absurdly predictable each line was, how nothing remotely *authentic* remained. They were just yelling what they were supposed to yell because it sounded like a good formula.

A producer relayed that story to me, laughing about how diluted reality had become since those early days when it was just a few trailblazers conceiving shows through a documentarian's lens, venerated legends like Bunim/Murray, the brains behind *The Real World.* But a lot of Bunim/Murray's success came long after *The Real World,* when they got in early on the Kardashian franchise, which was and still is seen as its own perversion of whatever authentic mode of expression *The Real World* had established.

I ask if that isn't also sort of scripted.

The producer tells me that the distinction is subtle. I mean, yeah, they have beats to hit and shit to cover; those scenarios are planned. But they're saying what they would say, you know? The personality is authentic; that's why it works. It's closer to the old days—just capturing people as they are.

Yet another producer, one who does his own casting, puts it

like this: The networks have been saying for a few years that they want authentic again, but that's not what they want. Authentic means you have to wait around for someone to be interesting. There's a lot of dead tape in authentic lives. And there isn't time for dead tape. In the old days, a week or two of footage would make for an episode. Now there's no patience. Now it's a day or two, turn it around, onto the next. It's asking a lot to make human beings interesting every day. Human beings don't do that.

"Look," he says, "you gotta make do with what you have. You gotta find a way to be compelling. Bro, what they're asking for is better people, people who can be interesting *and* authentic whenever you need them to be."

You turned thirty the other day. I wrote you a card. That's a full decade's worth of cards now—birthdays, anniversaries, Valentine's Days, a period of just-because cards that fell by the wayside fast. They are important because they are us trying to tell the story to each other, the story of the other one, the story we both know so well that it's rote, it's air, but we try to tell it like it's new, like no other story has ever been similar.

I woke up early on your birthday to write the card. It was more pressure than usual because this wasn't just a special-occasion card, it was a monumental-occasion card. When I tried to write it, the story felt like the story I'd told on previous cards, and I knew that I'd felt the same worry when writing each of those cards, that I was parroting myself and in doing so parroting so many things that I'd seen or heard or even just sort of absorbed about the ways to quantify love, the appropriate adjectives with which to say beauty, the register to adopt to give a sense that nobody has ever been like you. And nobody has. But how to say it? Or how to say it better, like I really *meant* it, even though

I did mean it, but how to make it sound that way? So many moments spent together, alone, in the same little space that is ours, seeing the same images flicker, seeing each other, too.

You said you liked the card. You emoted like you liked the card, and that was all I needed to emote back. I'm not trying to say this was all bullshit because it wasn't bullshit at all; it was just emoting. I made us smoothies and put a candle in a vegan cupcake I'd bought the night before and hidden in the back of the fridge. You were dressed for work, eating your cupcake, your smoothie next to you, and I took a picture of it and put it on Instagram with a caption marking the occasion and the hashtag "late capitalism," which I thought was hilarious. The likes trickled in. We tracked them together. You had a little time before work. We went to the couch, sat, watched for a moment, held each other.

I speak to Bruce David Klein, twenty-five years in the business, creator of the oddly popular *Restaurant Impossible* series, a week before he gives a highly anticipated conference speech titled "The Death of Reality TV."

"Buddy, you're late," is the first thing he says to me. Then he laughs.

He tells me it's only natural that all the stuff that was once exciting—the breathless tone, the *drama* of it all, even the precious on-the-fly-interviews—is getting a little long in the tooth. When novelty becomes formula, audiences become restless but also don't really know what else it is that they want. The past fifteen years have been about making people desire access and then subsequent manipulation to make that accessed material interesting—the screaming mess of manufactured real lives. But hear enough screaming and even that's a bore.

Now people can target their cable packages to just a few channels. Or they can avoid cable and seek out what they want online. Klein puts it like this: How many of these reality shows would you actually look for, as opposed to stumble upon, let wash over you until all of a sudden three hours have passed?

It's the perfect catch-22: audiences are showing signs of rejecting the heavily produced formula, too cynical now for all that, yet still demanding a loud bang. Nothing is real enough. Nothing is entertaining enough. We're pushing *reality* to the very edge of both its believability and its intrigue, until all that's left is a crater of disappointment.

"I mean, what about you?" Klein asks me. "When does this thing run its course?"

Yesterday was the first time in a while that we watched something and I felt like we shouldn't be watching it. The last time was the whole *Intervention* thing, years ago—my need to say something out loud about addiction not being a spectacle. Of course, that half-protest faded quickly, and soon I was doing impressions of a former piano prodigy smoking dust and talking to pigeons.

But yesterday. It was the season finale of *Sister Wives,* and Meri started stammering at dinner. The story had leaked on the blogs months before, but now the show had caught up with its gossip: Meri had to find a way to acknowledge that she'd been catfished into an online affair by a woman posing as a dreamy man, who'd saved all her voice mails and photos. I remember being so angry at the rumors, like how *dare* this asshole ruin everything?

I get it; that's a ridiculous reaction. But it had become important to believe that we'd been watching contented love, love in the way that we'd conditioned ourselves to want to see it—the little affects of affection that we recognized ourselves in. And I know that an Internet affair doesn't mean that there was never love, or still isn't. And I know that watching a show about a family was never going to give me any access into the quiet reality of that family's problems. Doesn't matter; it felt nice to watch them. That's such a tepid word, *nice,* but it did.

The episode was edited so that Meri's confession to the audience was interspersed with the dinner scene in which she could not find the words or nerve to fully confess to her family.

Kody and the wives were at a packed restaurant in a resort town in Alaska. The restaurant was startlingly loud, the lack of quiet staging a clear choice. We could hear dozens of other conversations, as the camera focused on Meri trying to push her voice beyond a quiver, then a sister wife to her left making a confused face. We could hear laughter from beyond the borders of the shot, glasses cheerfully clinking. The effect of this was near-profane. Meri was barely audible in the din. She fell silent again, looked down. She couldn't say it.

Then her voice began to intone over the silence, and then the image followed her into a small confessional room, alone, the camera maybe two feet away from her face. Her eyes were a stark, wet greenish blue. Her hair was newly feathered. The feel was of a cross between an audition and a deposition.

She stared at the camera and said, *I'm just in this place where I feel alone. Isolated. Lonely.*

In the restaurant again, she told her family that she . . . she just didn't know what to do. She trailed off. Another person laughed offscreen.

Then, back with us: *I wake up in the mornings . . . and, I turn the music on in my house just so I can have some noise. It's just. Quiet.*

She turned her eyes up, like when she heard herself say it, she realized how pitiful it might sound.

A pause, then: *It's just lonely. I'm just lonely. I'm just alone.*

She stopped talking and the camera lingered on her crying, actually alone, then went back to her at the dinner table, surrounded by the enormous apparatus of her family and the fame and the camera crew, eyes frozen, still alone. And I didn't want to be watching then. Well, I did and I didn't. I loved her confessional face, what I assume to be the conscious decision to add the makeup so that it could be cried through. And I loved the words, the depth of her emotion, the perfectly vulnerable way she looked up after describing the ritual of filling an empty home with music. And I loved the intimacy of being welcomed into this experience, along with you and 2.9 million others, the show's highest rating since its premiere.

But I couldn't shake the fact that part of the appeal was that Meri could vocalize this shame out to us millions more easily than she could to the ones we've watched her love and watched love her. And that the vividness of her loneliness, her breakdown, the thrill of being the ones to hear her explain it, was so seductive. As we watched, I had the thought that this was Meri at her best, that she had achieved peak connectivity, her performance never more articulate or more beautiful, and I didn't like that I thought that.

By the end of the episode, Meri was asking for forgiveness, her family's and ours. She told us she was sorry. She told us she could never fully explain. It felt like we didn't know her at all, and also like we knew her very well. She looked tired.

On one of the blogs I read the next day, the headline was *The truth is out!*

At the end of the article there was a poll: *What do we think, guys: Did Meri have a good reason for her betrayal?*

And then another: *Do you think she'll be back for more next season?*

I own buildings all over the place, model agencies, the Miss Universe pageant, jetliners, golf courses, casinos. . . . But it wasn't always so easy. About thirteen years ago, I was seriously in trouble. I was billions of dollars in debt. But I fought back and I won—big league. I used my brain, I used my negotiating skills, and I worked it all out. Now my company's bigger than it ever was and stronger than it ever was, and I'm having more fun than I ever had.

—*The Apprentice,* Season 1, Episode 1

It's a year or so later now than when I finished the first draft of most of these scenes and conducted most of these interviews, and many years since I watched some of these episodes, and since then Donald Trump has been elected president. Everything is more anxious now; every question of motivation is more shrill, more probing; every spectacle contains menace.

My editor has e-mailed asking for a postscript. (*For the republic?* I asked. *Ha-ha!*) In the e-mail he wrote: *Though I have never been an avid viewer of reality television shows, I now find that its latest incarnation is personally overwhelming and all-consuming. I have, as it were, a far greater appreciation of the genre. We are all prisoners now.*

I looked at the e-mail for a long time and tried to will myself to passionately disagree, but I couldn't. It does feel so dramatic—*We are all prisoners*—but then every feeling feels that way now; hyperbole seems impossible to achieve. In all that feeling my editor's point stands—if every word is a yell, every revelation a bombshell, every risk extreme, then it's easy to see the prison of a certain kind of manic, manufactured type of existence being built around us.

At a party last night, a guy told me he listens to political podcasts on 1.5x speed because normal pauses make him feel like he's not doing enough, or he's missing the thing he needs, like what could be changing in the world in the seconds that some wonk stops to say *Umm?*

I have begun leaving my phone plugged in downstairs before going up to bed, so that the only image I might see before sleep is blank ceiling, your face, each a smudgy suggestion in the dark. But so often you are still engaged, and the screen glow traces a little box (yes, fine, the obvious prison metaphor) on the white ceiling.

"Did you see what the fucking president did this time?" you say.

I did. And then in the morning, I get down to my phone, find something that makes me feel terror or righteousness or that kind of numb sadness that doesn't even bring the satisfaction of regular sadness, and I hold it out to you over coffee—Did you see?

Kristin Dombek's wonderful book *The Selfishness of Others* is about how we've fretted over the destructiveness of narcissism since Narcissus himself. She makes the point that people have always been terrified of a swelling narcissism epidemic, and have looked backward with desperate wistfulness for a better time. She ends up here, in this modern moment, and of course she points to the way we discuss reality TV, how what we see there is a performance of a type of humanity that *must* have not existed before the shows encouraged it.

Reality TV presents the worst of who we think we have the

capacity to be, she writes. And so when we watch we have to wonder, if we were coerced or empowered to defend or define ourselves out to a broadcast audience, would we sound the way that worst person sounds there on our screen? We don't want to be that person there; part of the role of that person there is to remind us that we don't want to be them. We want to be better than them. But the more we're drawn to watch them, the more complicit we are in the type of humanity they advertise.

Dombek published her book in early 2016, probably started working on it years before, so the sentiment was pre-Trumpian, but (like everything, I suppose) it feels even more vivid now, doesn't it? What does Trump display other than the empowered vocalization of unrelenting self-obsession? Which is something we've always loved to watch, and then wallow in—that stabbing, titillating anxiety of what the watching might say about us. But now every aspect of American discourse is dominated by a loud and unrepentant narcissist, the prick from *The Apprentice,* a ridiculed reality-TV buffoon. Now the object of scorn and fascination is causing constant, inarguable harm as we watch him. The anxiety of spectatorship keeps amplifying.

The call is out to rebel against reality TV. The call is out to move from guilty pleasure to just guilt—see the fevered piety of Jennifer Weiner in her *New York Times* op-ed, vowing to never again watch *The Bachelor* after the Trump presidency. The pressure feels greater now to be a decent person, a better person than the ever-displayed alternative, a person less concerned with his own petty pleasures, less concerned with petty pleasure in general. And I do want to be that person, but we still haven't stopped watching.

Now we watch *Vanderpump,* and it feels extrameaningless, but there's also the nagging fear that it's meaningful, which doesn't dull the pleasure. Mondays at ten, Jax is still there behaving in the awful way that we've always loved to watch him behave (*All I'm saying is I pay for everything, I paid for those tits, and it would be nice to get a sandwich when I want a sandwich*) and it feels more important to say to each other that he is awful, that we wish for his new girlfriend/costar to get away from that awfulness. Still, we watch. And when we do, we are at least slightly more inclined than ever before to reach toward the opposite consumptive desire in response to Jax, as though our interest in truth and empathy and connectivity might somehow absolve our interest in him: a crass, self-loving reality star who suddenly resembles the president.

I renewed my *New York Times* account, and we read what feels somber or urgent and talk about what we've read with somberness, with urgency. We click the monthly donation button (Planned Parenthood, the ACLU, all the hits) and commend each other for doing so and then say, No, to donate is not enough, we know that, we just read that. We join marches and then look at the pictures that we took of those marching around us and let the instant myth of that warm mutual empathy bathe us until we're momentarily soothed. When we fail to march, we hate ourselves for it, and then hate ourselves for getting wrapped up in our own feelings, so we scroll through others' march photos, liking, thanking them.

I'm not trying to mock these actions; I'm not trying to mock action at all, and I certainly don't buy any argument about protest not counting if you take a selfie in the middle of it. To engage in anything that approximates solidarity and action feels so absolutely necessary, at least in part because apathy and self-regard feel so much more disgusting. But apathy and self-regard have always felt disgusting; that's always been part of the equation: to hate it as you embody it. It's the sense of being trapped in yourself even when you want not to be, and how the wanting tightens the trap. Where to look? What to feel? How to be?

Dombek, in an excerpt published in *Harper's Magazine,* homes in on the moment of encountering a reality performer at their worst, when we are invited to think, briefly, that [*their*] *perfor-mance doesn't resemble ours.* It's the tension offered up every time we tune in. Trump is the worst performance come to life, empow-ered. Breathless, we watch him in barrages of clips at the end of the day, each displaying the affect of his disinterest for any interest other than his own, an affect so familiar. Fidgeting, we watch his face contort at the indignity of a question, marvel at how quickly he can seem so certain that he is under attack, the righteousness he conjures in his own defense. We say it's funny; we say it's tragic; we say it's scary; we say it's unbelievable.

Sometimes it feels like the whole act of watching balances on that little phrase of Dombek's, on that little precipice she sets up, teetering. That's what it feels like, but then that feeling is just a metaphor—I'm too safe to fall; I'm almost always sitting down.

All I have wanted to do lately is look at you. It feels good to do that—good because I know your face so well, and your body, and how each contorts with a different type of movement or mood, and how that feels like frankness, honesty, since I know it well enough to trust what I'm seeing and its beauty.

Solmaz Sharif's incredible poem "Look" begins like this: *It matters what you call a thing.*

It's a poem about pain and bigotry and terror, and the danger of America acting upon the poet's Iranian American body with-out looking, or looking at her body without seeing her. She traces the sixteen seconds that it might take between a button pressed in Las Vegas and a Hellfire missile hitting Mazar-e-Sharif, how casually and quietly our nation can kill a type of person we've decided to name an enemy. Then she ends with this:

> *Let it matter what we call a thing.*
> *Let it be the exquisite face for at least sixteen seconds.*

Let me LOOK at you.
Let me look at you in a light that takes years to get here.

I had forgotten about the poem until I read it in a coffee shop while trying to write about reality television. I was having a hard time focusing and I was on Twitter and I was scrolling and glancing and occasionally reading, and then Jia Tolentino, a writer I really admire, said that this was the poem that kept her sane in these times, and I wanted to be attached to her attempt, her wisdom, so I read the poem. And I was so moved—I *am* so moved writing this; tears on my fucking keyboard and all that, literal tears, no metaphor.

Look. I want to. *LOOK.*

When I see that word repeated—an invitation, a command— I want to be near you so I can look at you. Maybe that's all I'm crying for. Or, worse, maybe I'm crying about the idea of myself *LOOKING* at you, about the absolving power of intimacy, context fading like fog in wind, even as the poem demands that context be unavoidable.

I do believe that the personal is always political, and even if I sometimes waver in that belief I trumpet it loudly enough to my students that I start believing again. After the election I handed out photocopies of Arendt's "On Refugees," Orwell's "Why I Write," held them up as cajoling proof of the power and responsibility of a personal story in a dangerous world. Now I hear myself so often in class demanding the acknowledgment that the personal and political must run hand in hand, but usually my students' responses suggest that the political is a burden to their personal narratives as opposed to an opportunity. The political doesn't deepen what they want to say; it corrals it, it diffuses. Or defuses.

When my students write about love, they want it to be about just that, on the nose: love, and that should be enough. Or loss:

just loss, the only story to tell. Or pain, or rage, or triumph. And sometimes that's frustrating, and I know teachers who consider it their jobs to make a student leave their class with some diminished sense of his or her own importance in the face of the adult world. But sometimes I think, how can anything feel larger than their own feelings, their own heartbreaks? And in that way, what is intimate, what is entirely theirs to feel, blocks out everything; it's the shadow of an eclipse edging its way across a sun that is every important thing that is happening to and for and with everyone else in the world. All the rest is too bright to look at head-on, anyway.

And I see myself in them, of course. I return to myself and the poem, and the command to *look,* and I think that I am looking, but when I think of the power of looking, there I am looking at you and then looking at the idea of myself looking at you.

The exquisite face for sixteen seconds.

A light that takes years to get here.

It is so much more than two faces pressed close, love-lit, staring. But it's also that. And there is the shadow of an eclipse edging across the sun.

On Inauguration Day I was driving home to you through a leafy part of New Hampshire, from a reading I gave at a college. I was thinking about the impending overwhelm of the inaugural address, and I was feeling nauseous in anticipation. I was also feeling nauseous because at dinner the night before some other writers were saying I should do an op-ed about Trump's reality-TV rhetoric; maybe the *Times* would even run it. I was in the middle of convincing myself that I wouldn't write the piece out of some sense of decorum, not wanting to piggyback a personal victory on top of an international trauma, but really I was afraid that I had no insight to give other than general terror, and a pretty dull terror compared to that of most, what with the insulation of my privilege.

I turned on the radio right before he spoke, and, as for so many, I imagine, my internal monologue was subsumed by his external one. It's infamous now what he spoke of—nothing subtle, nothing true. But the images were vivid: abandoned factories, cities aflame; the husk of a place, this place, and what could that make you feel beyond desperate? And yes it was what I expected, and yes it was a lie, but it was also imagery. More than that, it was intimacy. It whittled away any context—fact, history, perspective. It whittled it all away to an emotion, one face, one voice so loud that it suffocates all other sound.

So many of the interviews that I did with reality producers now seem about as relevant as all the political podcasts I listened to in 2016. They were so certain that loud, mean, repetitive stageyness had oversaturated an audience until we were all ready to rebel into the arms of *authenticity*. But authenticity has proven too malleable a term to predict. Somebody can find Donald Trump authentic because he doesn't stop to bother with honesty; somebody can believe in him not because they believe the truth of what he's saying but because they believe the feeling of the pointlessness of factual belief. I recognize that vacillation, that rationalization, that pleasure.

When we watch him, we mutter the way we mutter at the most toxic cast members of our favorite shows. When he bullies a reporter—when he actually fucking yells at a reporter until they've been muted—he is reminiscent of any *Housewives* reunion episode, when warring stars are asked to explain themselves in the service of inevitable combustion. There's no direction or resolution or truth; just a contest, just a scream played on a loop.

I'm back to my editor's words about how we are all prisoners now. Part of me wants to say that this has nothing to do with reality TV, that reality TV is a convenient panacea for more serious questions—we're trapped in the consequences of stoked white rage, gerrymandering, and maybe treason, not the consequences of *The Apprentice.* And that's true. But there's also the sensation of watching, the one I know so well, when you're wracked in semibelief, staring at the face on-screen, and all you can do is match the volume of its emotion with your own.

Sometimes, next to me on the couch, you say, "I can't, I can't, I can't," and when I glance at you, you're shaking your hands a little, as if trying to push the unavoidability of his image away, a pose I recognize from a death-in-the-family phone call and a couple of our worst fights. You look like you really feel it, and you do really feel it, but it's also a performance of that feeling, the anxiety of how to frame oneself in relationship to the image on the screen. I do it, too, with my own little affects. We do it back and forth at each other, and it's so exhausting to watch that it begins to feel like action.

It is routine, now, to read and see political journalists yelling about a reality-TV world and turning to reality-TV producers to explain what the hell is happening. I hear the kinds of people I interviewed using the same language to describe the president— It's just storytelling; he's just a storyteller; people have always wanted a simple, close-up story to react to. And sure, that seems true, so true that it's obvious, but also: so what? What's next? Where does that explanation leave us, except back in the echo? The rush to point out the trick becomes part of the panic and self-definition and stagnation. What's left to point out? I don't know. All I really know is how it feels—that's the truth and that's also the problem.

I called you short of breath, sitting there in my car, hearing him. On the other end of the line you were crying. A scene: intimate, familiar.

———

The issue remains that I'm trying to write you, or at least us, through all this noise, or maybe rising out of all this noise, but I worry that I'm drowning you out. And I worry that's all I do. I worry that there are built-in limits and corrosive flaws to the act of ascribing meaning. The act of storytelling. I tell and tell and tell and I ascribe and ascribe and ascribe the best-intended meaning, but that turns into a kind of muting.

I'm still unsure if the epistolary form is right, this pretense of me confessing moments that you were there for. It's starting to feel like mansplaining again, hiding the smallness of my *I* by telling you about what *we* do and believe. Pontificating on a subject again—saying that there must be value in the crevasses of sex or sadness or meanness or stupidity or routine or simple care—but this time the subject is us. All the time, the subject is us. All the time, the subject is me.

What starts as cultural or sociological, what starts as inquiry, becomes personal, which then becomes some fantasy of you and me that I also don't quite understand, can't quite express. What I do know is this: There is violence in the passivity of watching. Of being able to feel that close. Like you can fade into someone else's story if you want to, or you can absorb them into yours. That's the feeling to chase, that's being made and sold over and over: to be a semipermeable vessel lying in a warm bath, swelling.

Or maybe it's just that you have to look away from the actual subject, at objects that can be turned into metaphor. And that's what all these flickering stories are, in the background but sneaking into the foreground, too. At their best I convince myself that the shows we watch are offerings, little talismans of gnawing, insatiable desire piling up in our living room. I look at you over the pile—panicked, miniscule, ordinary, in love.

Author's Note

This book moves through a series of scenes, both from my own life and from an array of reality TV shows. The narrative covers many years and often bounces around in nonchronological order. Some of the episodes I write about are very recent and some are many years old, and in each instance, I write what I thought and felt about the show at the time and the role it played in my own narrative. This book is not meant to provide an up-to-date account of every show, or even the genre, as a whole. For example, since I wrote about Rob Kardashian, he has returned to TV in his own show and exhibited horrifying, abusive behavior toward the mother of his child; since I wrote about *Here Comes Honey Boo Boo,* Mama June lost 300 pounds. The book doesn't trace these developments or any others that have arisen (or may be arising right now). The plots and trends change so quickly and often in such extreme ways. That's part of the experience of watching— a fragmented, fast-cutting, incomplete, personal experience— and that's what I hope to chronicle here.